The Tragedies

SOPHOCLES

The Tragedies, Sophocles
Jazzybee Verlag Jürgen Beck
86450 Altenmünster, Loschberg 9
Deutschland

ISBN: 9783849671822

Translated by Richard Claverhouse Jebb

www.jazzybee-verlag.de
admin@jazzybee-verlag.de

Printed by Createspace, North Charleston, SC, USA

CONTENTS:

The Genius Of Sophocles.. 1

Oedipus The King... 18

Oedipus At Colonus 45

Antigone..74

Ajax 95

Electra..117

Trachiniae..141

Philoctete...162

THE GENIUS OF SOPHOCLES

By Richard Claverhouse Jebb

The most brilliantly joyous of all comedies were brought out in a city vexed during the years that gave them birth by every kind of misery in turn; by want and pestilence, by faction and the mutual distrust of citizens, by defeat on land and sea, by the sense of abasement and the presage of ruin. During more than twenty years of war Aristophanes was the best public teacher of Athens; but there were times when distraction was more needed than advice. One of the best of his plays belongs to the number of those which were meant simply to amuse the town at a time when it would have been useless to lash it. The comedy of the "Frogs" came out in a season of gloomy suspense—just after Athens had made a last effort in equipping a fleet, and was waiting for decisive news from the seat of war; in January of 405 B.C., eight months before Ægospotami and about fifteen months before the taking of Athens by Lysander. A succession of disasters and seditions had worn out the political life of the city; patriotic satire could no longer find scope in public affairs, for there were no longer any vital forces which it could either stimulate or combat. Nor could the jaded minds of men at such a time easily rise into a region of pure fancy, as when nine years before, on the eve of the last crisis in the war, Aristophanes had helped them to forget scandals of impiety and misgovernment on a voyage to his city in the clouds. What remained was to seek comfort or amusement in the past; and since the political past could give neither, then in the literary past—in the glories, fading now like other glories, of art and poetry.

It was now just fifty years since the death of Æschylus. It was only a few months since news had come from Macedonia of the death of Euripides. More lately still, at the end of the year before, Sophocles had closed a life blessed from its beginning by the gods and now happy in its limit; for, as in his boyhood he had led the pæan after Salamis, so he died too soon to hear the dirge of Imperial Athens—the cry, raised in the Peiræus and caught up from point to point through the line of the Long Walls, which carried up from the harbour to the town the news of the overthrow on the Hellespont.

With the death of Euripides and the death of Sophocles so recent, and no man living who seemed able to replace them, it might well seem to an Athenian that the series of the tragic masters was closed. In the "Frogs" Aristophanes supposes Dionysus, the god of dramatic inspiration, going down to the shades, to bring back to Athens, beggared of poets and unable to live without them, the best poet that could be found below. It is hard to imagine anything more pathetic than an Athenian audience listening, at just that time, to that comedy in the theatre of Dionysus; in view of the sea over which their empire was even then on its last trial; surrounded by the monuments of an empire over art which had already declined—in the building, at once theatre and temple, which the imagination of the poets lately dead had long peopled with the divine or heroic shapes known to them and their fathers, but in which, they might well forebode, the living inspiration of the god would never be so shown forth again.

The interest of the comedy does not depend, however, merely on its character of epilogue to a school of tragic drama so masterly, of so short an actual life, of so

1

perpetual an influence; it takes another kind of interest from the justness of its implicit criticism; the criticism of a man whose wit would not have borne the test of centuries and the harder test of translation, if he had not joined to a quick fancy the qualities which make a first-rate critic.

When Dionysus reaches the lower world, an uproar is being raised among the dead. It has been the custom that the throne of Tragedy, next to Pluto's own, shall be held by a laureate for the time being, subject to removal on the coming of a better. For some time Æschylus has held the place of honour. Euripides, however, has just come down; the newer graces of his style, which he lost no time in showing off, have taken the crowd; and their applause has moved him to claim the tragic throne. Æschylus refuses to yield. As the only way of settling the dispute, scales are brought; the weightiest things which the rivals can offer are compared; and at last the balance inclines for Æschylus. But where, in the meantime, is Sophocles? He, too, is in the world of the dead, having come down just after Euripides. "Did he" (asked Xanthias, the slave of Dionysus) "lay no claim to the chair?" "No, indeed, not he," answers Æacus: "No—he kissed Æschylus as soon as he came down, and shook hands with him; and Æschylus yielded the throne to him. But just now he meant, Cleidemides said, to hold himself in reserve, and, if Æschylus won, to stay quiet; if not, he said he would try a bout with *Euripides.*"

It is in this placing of Sophocles relatively to the disputants, even more than in the account of the contest, that Aristophanes has shown his appreciativeness. While he seems to aim merely at marking by a passing touch the good-humoured courtesy of Sophocles, he has, with the happiness of a real critic, pointed out his place as a poet. The behaviour of Sophocles in the "Frogs" just answers to his place in the literary history of his age. This place is fixed chiefly by the fact that Sophocles was a poet who did not seek to be a prophet; who was before all things an artist; and who, living in the quiet essence of art, represented the mind of his day less by bringing into relief any set tendencies than by seizing in its highest unity the total spirit of the world in which he lived and of the legendary world in which his fancy moved, and bringing the conflicts of this twofold world into obedience, as far as possible, to the first law of his own nature—harmony. The workings of this instinct of harmony will be best seen, first, by viewing Sophocles as a poet in two broad aspects—in regard to his treatment of the heroic legends and in his relation to the social ideas of the age of Pericles; next, by considering two of his special qualities—the quality which has been called his irony, and his art of drawing character.

The national religion of Greece was based upon genealogy. It carried back the mind by an unbroken ascent from living men to heroes or half-gods who had been their forefathers in the flesh, and thence to gods from whom these heroes had sprung. The strength of a chain is the strength of its weakest part; enfeeblement of belief in the heroes implied enfeeblement of belief in the gods. The decreasing vividness of faith in the heroes is the index of failing life in the Greek national religion.

At the beginning of the fifth century before Christ this belief in the heroes was real and living. The Persian Wars were wars of race, the first general conflict of Hellene with barbarian; and it was natural that in such a conflict the Greek mind should turn with longing and trust towards those kindred heroes of immortal blood who long ago had borne arms for Achaia against Asia. It was told how, on the day of Marathon, the Athenian ranks had been cheered by the sudden presence among them of Theseus; while through the press of battle two other combatants had been seen to pass in more than earthly strength, the hero Echetlus and he who had given his name to the field. Just before the fight at Salamis a Greek ship was sent with offerings to the tombs of the Æacidae in Ægina; and when the pæan sounded and the fleets closed, the form of a colossal warrior was seen to move over the battle, and the Greeks knew that the greatest of the Æacid line, the Telamonian Ajax, was with them that day, as he had been with their fathers at Troy.

But from the moment when the united Greek effort against Persia was over, the old belief which it had made to start up in a last glow began to die out. The causes of this decline were chiefly three. First, the division of once-united Greece into two camps—the Athenian and the Spartan,—a division which tended to weaken all sentiments based on the idea of a common blood; and the belief in the heroes as an order was one of these sentiments. Secondly, the advance of democracy, which tended to create a jealous feeling and a sarcastic tone in regard to the claims of the old families; chief among which claims was that of kinship with the gods through the heroes. Thirdly, the birth of an historical sense. Before the Persian crisis history had been represented among the Greeks only by local or family traditions. The Wars of Liberation had given to Herodotus the first genuinely historical inspiration felt by a Greek. These wars showed him that there was a corporate life, higher than that of the city, of which the story might be told; and they offered to him as a subject the drama of the collision between East and West. With him, the spirit of history was born into Greece; and his work, called after the nine Muses, was indeed the first utterance of Clio. The historical spirit was the form in which the general scepticism of the age acted on the belief in the heroic legends. For Herodotus himself, the heroes are still godlike. But for Thucydides, towards the end of the century, the genuine hero-ship of Agamemnon and Pelops is no more; he criticises their probable resources and motives as he might have discussed the conduct or the income of a contemporary. They are real to him; but they are real as men; and, for that very reason, unreal as claimants of a half-divine character.

The great cycles of heroic legends furnished the principal subjects of Attic tragedy. Three distinct methods of treating these legends appear in Æschylus, Sophocles, and Euripides.

The spirit of Æschylus is in all things more Hellenic than Athenian. The Pan-hellenic heroism of which in the struggle with Persia he had himself been a witness and a part is the very inspiration of his poetry. For him those heroes who were the common pride of the Greek race are true demigods. In his dramas they stand as close to the gods as in the Iliad; and more than in the Iliad do they tower above men. With him their distinctive attribute is majesty; a majesty rather Titanic than in the proper Greek sense heroic. What, it may be asked, is the basis of this Titanic majesty? It would be easy to say that the effect is wrought partly by pomp and weight of language, partly by vagueness of outline. But the essential reason appears to be another. The central idea of Greek tragedy is the conflict between free-will and fate. In Æschylus this conflict takes its simplest and therefore grandest form. No subtle contrivance, no complexity of purposes, breaks the direct shock of the collision between man and destiny. Agamemnon before the Fury of his house is even as Prometheus facing Zeus.

3

In thus imagining the heroes as distinctly superhuman, and as claiming the sympathy of men rather by a bare grandeur of agony than by any closely-understood affinity of experience, Æschylus was striving to sustain a belief which had not gone out of his age, but which was dying. In his mid-career, about ten years before his Oresteia, the so-called relics of Theseus found at Scyros were brought to Athens by Cimon and laid in a shrine specially built for them. The distinctly religious enthusiasm then shown implies the old faith. It is hard to suppose that a like incident could have brought out a like public feeling even thirty years later.

Euripides, towards the end of the century, stood in nearly the same relation to his contemporaries as that of Æschylus to his at the beginning: that is, he was in general agreement with their beliefs, but held to some things from which they were going further and further away. The national religion was now all but dead. By the side of philosophic scepticism had come up the spurious scepticism which teachers of rhetoric had made popular. The devotional need, so far as it was felt, was usually satisfied by rituals or mysteries brought in from abroad; the old creed was not often attacked, but there was a tacit understanding among "able" men that it was to be taken allegorically; and a dim, silently spreading sense of this had further weakened its hold upon the people. What, then, was a tragic poet to do? The drama was an act of worship; the consecrated mythology must still supply the greatest number of its subjects. Euripides solved the problem partly by realism, partly by antiquarianism. He presented the hero as a man, reflecting the mind as well as speaking the dialect of the day; and he made the legend, where he could, illustrate local Attic tradition. The reason why this treatment failed, so far as it failed, has not always been accurately stated. Euripides has sometimes been judged as if his poetical fault had been in bringing down half-gods to the level of men and surrounding them with mean and ludicrous troubles. Probably this notion has been strengthened by the scene in the "Acharnians" (the really pointed criticisms of Aristophanes upon Euripides are to be found elsewhere), in which the needy citizen calls on Euripides and begs for some of the rags in which he has been wont to clothe his heroes; and the tragic poet tells his servant to look for the rags of Telephus between those of Thyestes and those of Ino. But the very strength of Euripides lay in a deep and tender compassion for human suffering: if he had done nothing worse to his heroes than to give them rags and crutches, his power could have kept for them at least the sympathy due to the sordid miseries of men; he would only have substituted a severely human for an ideal pathos. His real fault lay in the admission of sophistic debate. A drama cannot be an artistic whole in which the powers supposed to control the issues of the action represent a given theory of moral government, while the agents are from time to time employing the resources of rhetorical logic to prove that this theory is either false or doubtful.

Between these two contrasted conceptions—the austere transcendentalism of Æschylus and the sophistic realism of Euripides—stands the conception of Sophocles. But Sophocles is far nearer to Æschylus than to Euripides; since Sophocles and Æschylus have this affinity, that the art of both is ideal. The heroic form is in outline almost the same for Sophocles as for Æschylus; but meanwhile there has passed over it such a change as came over the statue on which the sculptor gazed until the stone began to kindle with the glow of a responsive life, and what just now was a blank faultlessness of beauty became loveliness warmed by a human soul.

4

Sophocles lived in the ancestral legends of Greece otherwise than Æschylus lived in them. Æschylus felt the grandeur and the terror of their broadest aspects, their interpretation of the strongest human impulses, their commentary on problems of destiny: Sophocles dwelt on their details with the intent, calm joy of artistic meditation; believing their divineness; finding in them a typical reconciliation of forces which in real life are never absolutely reconciled—a concord such as the musical instinct of his nature assured him must be the ultimate law; recognizing in them, too, scope for the free exercise of imagination in moral analysis, without breaking the bounds of reverence; for, while these legends express the conflict between necessity and free-will, they leave shadowy all that conflict within the man himself which may precede the determination of the will.

The heroic persons of the Sophoclean drama are at once human and ideal. They are made human by the distinct and continuous portrayal of their chief feelings, impulses, and motives. Their ideality is preserved chiefly in two ways. First, the poet avoids too minute a moral analysis; and so each character, while its main tendencies are exhibited, still remains generic, a type rather than a portrait. Secondly—and this is of higher moment—the persons of the drama are ever under the directly manifested, immediately felt control of the gods and of fate. There is, indeed, no collision of forces so abrupt as in Æschylus; since the ampler unfolding of character serves to foreshow, and sometimes to delay, the catastrophe. On the other hand, there is no trace of that competition between free thought and the principle of authority which is often so jarring in the plots of Euripides. In the dramas of Sophocles there is perfect unity of moral government; and the development of human motives, while it heightens the interest of the action, serves to illustrate the power of the gods.

The method by which Sophocles thus combines humanity with idealism may be seen in the cases of Ajax, of Œdipus, and of Heracles.

Ajax had been deprived of the arms of Achilles by the award of the Atreidæ. The goddess Athene, whom he had angered by arrogance, had seized the opportunity of his disappointment and rage to strike him with madness. In this frenzy he had fallen upon the flocks and herds of the Greek army on the plain of Troy, and had butchered or tortured them, thinking that he was wreaking vengeance on his enemies. When he comes to his senses, he is overpowered by a sense of his disgrace, and destroys himself.

The central person of this drama becomes human in the hands of Sophocles by the natural delineation of his anguish on the return to sanity. Ajax feels the new shame added to his repulse as any man of honour would feel it. At the same time he stands above men. An ideal or heroic character is lent to him, partly by the grandeur with which two feelings—remorse, and the sense that his dishonour must be effaced by death—absolutely predominate over all other emotions, as over pity for Tecmessa and his son; chiefly by his terrible nearness to Athene, as one whom with her own voice she had once urged to battle, promising her aid—when, face to face with her, he vaunted his independence of her, and provoked her anger;—then, as the blinded victim whom she, his pretended ally, had stung into the senseless slaughter—lastly, as the conscious, broken-hearted sufferer of her chastisement.

In the farewell of Ajax to Tecmessa and the seamen who had come with him from Salamis to Troy—a farewell really final, but disguised as temporary under a sustained (though possibly unconscious) irony—the human and the heroic elements are thus blended:—

"All things the long and countless years first draw from darkness, then bury from light; and nothing is past hope, but there is confusion even for the dreadful oath and for the stubborn will. For even I, I once so wondrous firm, like iron in the dipping felt my keen edge dulled by yon woman's words; and I have ruth to leave her a widow with my foes, and the boy an orphan. But I will go to the sea-waters and the meadows by the shore, that in the purging of my stains I may flee the heavy anger of the goddess....Henceforth I shall know how to yield to the gods and learn to revere the Atreidæ: they are rulers, so we must submit. Of course, dread things and things most potent bow to office. Thus it is that the snow-strewn winters give place to fruitful summer; and thus Night's weary round makes room for Day with her white horses to kindle light; and the breath of dreadful winds at last gives slumber to the groaning sea; and, like the rest, almighty Sleep looses whom he has bound, nor holds with an eternal grasp. And *we*, shall we not learn discretion? I chiefly, for I have newly learned that our enemy is to be hated but so far as one who will hereafter be a friend; and towards a friend I would wish so far to show aid and service as knowing that he will not always abide. For to most men the haven of friendship is false. But all this will be well.—Woman, go thou within, and pray to the gods that in all fulness the desires of my heart may be fulfilled. And do ye, friends, honour my wishes even as she does, and bid Teucer, when he come, have care for me and good-will to you as well. For I will go whither I must pass,—but do ye what I bid; and perchance, perchance, though now I suffer, ye will hear that I have found rest."

The story of Œdipus is more complex; alternations of alarm and relief, of confidence and despair, attend the gradual unravelling of his history; the miseries which crowd upon him at the last discovery seem to exhaust the possibilities of sorrow. A character so variously tried is necessarily laid open; and Œdipus is perhaps the best known to us of all the persons of Sophocles. Antigone, Electra, Philoctetes are not less human; but no such glare of lightning flashes in the depths of their natures. At the opening of the play how perfect an embodiment of assured greatness is Œdipus the King, bending with stately tenderness to the trouble of the Theban folk:—

"O my children, latest-born to Cadmus who was of old, why bow ye to me thus beseeching knees, with the wreathed bough of the suppliant in your hands, while the city reeks with incense, rings with prayers for health and cries of woe? I deemed it unmeet, my children, to learn of these things from the mouth of others, and am come here myself, I, whom all men call Œdipus the famous."

And how thoroughly answering to this is the tone in which the priest, the leader of the suppliants, tells the trouble and the faith of Thebes:—

"A blight is on it in the fruit-guarding blossoms of the land, in the herds among the pastures, in the barren pangs of women; and withal that fiery god, the dreadful Plague, has swooped on us, and ravages the town; by whom the house of Cadmus is made waste, but dark Hades rich in groans and tears.

"It is not that we deem thee ranked with gods that I and these children are suppliants at thy hearth; but as deeming thee first of men, not only in life's common chances, but when men have to do with the immortals; thou who earnest to the town of Cadmus and didst rid us of the tax that we paid to the hard songstress,—and this, though thou knewest nothing from us that could help thee, nor hadst been schooled; no, with a god's aid, as we say and deem, didst thou uplift our life.

"And now, Œdipus, name glorious in all eyes, we beseech thee, all we suppliants, to find for us some succour; whether thou wottest of it by the whisper of a god, or knowest it in the power of man."

Then comes the oracle, announcing that the land is thus plagued because it harbours the unknown murderer of Laius; the pity of Œdipus is quickened into a fiery zeal for discovery and atonement; and he appeals to the prophet Teiresias:—

"Teiresias, whose soul grasps all things, the lore that may be told and the unspeakable, the secrets of heaven and the low things of the earth,—thou feelest, though thou canst not see, what a plague doth haunt our state,—from which, great prophet, we find in thee our protector and only saviour. Now, Phœbus—if perchance thou knowest it not from the messengers—sent answer to our question that the only riddance from this pest which could come to us was if we should learn aright the slayers of Laius, and slay them, or send them into exile from our land. Do thou, then, grudge neither voice of birds nor any other way of seer-lore that thou hast, but save thyself and the state and me, and take away all the taint of the dead. For in thee is our hope; and a man's noblest task is to help others by his best means and powers."

Teiresias is silent: the taunts of Œdipus at last sting him into uttering his secret—*Œdipus* is the murderer: and thenceforward, through indignation, scorn, agonized suspense, the human passion mounts until it bursts forth in the last storm.

And now the human element of the history has been worked out. Œdipus has passed to the limit of earthly anguish; and, as if with his self-inflicted blindness had come clearer spiritual sight, he begins to feel a presentiment of some further, peculiar doom. "Suffer me to dwell on the hills," he asks of Creon, "that there I may die. And yet thus much I know, that neither sickness nor aught else shall destroy me; for I should never have been saved on the verge of death except for some *strange* ill." The second play of Sophocles—"Œdipus at Colonus"—has pervading it the calm of an assurance into which this first troubled foreboding has settled down: Œdipus, already in spirit separate from men, has found at Colonus the destined haven of his wanderings, and only awaits the summons out of life. At last from the darkness of the sacred cavern the voice long-waited for is heard,—"Œdipus, Œdipus, why do we tarry?" And the eye-witness of his passing says, "Not the fiery bolt of the god took him away, nor the tumult of sea-storm in that hour, but either a summoner from heaven, or the deep place of the dead opened to him in love, without a pang. For the man was ushered forth, not with groans nor in sickness or pain, but beyond all mortals, wondrously."

As Œdipus, first shown in the vividness of a tortured humanity, is then raised above men by keen spiritual anguish, so it is earthly passion and bodily suffering which give a human interest to Heracles the very son of Zeus. He stands by the altar on Mount Cenæum, doing sacrifice to his Olympian Father for the taking of Œchalia; clad in the robe which his messenger, Lichas, has just brought him as the gift of Deianeira; the robe which she has secretly anointed with the blood of the Centaur Nessus, believing this to be a charm which shall win back to her the love of Heracles. What follows is thus told:—

"At first, hapless one, he prayed with cheerful heart, rejoicing in his comely garb. But when the flame of sacrifice began to blaze from the holy offerings and from the resinous wood, sweat broke out upon his flesh, and the tunic clung to his sides, and at every joint, close-glued as if by workman's hand; and there came a biting pain twitching at his bones; and then the venom as of a deadly, cruel adder began to eat him.

"Then it was that he cried out on the unhappy Lichas, in nowise guilty for *thy* crime, asking with what thoughts he brought this robe; and he, knowing nothing, hapless man, said that he had only brought thy gift, as he was charged. Then Heracles, as he heard it, and as a piercing spasm clutched his lungs, caught him by the foot, where the ankle hinges in the socket, and flung him at a rock washed on both sides by the sea; and Lichas has his white brain oozing through his hair, as the skull is cloven and the blood scattered therewith.

"But all the people lifted up a voice of anguish and of awe, since one was frenzied and the other slain; and no one dared to come before the man. For he was twitched to the ground and into the air, howling, shrieking; and the rocks rang around,—the steep Locrian headlands and Eubœa's capes. But when he was worn out with ofttimes throwing himself in his misery on the ground and often making loud lament, while he reviled his ill-starred wedlock with thee and his marriage into the house of Œneus, saying how he had found in it the ruin of his life—then, out of the flame and smoke that beset him, he lifted his distorted eye and saw me in the great host, weeping; and he looked at me, and called me, 'Son, come here, do not flee my woe, even if thou must die with me—come, bear me out of the crowd, and set me, if thou canst, in a place where no man shall see me; or, if thou hast any pity, at least convey me with all speed out of this land, and let me not die on this spot.'"

Presently Heracles himself is brought before the eyes of the spectators. In the lamentation wrung from him by his torment two strains are clear above the rest, and each is a strain of thoroughly human anguish. He contrasts the strength in which, through life, he has been the champion of helpless men—"ofttimes on the sea and in all forests ridding them of plagues"—with his own helpless misery in this hour; and he contrasts the greatness of the work to which he had seemed called with the weakness of the agent who has arrested it:—

"Ah me, whose hands and shoulders have borne full many a fiery trial and evil to tell! But never yet hath the wife of Zeus or the hated Eurystheus laid on me aught so dreadful as this woven snare of the Furies, which the daughter of Œneus, falsely fair, hath fastened on my shoulders, and by which I perish. Glued to my sides, it has eaten away my flesh to the bone; it is ever with me, sucking the channels of my breath; already it has drained my vigorous blood, and in all my body I am marred, the thrall of these unutterable bonds. Not the warrior on the battle-field, not the giant's earthborn host, nor the might of wild beasts, nor Hellas, nor the land of the alien, nor all the lands that I have visited and purged, have done unto me thus; but a woman, a weak woman, born not to the strength of man, alone, alone has struck me down without a sword.

"O King Hades, receive me!—Smite me, O flash of Zeus! O King, O Father, dash, hurl thy thunderbolt upon me! Again the pest eats me—it has blazed up, it has started into fury! O hands, hands, O shoulders and breast and trusty arms, ye, ye in this plight, are they who once tamed by force the haunter of Nemea, the scourge of herdsmen, the lion whom no man might approach or face—who tamed the hydra of Lerna and the host of monsters of double form, man joined to horse, with whom none might mingle, fierce, lawless, of surpassing might—tamed the Erymanthian beast and the three-headed dog of Hades underground, an appalling foe, offspring of the dread Echidna,—tamed the serpent who guards the golden apples in earth's utmost clime. And of other toils ten thousand I had taste, and no man got a trophy from my hands. But now with joint thus wrenched from joint, with frame torn to shreds, I have been wrecked by this blind curse—I, who am named son of noblest mother—I, who was called the offspring of starry Zeus!"

Anon he learns that the venom which is devouring him is the poisoned blood of his old enemy, the Centaur Nessus. That knowledge gives him at once the calm certainty of death; and now, in the nearness of the passage to his Father, there arises, triumphant over bodily torment, the innate, tranquil strength of his immortal origin. He sees in this last chapter of his earthly ordeal the foreordained purpose of Zeus:—

"It was foreshown to me by my Father of old that I should die by no creature that had the breath of life, but by one who was dead and a dweller in Hades. So this monster, the Centaur, even as the god's will had been foreshown, slew me, a living man, when he was dead."

He directs that he shall be carried to the top of Mount Œta, above Trachis, sacred to Zeus; that a funeral pyre shall there be raised, and he, while yet living, laid upon it; that so the flame which frees his spirit from the flesh may in the same moment bear it up to Zeus. No one of the sacred places of Greece was connected with a legend of such large meaning, with one which was so much a world-legend, as this mountain-summit looking over the waters of the Malian Gulf. As generation after generation came to the struggle with plagues against which there arose no new deliverer, weary eyes must often have been turned to the height on which the first champion of men had won his late release from the steadfast malignity of fate; where, in the words of the Chorus foreboding the return of Philoctetes to Trachis, "the great warrior, wrapt in heavenly fire, drew near to all the gods." It is Sophocles in the "Trachiniæ" who has given the noblest and the most complete expression to this legend; showing Heracles, first, as the son of Zeus suffering for men and sharing their pain; then, towards the end of his torments, as already god-like in the clear knowledge of his Father's will and of his own coming change to perfect godhead.

One aspect of the poetry of Sophocles has now been noticed; the character of the treatment applied by him to those legends which supplied the chief material of Greek tragedy. It has been pointed out that the heroes of Æschylus are essentially superhuman; that the heroes of Euripides are essentially human, and often of a low human type; that the heroes of Sophocles are at once human and superhuman: human generically, by the expression of certain general human qualities; superhuman, partly by the very strength in which these qualities are portrayed, partly by the direct relation of the persons with supernatural powers. It has been seen further that these three styles of handling correspond with successive phases of contemporary belief; the tendency of Greek thought in the fifth century B.C. having been gradually to lower the ideal stature of the ancestral demigods.

But this change of feeling towards the myths is not the only change of which account has to be taken. The spirit of dramatic poetry was influenced, less directly, yet broadly, by the current of political change.

9

At the beginning of the fifth century B.C. Athens was a limited democracy; at the close of the century it was an absolute democracy. Three periods may be marked in the transition. The first includes the new growth of democracy at Athens, springing from the common effort against Persia— the reform of Aristeides and the reform of Pericles. Its net result was the formal maturing of the democracy by the removal of a few old limitations. The second period is one of rest. It covers those thirty years during which the recent abolition of conservative checks was compensated by the controlling power of Pericles, and there was "in name a democracy, but in fact government by the leading man." The third period, beginning at the death of Pericles, at last shows the mature democracy in its normal working. The platform for a leader of the people which Pericles had first set up remains; it is held by a series of men subservient to the people; and the result is the sovereignty of the ecclesia. Æschylus, Sophocles, and Euripides represent respectively the first, second, and third of these periods.

Æschylus, whose mind was heated to its highest glow by the common Greek effort against Persia and thenceforth kept the impress of that time, was through life democratic just so far as Athens was democratic at the end of the Persian Wars. On the one hand, he shared the sense of civic equality created by common labours and perils. On the other hand, he held to the old religion of Greece and Athens, to the family traditions bound up with it and to the constitutional forms consecrated by both. His greatest trilogy, the Oresteia, marks the end of the first period just defined; and its third play, the "Eumenides," is a symbol of his political creed. On the one hand, it exalts Theseus, peculiarly the hero of the democracy; on the other, it protests against the withdrawal of a moral censorship from the Areiopagus.

Euripides, in the last third of the century, is a democrat living under a democracy which disappointed his theory. His constant praise of the farmer-class is meaning; he liked them because they were the citizens who had least to do with the violence of the ecclesia. It was the sense of this violence—the hopeless bane, as he thought it, of the democracy—which hindered him from having a thorough interest in the public affairs of the city and from drawing any vigorous or continuous life for his poetry from that source. It was natural that he should have been one of the literary men who towards the end of the war emigrated from Athens to Macedonia. The strain of social criticism, often rather querulous, which runs through his plays gives them, in one respect, a tone strange to Attic tragedy. An Athenian dramatist at the festivals was a citizen addressing fellow-citizens; not only a religious but a certain political sympathy was supposed to exist between them, Æschylus and Sophocles, in their different ways, both make this political sympathy felt as part of their inspiration; Euripides has little or nothing of it. He shares the pride of his fellow-citizens in the historical or legendary glories of the city; as for the present, he is a critic standing apart.

More thoroughly than Æschylus in the first period or Euripides in the third, is Sophocles a representative poet in the second period of the century. The years from about 460 to about 430 B.C. have been called the Age of Pericles. The chief external characteristic of the time so called is plain enough. It was the age of the best Athenian culture; a moment for Greece such as the Florentine renaissance was for Europe; the age especially of sculpture, of architecture, and of the most perfect dramatic poetry. But is there any general intellectual characteristic, any distinctive idea, which can be recognized as common to all the various efforts of that age? The distinctive idea of the Periclean age seems to have been that of Pericles himself; the desire to reconcile progress with tradition. Pericles looked forward and backward: forward, to the development of knowledge and art; backward, to the past from which Athens had derived an inheritance of moral and religious law. He had the force both to make his own idea the ruling idea in all the intellectual activity of his age, and to give to his age the political rest demanded for this task of harmonizing the spiritual past and future of a people. Thucydides—a trustworthy witness for the leading thoughts if not for the words of Pericles—makes him dwell on the way in which two contrasted elements had come to be tempered in the life of Athens. After describing the intellectual tolerance, the flexibility and gladness of Athenian social life, Pericles goes on: "Thus genial in our private intercourse, in public things we are kept from lawlessness mainly by fear, obedient to the magistrates of the time and to the laws—especially to those laws which are set for the help of the wronged, *and to those unwritten laws of which the sanction is a tacit shame.*"

It is by this twofold characteristic—on the one hand, sympathy with progressive culture, on the other hand, reverence for immemorial, unwritten law—that Sophocles is the poet of the Periclean Age. There are two passages which, above all others in his plays, are expressive of these two feelings. One is a chorus in the "Antigone"; the other is a chorus in the "Œdipus Tyrannus." One celebrates the inventiveness of man; the other insists upon his need for purity.

In the "Antigone" the Chorus exalts the might of the gods by measuring against it those human faculties which it alone can overcome:—

"Wonders are many, but nothing is more wonderful than Man; that power which walks the whitening sea before the stormy south, making a path amid engulfing surges; and Earth, the eldest of the gods, the immortal, the unwearied, doth it wear, turning the soil with the race of horses as the ploughs go to and fro from year to year.

"And the careless tribe of birds, the nations of the angry beasts, the deep sea's ocean-brood he snares in the meshes of his woven wiles, he leads captive, man excellent in wit. He conquers by his arts the beast that walks in the wilds of the hills, he tames the horse with shaggy mane, he puts its yoke on its neck, he tames the stubborn mountain-bull.

"And speech, and wind-swift thought, and all the moods that mould a state hath he taught himself; and how to flee the shafts of frost beneath the clear, unsheltering sky, and the arrows of the stormy rain.

"All-providing is he; unprovided he meets nothing that must come. Only from death shall he not win deliverance; yet from hard sicknesses hath he devised escapes.

"Cunning beyond fancy's dreams is that resourceful skill which brings him now to evil, anon to good. When he honours the laws of the land, proudly stands his city: no city hath he who in his rashness harbours sin. Never may he share my hearth, never think my thoughts, who doth these things!"

In the "Œdipus Tyrannus" the Chorus is indirectly commenting on the scorn for oracles just expressed by Iocastê:—

"Mine be the lot to win a reverent purity in all words and deeds sanctioned by those laws of sublime range, brought forth in the wide, clear sky, whose birth is of

11

Olympus alone; which no brood of mortal men begat; which forgetfulness shall never lay to sleep. Strong in these is the god, and grows not old.

"Insolence breeds the tyrant; Insolence, once blindly gorged with plenty, with things which are not fit or good, when it hath scaled the crowning height leaps on the abyss of doom, where it is served not by the service of the foot. But that rivalry which is good for the state I pray that the god may never quell: the god ever will I hold my champion.

"But whoso walks haughtily in deed or word, unterrified by Justice, revering not the shrines of gods, may an evil doom take him for his miserable pride, if he will not gain his gains fairly, if he will not keep himself from impieties, but must lay wanton hands on things inviolable.

"In such case, what man can boast any more that he shall ward the arrows of anger from his life? Nay, if such deeds are honoured, what have I more to do with dance and song?

"No more will I go, a worshipper, to the awful altar at Earth's centre, no more to Abæ's shrine or to Olympia, if these oracles fit not the issue so that all men shall point at them with the finger. Nay, King—if thou art rightly called—Zeus, all-ruling, let it not escape thee and thy deathless power!"

We have now looked at a second general aspect of the poetry of Sophocles. As in his treatment of the heroic legends he interprets, but is above, the religious spirit of his age, so in his reconciliation of enterprise and reverence he gives an ideal embodiment to the social spirit of his age.

Æschylus is a democratic conservative; Euripides is the critic of a democracy which he found good in theory but practically vicious; Sophocles sets upon his work no properly political stamp, but rather the mark of a time of political rest and of manifold intellectual activity; an activity which took its special character from the idea of an elastic development reconciled with a restraining moral tradition.

As the general spirit of Sophocles is perhaps best seen in these two phases, so among the special qualities of his work there are two which may be taken as the most distinctive—his "irony," to give it the name which Bishop Thirlwall's Essay has made familiar; and his delineation of character.

The practical irony of drama depends on the principle that the dramatic poet stands aloof from the world which he creates. It is not for him to be an advocate or a partisan. He describes a contest of forces, and decides the issue as he conceives that it would be decided by the powers which control human life. The position of a judge in reference to two litigants, neither of whom has absolute right on his side, is analogous to the position of a dramatic poet in reference to his characters. Every dramatic poet is necessarily in some degree ironical. In speaking, then, of the dramatic irony of Sophocles it is not meant that this quality is peculiar to him. It is only meant that in him this quality is especially noticeable and especially artistic.

Irony depends on a contrast; the irony of tragedy depends mainly on a contrast between the beliefs or purposes of men and those issues to which their actions are overruled by higher powers. Sophocles has the art of making this contrast, throughout the whole course of a drama, peculiarly suggestive and forcible. In his seven extant plays, the contrasts thus worked out have different degrees of complexity. The "Trachiniæ" and "Electra" may be taken as those in which the dramatic irony is simplest. In the "Trachiniæ" there is a twofold contrast of a direct kind: first, between the love of Deianeira for Heracles and the mortal agony into which she unwittingly throws him; then, between the meaning of the oracle (promising rest to Heracles), as understood by him and Deianeira, and its real import. In the "Electra" there is a particular and a general contrast, both direct; the sister is mourning the supposed death of her brother at the very moment when he is about to enter the house as an avenger; and the situation with which the play ends is the exact reversal of that with which it opened.

The "Ajax" and the two Œdipus plays, again, might be classed together in respect of dramatic irony; in each case suffering is inflicted by the gods, but through this the sufferer passes to a higher state. Athene, the pretended ally of Ajax, humbles him even to death; but this death is a complete atonement, and his immortal fame as a canonized hero begins from the burial with which the drama closes. In the "Œdipus Tyrannus" the primary contrast is between the seeming prosperity and the really miserable situation of the king. A secondary contrast runs through the whole process of inquiry which leads up to the final discovery. The truth is gradually evolved from those very incidents which display or even exalt the confidence of Œdipus. In the "Œdipus at Colonus" this contrast is reversed. The Theban king is old, blind, poor, an outcast, a wanderer. But he has the inward sense of a strength which can no more be broken; of a vision clearer than that of the bodily eye; of a spiritual change which has made a sorrow a possession; of approach to final rest.

It is, however, in the two remaining plays, the "Antigone" and the "Philoctetes," that this irony of drama takes its most subtle and most artistic form. Antigone buries Polyneices against the law of the land; Creon dooms her to death, and thereby drives his own son to suicide. But the issue is not a simple conflict between state-law and religious duty. It is a conflict between state-law too harshly enforced and natural affection set above the laws. Creon is right in the letter and wrong in the spirit; Antigone is right in the spirit and wrong in the letter. Creon carries his point, but his victory becomes his misery; Antigone incurs death, but dies with her work done. In the "Philoctetes," again, there is an antithesis of a like kind. Philoctetes is injured and noble; Odysseus is dishonest but patriotic. Odysseus wishes to capture Philoctetes in the public interests of the army at Troy. He urges on Neoptolemus that the end sanctifies the means. Neoptolemus at first recoils; then consents; finally deserts the plot in a passion of generous pity for Philoctetes. The result is that Philoctetes is brought back to Troy, but by fair means. He eventually agrees to do that of which he had loathed the thought, and goes back to his hated enemies under circumstances which make that return the happiest event of his life. Odysseus, on the other hand, gains his end; but not by the means which he had proposed to himself. He carries Philoctetes back to Troy; but only after his stratagems have been foiled. Neoptolemus, meanwhile—true, after his first lapse, to honour—conquers without a change of front.

It is that same instinct of harmony which has already been seen to rule the work of Sophocles in its largest phases, which gives its motive and its delicate precision to his management of dramatic irony. He works out the contrasts of drama so clearly and with such fineness because he aims at showing how a beneficent power at last solves them; not, as in Æschylus, by victory over a supernatural evil power, nor, as in Euripides, by abrupt intervention; but through those natural workings of human character and action over which the gods watch.

13

The accurate delineation of human character has therefore a special importance for Sophocles. It has already been said that in the primary or heroic persons of the Sophoclean drama human character is delineated only broadly, with a deliberate avoidance of fine shading. It is therefore in the secondary or subordinate persons of the drama that we must look for the more delicate touches of ethical portraiture.

Sophocles shows his psychological skill especially in two ways: in following the process by which a sensitive and generous nature passes from one phase of feeling to another; and in tracing the action upon each other of dissimilar or opposite natures. Philoctetes, first rejoiced by the arrival of the Greeks on his island,—then suspicious,—then reassured,—then frenzied with anger,—then finally conciliated; Tecmessa, agitated successively by fear, by hope, by despair concerning Ajax; Electra, at first heroically patient in the hope that her brother will return as an avenger, then broken-hearted at the news of his death, at last filled with rapture by his sudden living presence; Deianeira, by turns anxious, elated, jealous, horror-stricken—these are examples of the power with which Sophocles could trace a chapter of spiritual history.

A closer examination of the character of Deianeira will help to set this power in a clearer light. When the herald Lichas arrives at Trachis with the prisoners taken by Heracles at Œchalia, Iolê, beautiful and dejected, at once arouses the interest of Deianeira; but it is the interest of compassion merely, with a touch of condescension in its kindness. "Ah, unhappy girl, who art thou among women...?" "Lichas, from whom is this stranger sprung?" Lichas does not know; Iolê will not speak;—nor has she spoken, adds the herald, since they left Eubœa. So Deianeira says: "Then let her be left at peace and go into the house as best it pleases her, and not find a new pain at my hands beside her present ills; they are enough. And now let us all move towards the house."

Presently Deianeira is told by a man of Trachis, who had heard it from Lichas himself in the marketplace, that Iolê is the daughter of Eurytus, King of Œchalia; and that it was to win Iolê that Heracles had stormed and sacked that town. "Ah me unhappy," she cries, "in what a plight do I stand! What hidden bane have I taken under my roof?" Her informant and Lichas are confronted with each other; Lichas is put to confusion; and then Deianeira turns to him with this appeal:—

"Do not, I pray thee by Zeus who sends forth his lightnings over the high Œtean glen, do not use deceitful speech. For thou wilt tell thy news not to a base woman, nor to one who knows not the estate of men, and how it is not in their nature always to take joy in the same things. Now whosoever stands up against Love, as a boxer to change buffets, is not wise. For Love rules the gods as he will, and me also—why should he not?—yes, and many another such as I. So that I am quite mad if I blame my husband for being taken with this malady, or blame this woman, who has had part in a thing nowise shameful, and not in any wrong to me....Come, tell the whole truth; it is a foul blight on a free man to be called a liar."

Lichas confesses all, and ends with this advice—"For both your sakes, for his and for thine own as well, bear with the woman;" and Deianeira pretends to have adopted his counsel: "Nay," she says, "even thus am I minded to do. Believe me, I will not bring on myself a self-sought bane by waging fruitless war with the gods."

But how different is the feeling which she presently avows to the chorus of Trachinian maidens: "Of anger against the man I have no thought; but to live in the same house with this girl—what woman could bear it?" Then she remembers the love-charm given her long ago by Nessus. There is a moment of feverish hope while she is preparing and despatching the robe for Heracles. But hardly has it gone when an accident reveals to her that she has anointed the robe with some poison of fearful virulence. In a moment, her thoughts rush forward to the worst; and her own words, in telling the story to the Chorus, foreshow the death to which she presently gives herself on hearing the tidings from Eubœa—"Life with a bad name must not be borne by her who glories to have been born not base."

The second special form in which Sophocles shows his power of drawing character consists in exhibiting the action upon each other of natures broadly or at least distinctly different. He loved to display this mutual action in an interview at which the two speakers exchange arguments. The sisters Electra and Chrysothemis, the sisters Antigone and Ismene, hold conversations of this kind. It might be objected that in these cases the influence can scarcely be called mutual; and that, while Electra makes Chrysothemis angry and Antigone makes Ismene feel ashamed, Chrysothemis produces no impression upon Electra nor Ismene upon Antigone. But it should be observed that in each case the weak sister had this important influence upon the strong sister;—she made her feel alone. The selfishness of Chrysothemis isolates Electra in the task of avenging their father, as the feminine timidity of Ismene isolates Antigone in the task of burying their brother. In each case, the heroine agitates the less courageous sister, and on the other hand the defection of a natural ally braces the heroine.

But the finest examples of such juxtaposition are to be found in the "Philoctetes": a tragedy which for artistic finish has often, and perhaps justly been ranked as its author's masterpiece; and in which the absence of much incident permitted or exacted the utmost exercise of skill in delineating character. From many good passages in the play one may be chosen as a specimen—the opening scene between Odysseus and Neoptolemus. Odysseus, holding that the public interest of the army at Troy justifies recourse to fraud, proposes to take Philoctetes by a stratagem. Neoptolemus, a young and generous man, is at first shocked; but Odysseus succeeds in making ambition conquer the sense of honour. The dialogue itself alone can give an idea of the fineness with which this is managed:—

"*Neoptolemus.* What wouldst thou?

Odysseus. The mind of Philoctetes must be snared by thee with a well-told tale. When he asks thee who and whence thou art, say—'The son of Achilles,'—*that* must not be garbled; but thou art homeward bound, having quitted the Greek armada, and conceived for them a deadly hatred....The thing to be plotted is just this—how thou mayest compass to *steal* the unconquerable arms. I well know, my son, that by nature thou art unapt to utter or to frame such wiles. Yet victory, we know, is a sweet prize to win. Take heart: our honesty shall be proved another time. But now lend thyself to me for one little roguish day; and then, for all the rest of thy days, be called the most virtuous of men.

N. Son of Laertes, whatever counsels pain my ear, to the same I abhor to lend my hand. It is not in my nature to compass aught by knavery—neither in mine nor, as they say, in my father's. I am ready to take the man by force, not by fraud; with the use of only one foot he will never worst all of us in open fight. And yet, having

15

been sent to aid thee, I am loth to be called traitor. But I wish, Prince, to miss my mark by doing right rather than to win by baseness.

O. Son of a gallant sire, time was when I, too, in my youth had a slow tongue and an active hand. But now, when I come out to the proof, I see that words, not deeds, always come to the front with men.

N. In short, what dost thou bid me but to lie?

O. I bid thee take Philoctetes by guile.

N. And why by guile more than by persuasion?

O. He will never be persuaded; and by force thou art not likely to take him.

N. Hath he a strength so defiant, so dreadful?

O. Arrows inevitable and winging death.

N. One cannot dare, then, even to go near *him*?

O. No, unless thou snare him, as I bid.

N. So thou thinkest it no shame to lie?

O. None, if the lie is fraught with health.

N. And how shall a man have the face to utter it?

O. When thou dost aught for gain, it is unmeet to shrink.

N. And what gain for me is his coming to Troy?

O. Troy can be taken by these arrows alone.

N. Then *I* am not, as ye said, to be the captor?

O. Not thou apart from these, nor these from thee.

N. It seems, then, they must be won, if so it stands?

O. I tell thee by this deed thou shalt gain two gifts.

N. What are they? If I knew, I would not shrink.

O. Thou wilt be known as wise and brave.

N. Enough; I'll do it, and put away all shame."

I have attempted to show what is distinctive of the genius of Sophocles in a fourfold manifestation: in his blending of a divine with a human character in the heroes; in his expression of the effort to reconcile progress with tradition; in his dramatic irony—that is, in the precision with which he brings out contrasts, especially between the purposes of men and of the gods, in order that the final solution may be more impressive; lastly, in his portrayal of character—not in a series of situations, but continuously through chapters of spiritual history. It has been seen that the instinct which rules his work under each of these aspects is what may be called in the largest sense the instinct of harmony. His imagination has a tranquil mastery of the twofold realm of Tragedy—the natural and the supernatural—and tempers the conflicting elements of each or both with a sure sense of fitness and just proportion.

It is for this reason—because of all the Greek poets he is the most perfectly an artist—that his poetry has a closer significance than any other for that form of plastic art which stands nearest to drama. It is the best interpreter of those pieces of Greek sculpture, such as the groups of Niobe and Laocoon, which express a moment of conflict between human and superhuman force. It has been said that for the Greeks beauty was the index on the balance of expression—that is, a central control governing the equipoise between terror and pity. The terror inspired by Niobe and by Laocoon, accusing with upturned eyes the destroying power; the pity inspired by their children, clinging to the shelter which cannot protect them: these are harmonized by the beauty, at once terrible and tender, of the whole. Just such is the harmony between the human and superhuman elements in the agony of Œdipus and of Heracles.

Again, it is chiefly because Sophocles had supremely this most Greek of instincts, the instinct of just proportion, that his mind was so perfectly attempered to the genius of Greek polytheism—a religion of which the piety was a reverent sense of beauty and of measure. He lived just when this religion had shed upon it the greatest strength of intellectual light which it could bear without fading; he is, perhaps, the highest type of its votary—the man for whom, more than for any other who could be named, the old national religion of Greece was a self-sufficing, thoughtful, and ennobling faith. Sophocles was, indeed, the perfect Greek ideal of a man who loved the gods and was loved by them—one, the work of whose life was their service under their direct inspiration; to whom they gave victory not followed by insolence, long years and opportuneness of death; and whom the most imaginative of satirists could not imagine, even among the boundless rivalries of the dead, less good-humoured than he had been upon earth.

OEDIPUS THE KING

PERSONS OF THE DRAMA.

Oedipus, King of Thebes.
Priest of Zeus.
Creon, *brother of Iocasta.*
Teiresias, *the blind prophet.*
Iocasta.
First Messenger, *a shepherd from Corinth.*
A Shepherd, *formerly in the service of Laius.*
Second Messenger, *from the house.*
Chorus of Theban Elders.

MUTE PERSONS.

A train of Suppliants (old men, youths, and children). The children Antigone and Ismene, daughters of Oedipus and Iocasta.

Scene: Before the Royal Palace at Thebes.

Laius, son of Labdacus, King of Thebes, had been told at Delphi by the oracle that a son would be born to him who should slay him. When his wife Iocasta bore a son, the babe was given by its mother to a Theban shepherd, to expose on Mount Cithaeron. This man, in pity, gave it to a Corinthian shepherd whom he met in the hills, who took it to Corinth; and there the child was brought up as the son of King Polybus and his wife Merope.

Years went by. Once at a feast the young Oedipus was taunted with not being really the son of Polybus. He went to ask the oracle at Delphi; and was told that it was his destiny to slay his father and to wed his mother. He resolved never to go near Corinth again, and took the road leading eastwards into Boeotia. On his way he met Laius, King of Thebes, at the 'Branching Roads' in Phocis, without knowing who he was. A quarrel occurred: Oedipus slew Laius, and three of his four attendants. The fourth, who escaped, was the Theban shepherd who in old days had received the infant from Iocasta.

Oedipus continued his journey, and reached Thebes at the time when it was being plagued by the Sphinx. He guessed the monster's riddle, and the Sphinx hurled herself from a rock. Oedipus was made King of Thebes, and married Iocasta. Soon afterwards the shepherd sought an audience of the Queen, and earnestly prayed that he might be sent to tend flocks in certain distant pastures. She readily granted the boon; it was a small thing for an old and faithful servant to ask.

About sixteen years have passed since then, and Iocasta has borne two sons and two daughters to Oedipus.

But now a great calamity has visited Thebes: there is a blight on the fruits of the earth; a pestilence is desolating the city. While offerings are made at the altars, a band of suppliants, old and young, is led by the Priest of Zeus into the presence of the wise King. He, if any mortal, can help them.

OEDIPUS.

My children, latest-born to Cadmus who was of old, why are ye set before me thus with wreathed branches of suppliants, while the city reeks with incense, rings with prayers for health and cries of woe? I deemed it unmeet, my children, to hear these things at the mouth of others, and have come hither myself, I, Oedipus renowned of all.

Tell me, then, thou venerable man—since it is thy natural part to speak for these—in what mood are ye placed here, with what dread or what desire? Be sure that I would gladly give all aid; hard of heart were I, did I not pity such suppliants as these.

PRIEST OF ZEUS.

Nay, Oedipus, ruler of my land, thou seest of what years we are who beset thy altars,—some, nestlings still too tender for far flights,—some, bowed with age, priests, as I of Zeus,—and these, the chosen youth; while the rest of the folk sit with wreathed branches in the market-places, and before the two shrines of Pallas, and where Ismenus gives answer by fire.

For the city, as thou thyself seest, is now too sorely vexed, and can no more lift her head from beneath the angry waves of death; a blight is on her in the fruitful blossoms of the land, in the herds among the pastures, in the barren pangs of women; and withal the flaming god, the malign plague, hath swooped on us, and ravages the town; by whom the house of Cadmus is made waste, but dark Hades rich in groans and tears.

It is not as deeming thee ranked with gods that I and these children are suppliants at thy hearth, but as deeming thee first of men, both in life's common chances, and when mortals have to do with more than man: seeing that thou camest to the town of Cadmus, and didst quit us of the tax that we rendered to the hard songstress; and this, though thou knewest nothing from us that could avail thee, nor hadst been schooled; no, by a god's aid, 'tis said and believed, didst thou uplift our life.

And now, Oedipus, king glorious in all eyes, we beseech thee, all we suppliants, to find for us some succour, whether by the whisper of a god thou knowest it, or haply as in the power of man; for I see that, when men have been proved in deeds past, the issues of their counsels, too, most often have effect.

On, best of mortals, again uplift our State! On, guard thy fame,—since now this land calls thee saviour for thy former zeal; and never be it our memory of thy reign that we were first restored and afterward cast down: nay, lift up this State in such wise that it fall no more!

With good omen didst thou give us that past happiness; now also show thyself the same. For if thou art to rule this land, even as thou art now its lord, 'tis better to be lord of men than of a waste: since neither walled town nor ship is anything, if it is void and no men dwell with thee therein.

Oe. Oh my piteous children, known, well known to me are the desires wherewith ye have come: well wot I that ye suffer all; yet, sufferers as ye are, there is not one of you whose suffering is as mine. Your pain comes on each one of you for himself alone, and for no other; but my soul mourns at once for the city, and for myself, and for thee.

So that ye rouse me not, truly, as one sunk in sleep: no, be sure that I have wept full many tears, gone many ways in wanderings of thought. And the sole remedy which, well pondering, I could find, this I have put into act. I have sent the son of Menoeceus, Creon, mine own wife's brother, to the Pythian house of Phoebus, to learn by what deed or word I might deliver this town. And already, when the lapse of days is reckoned, it troubles me what he doth; for he tarries strangely, beyond the fitting space. But when he comes, then shall I be no true man if I do not all that the god shows.

Pr. Nay, in season hast thou spoken; at this moment these sign to me that Creon draws near.

Oe. O king Apollo, may he come to us in the brightness of saving fortune, even as his face is bright!

Pr. Nay, to all seeming, he brings comfort; else would he not be coming crowned thus thickly with berry-laden bay.

Oe. We shall know soon: he is at range to hear.—Prince, my kinsman, son of Menoeceus, what news hast thou brought us from the god?

CREON.

Good news: I tell thee that even troubles hard to bear,—if haply they find the right issue,—will end in perfect peace.

Oe. But what is the oracle? So far, thy words make me neither bold nor yet afraid.

Cr. If thou wouldest hear while these are nigh, I am ready to speak; or else to go within.

Oe. Speak before all: the sorrow which I bear is for these more than for mine own life.

Cr. With thy leave, I will tell what I heard from the god. Phoebus our lord bids us plainly to drive out a defiling thing, which (he saith) hath been harboured in this land, and not to harbour it, so that it cannot be healed.

Oe. By what rite shall we cleanse us? What is the manner of the misfortune?

Cr. By banishing a man, or by bloodshed in quittance of bloodshed, since it is that blood which brings the tempest on our city.

Oe. And who is the man whose fate he thus reveals?

Cr. Laïus, king, was lord of our land before thou wast pilot of this State.

Oe. I know it well—by hearsay, for I saw him never.

Cr. He was slain; and the god now bids us plainly to wreak vengeance on his murderers—whosoever they be.

Oe. And where are they upon the earth? Where shall the dim track of this old crime be found?

Cr. In this land,—said the god. What is sought for can be caught; only that which is not watched escapes.

Oe. And was it in the house, or in the field, or on strange soil that Laïus met this bloody end?

Cr. 'Twas on a visit to Delphi, as he said, that he had left our land; and he came home no more, after he had once set forth.

Oe. And was there none to tell? Was there no comrade of his journey who saw the deed, from whom tidings might have been gained, and used?

Cr. All perished, save one who fled in fear, and could tell for certain but one thing of all that he saw.

Oe. And what was that? One thing might show the clue to many, could we get but a small beginning for hope.

Cr. He said that robbers met and fell on them, not in one man's might, but with full many hands.

Oe. How, then, unless there was some trafficking in bribes from here, should the robber have dared thus far?

Cr. Such things were surmised; but, Laïus once slain, amid our troubles no avenger arose.

Oe. But, when royalty had fallen thus, what trouble in your path can have hindered a full search?

Cr. The riddling Sphinx had made us let dark things go, and was inviting us to think of what lay at our doors.

Oe. Nay, I will start afresh, and once more make dark things plain. Right worthily hath Phoebus, and worthily hast thou, bestowed this care on the cause of the dead; and so, as is meet, ye shall find me too leagued with you in seeking vengeance for this land, and for the god besides. On behalf of no far-off friend, no, but in mine own cause, shall I dispel this taint. For whoever was the slayer of Laïus might wish to take vengeance on me also with a hand as fierce. Therefore, in doing right to Laïus, I serve myself.

Come, haste ye, my children, rise from the altarsteps, and lift these suppliant boughs; and let some other summon hither the folk of Cadmus, warned that I mean to leave nought untried; for our health (with the god's help) shall be made certain— or our ruin.

Pr. My children, let us rise; we came at first to seek what this man promises of himself. And may Phoebus, who sent these oracles, come to us therewith, our saviour and deliverer from the pest.

CHORUS.

str. 1.O sweetly-speaking message of Zeus, in what spirit hast thou come from golden Pytho unto glorious Thebes? I am on the rack, terror shakes my soul, O thou Delian healer to whom wild cries rise, in holy fear of thee, what thing thou wilt work for me, perchance unknown before, perchance renewed with the revolving years: tell me, thou immortal Voice, born of Golden Hope!

ant. 1.First call I on thee, daughter of Zeus, divine Athena, and on thy sister, guardian of our land, Artemis, who sits on her throne of fame, above the circle of our Agora, and on Phoebus the far-darter: O shine forth on me, my three-fold help against death! If ever aforetime, in arrest of ruin hurrying on the city, ye drove a fiery pest beyond our borders, come now also!

str. 2.Woe is me, countless are the sorrows that I bear; a plague is on all our host, and thought can find no weapon for defence. The fruits of the glorious earth grow not; by no birth of children do women surmount the pangs in which they shriek; and life on life mayest thou see sped, like bird on nimble wing, aye, swifter than resistless fire, to the shore of the western god.

ant. 2.By such deaths, past numbering, the city perishes: unpitied, her children lie on the ground, spreading pestilence, with none to mourn: and meanwhile young wives, and gray-haired mothers with them, uplift a wail at the steps of the altars, some here, some there, entreating for their weary woes. The prayer to the Healer rings clear, and, blent therewith, the voice of lamentation: for these things, golden daughter of Zeus, send us the bright face of comfort.

str. 3.And grant that the fierce god of death, who now with no brazen shields, yet amid cries as of battle, wraps me in the flame of his onset, may turn his back in speedy flight from our land, borne by a fair wind to the great deep of Amphitritè, or to those waters in which none find haven, even to the Thracian wave; for if night leave aught undone, day follows to accomplish this. O thou who wieldest the powers of the fire-fraught lightning, O Zeus our father, slay him beneath thy thunderbolt!

ant. 3.Lycean King, fain were I that thy shafts also, from thy bent bow's string of woven gold, should go abroad in their might, our champions in the face of the foe; yea, and the flashing fires of Artemis wherewith she glances through the Lycian hills. And I call him whose locks are bound with gold, who is named with the name of this land, ruddy Bacchus to whom Bacchants cry, the comrade of the Maenads, to draw near with the blaze of his blithe torch, our ally against the god unhonoured among gods.

Oe. Thou prayest: and in answer to thy prayer,—if thou wilt give a loyal welcome to my words and minister to thine own disease,—thou mayest hope to find succour and relief from woes. These words will I speak publicly, as one who has been a stranger to this report, a stranger to the deed; for I should not be far on the track, if I were tracing it alone, without a clue. But as it is,—since it was only after the time of the deed that I was numbered a Theban among Thebans,—to you, the Cadmeans all, I do thus proclaim.

Whosoever of you knows by whom Laius son of Labdacus was slain, I bid him to declare all to me. And if he is afraid, I tell him to remove the danger of the charge from his path by denouncing himself; for he shall suffer nothing else unlovely, but only leave the land, unhurt. Or if any one knows an alien, from another land, as the assassin, let him not keep silence; for I will pay his guerdon, and my thanks shall rest with him besides.

But if ye keep silence—if any one, through fear, shall seek to screen friend or self from my behest—hear ye what I then shall do. I charge you that no one of this land, whereof I hold the empire and the throne, give shelter or speak word unto that murderer, whosoever he be,—make him partner of his prayer or sacrifice, or serve him with the lustral rite; but that all ban him their homes, knowing that *this* is our defiling thing, as the oracle of the Pythian god hath newly shown me. I then am on this wise the ally of the god and of the slain. And I pray solemnly that the slayer, whoso he be, whether his hidden guilt is lonely or hath partners, evilly, as he is evil, may wear out his unblest life. And for myself I pray that if, with my privity, he should become an inmate of my house, I may suffer the same things which even now I called down upon others. And on you I lay it to make all these words good, for my sake, and for the sake of the god, and for our land's, thus blasted with barrenness by angry heaven.

For even if the matter had not been urged on us by a god, it was not meet that ye should leave the guilt thus unpurged, when one so noble, and he your king, had perished; rather were ye bound to search it out. And now, since 'tis I who hold the powers which once he held, who possess his bed and the wife who bare seed to him; and since, had his hope of issue not been frustrate, children born of one mother would have made ties betwixt him and me—but, as it was, fate swooped upon his head; by reason of these things will I uphold this cause, even as the cause of mine own sire, and will leave nought untried in seeking to find him whose hand shed that blood, for the honour of the son of Labdacus and of Polydorus and elder Cadmus and Agenor who was of old.

And for those who obey me not, I pray that the gods send them neither harvest of the earth nor fruit of the womb, but that they be wasted by their lot that now is, or by one yet more dire. But for all you, the loyal folk of Cadmus to whom these things seem good, may Justice, our ally, and all the gods be with you graciously for ever.

Ch. As thou hast put me on my oath, on my oath, O king, I will speak. I am not the slayer, nor can I point to him who slew. As for the question, it was for Phoebus, who sent it, to tell us this thing—who can have wrought the deed.

Oe. Justly said; but no man on the earth can force the gods to what they will not.

Ch. I would fain say what seems to me next best after this.

Oe. If there is yet a third course, spare not to show it.

Ch. I know that our lord Teiresias is the seer most like to our lord Phoebus; from whom, O king, a searcher of these things might learn them most clearly.

Oe. Not even this have I left out of my cares. On the hint of Creon, I have twice sent a man to bring him; and this long while I marvel why he is not here.

Ch. Indeed (his skill apart) the rumours are but faint and old.

Oe. What rumours are they? I look to every story.

Ch. Certain wayfarers were said to have killed him.

Oe. I, too, have heard it, but none sees him who saw it.

Ch. Nay, if he knows what fear is, he will not stay when he hears thy curses, so dire as they are.

Oe. When a man shrinks not from a deed, neither is he scared by a word.

Ch. But there is one to convict him. For here they bring at last the godlike prophet, in whom alone of men doth live the truth.

Enter Teiresias, *led by a Boy.*

Oe. Teiresias, whose soul grasps all things, the lore that may be told and the unspeakable, the secrets of heaven and the low things of earth,—thou feelest, though thou canst not see, what a plague doth haunt our State,—from which, great prophet, we find in thee our protector and only saviour. Now, Phoebus—if indeed thou knowest it not from the messengers—sent answer to our question that the only riddance from this pest which could come was if we should learn aright the slayers of Laïus, and slay them, or send them into exile from our land. Do thou, then, grudge neither voice of birds nor any other way of seer-lore that thou hast, but rescue thyself and the State, rescue me, rescue all that is defiled by the dead. For we are in thy hand; and man's noblest task is to help others by his best means and powers.

TEIRESIAS.

Alas, how dreadful to have wisdom where it profits not the wise! Aye, I knew this well, but let it slip out of mind; else would I never have come here.

Oe. What now? How sad thou hast come in!

Te. Let me go home; most easily wilt thou bear thine own burden to the end, and I mine, if thou wilt consent.

Oe. Thy words are strange, nor kindly to this State which nurtured thee, when thou withholdest this response.

Te. Nay, I see that thou, on thy part, openest not thy lips in season: therefore I speak not, that neither may I have thy mishap.

Oe. For the love of the gods, turn not away, if thou hast knowledge: all we suppliants implore thee on our knees.

Te. Aye, for ye are all without knowledge; but never will I reveal my griefs—that I say not thine.

Oe. How sayest thou? Thou knowest the secret, and wilt not tell it, but art minded to betray us and to destroy the State?

Te. I will pain neither myself nor thee. Why vainly ask these things? Thou wilt not learn them from me.

Oe. What, basest of the base,—for thou wouldest anger a very stone,—wilt thou never speak out? Can nothing touch thee? Wilt thou never make an end?

Te. Thou blamest my temper, but seest not that to which thou thyself art wedded: no, thou findest fault with me.

Oe. And who would not be angry to hear the words with which thou now dost slight this city?

Te. The future will come of itself, though I shroud it in silence.

Oe. Then, seeing that it must come, thou on thy part shouldst tell me thereof.

Te. I will speak no further; rage, then, if thou wilt, with the fiercest wrath thy heart doth know.

Oe. Aye, verily, I will not spare—so wroth I am—to speak all my thought. Know that thou seemest to me e'en to have helped in plotting the deed, and to have done it, short of slaying with thy hands. Hadst thou eyesight, I would have said that the doing, also, of this thing was thine alone.

Te. In sooth?—I charge thee that thou abide by the decree of thine own mouth, and from this day speak neither to these nor to me: *thou* art the accursed defiler of this land.

Oe. So brazen with thy blustering taunt? And wherein dost thou trust to escape thy due?

Te. I have escaped: in my truth is my strength.

Oe. Who taught thee this? It was not, at least, thine art.

Te. Thou: for thou didst spur me into speech against my will.

Oe. What speech? Speak again that I may learn it better.

Te. Didst thou not take my sense before? Or art thou tempting me in talk?

Oe. No, I took it not so that I can call it known:—speak again.

Te. I say that thou art the slayer of the man whose slayer thou seekest.

Oe. Now thou shalt rue that thou hast twice said words so dire.

Te. Wouldst thou have me say more, that thou mayest be more wroth?

Oe. What thou wilt; it will be said in vain.

Te. I say that thou hast been living in unguessed shame with thy nearest kin, and seest not to what woe thou hast come.

Oe. Dost thou indeed think that thou shalt always speak thus without smarting?

Te. Yes, if there is any strength in truth.

Oe. Nay, there is,—for all save thee; for thee that strength is not, since thou art maimed in ear, and in wit, and in eye.

Te. Aye, and thou art a poor wretch to utter taunts which every man here will soon hurl at thee.

Oe. Night, endless night hath thee in her keeping, so that thou canst never hurt me, or any man who sees the sun.

Te. No, thy doom is not to fall by *me:* Apollo is enough, whose care it is to work that out.

Oe. Are these Creon's devices, or thine?

Te. Nay, Creon is no plague to thee; thou art thine own.

Oe. O wealth, and empire, and skill surpassing skill in life's keen rivalries, how great is the envy that cleaves to you, if for the sake, yea, of this power which the city hath put into my hands, a gift unsought, Creon the trusty, Creon mine old friend, hath crept on me by stealth, yearning to thrust me out of it, and hath suborned such a scheming juggler as this, a tricky quack, who hath eyes only for his gains, but in his art is blind!

Come, now, tell me, where hast thou proved thyself a seer? Why, when the Watcher was here who wove dark song, didst thou say nothing that could free this folk? Yet the riddle, at least, was not for the first comer to read; there was need of a seer's skill; and none such thou wast found to have, either by help of birds, or as known from any god: no, I came, I, Oedipus the ignorant, and made her mute, when I had seized the answer by my wit, untaught of birds. And it is I whom thou art trying to oust, thinking to stand close to Creon's throne. Methinks thou and the plotter of these things will rue your zeal to purge the land. Nay, didst thou not seem to be an old man, thou shouldst have learned to thy cost how bold thou art.

Ch. To our thinking, both this man's words and thine, Oedipus, have been said in anger. Not for such words is our need, but to seek how we shall best discharge the mandates of the god.

Te. King though thou art, the right of reply, at least, must be deemed the same for both; of that I too am lord. Not to thee do I live servant, but to Loxias; and so I shall not stand enrolled under Creon for my patron. And I tell thee—since thou hast taunted me even with blindness—that thou hast sight, yet seest not in what misery thou art, nor where thou dwellest, nor with whom. Dost thou know of what stock thou art? And thou hast been an unwitting foe to thine own kin, in the shades, and on the earth above; and the double lash of thy mother's and thy father's curse shall one day drive thee from this land in dreadful haste, with darkness then on the eyes that now see true.

And what place shall not be harbour to thy shriek, what of all Cithaeron shall not ring with it soon, when thou hast learnt the meaning of the nuptials in which, within that house, thou didst find a fatal haven, after a voyage so fair? And a throng of other ills thou guessest not, which shall make thee level with thy true self and with thine own brood.

Therefore heap thy scorns on Creon and on my message: for no one among men shall ever be crushed more miserably than thou.

Oe. Are these taunts to be indeed borne from *him?*—Hence, ruin take thee! Hence, this instant! Back!—away!—avaunt thee from these doors!

Te. I had never come, not I, hadst thou not called me.

Oe. I knew not that thou wast about to speak folly, or it had been long ere I had sent for thee to my house.

Te. Such am I,—as thou thinkest, a fool; but for the parents who begat thee, sane.

Oe. What parents? Stay...and who of men is my sire?

Te. This day shall show thy birth and shall bring thy ruin.

Oe. What riddles, what dark words thou always speakest!

Te. Nay, art not thou most skilled to unravel dark speech?

Oe. Make that my reproach in which thou shalt find me great.

Te. Yet 'twas just that fortune that undid thee.

Oe. Nay, if I delivered this town, I care not.

Te. Then I will go: so do thou, boy, take me hence.

Oe. Aye, let him take thee: while here, thou art a hindrance, thou, a trouble: when thou hast vanished, thou wilt not vex me more.

Te. I will go when I have done mine errand, fearless of thy frown: for thou canst never destroy me. And I tell thee—the man of whom thou hast this long while been in quest, uttering threats, and proclaiming a search into the murder of Laïus—that man is here,—in seeming, an alien sojourner, but anon he shall be found a native Theban, and shall not be glad of his fortune. A blind man, he who now hath sight, a beggar, who now is rich, he shall make his way to a strange land, feeling the ground before him with his staff. And he shall be found at once brother and father of the children with whom he consorts; son and husband of the woman who bore him; heir to his father's bed, shedder of his father's blood.

So go thou in and think on that; and if thou find that I have been at fault, say thenceforth that I have no wit in prophecy.

[Teiresias *is led out by the Boy.*—Oedipus *enters the palace.*

CHORUS.

str. 1.Who is he of whom the divine voice from the Delphian rock hath spoken, as having wrought with red hands horrors that no tongue can tell?

It is time that he ply in flight a foot stronger than the feet of storm-swift steeds: for the son of Zeus is springing on him, all armed with fiery lightnings, and with him come the dread, unerring Fates.

ant. 1.Yea, newly given from snowy Parnassus, the message hath flashed forth to make all search for the unknown man. Into the wild wood's covert, among caves and rocks he is roaming, fierce as a bull, wretched and forlorn on his joyless path, still seeking to put from him the doom spoken at Earth's central shrine: but that doom ever lives, ever flits around him.

str. 2.Dreadly, in sooth, dreadly doth the wise augur move me, who approve not, nor am able to deny. How to speak, I know not; I am fluttered with forebodings; neither in the present have I clear vision, nor of the future. Never in past days, nor

26

in these, have I heard how the house of Labdacus or the son of Polybus had, either against other, any grief that I could bring as proof in assailing the public fame of Oedipus, and seeking to avenge the line of Labdacus for the undiscovered murder.

ant. 2.Nay, Zeus indeed and Apollo are keen of thought, and know the things of earth; but that mortal seer wins knowledge above mine, of this there can be no sure test; though man may surpass man in lore. Yet, until I see the word made good, never will I assent when men blame Oedipus. Before all eyes, the winged maiden came against him of old, and he was seen to be wise; he bore the test, in welcome service to our State; never, therefore, by the verdict of my heart shall he be adjudged guilty of crime.

CREON.

Fellow-citizens, having learned that Oedipus the king lays dire charges against me, I am here, indignant. If, in the present troubles, he thinks that he has suffered from *me*, by word or deed, aught that tends to harm, in truth I crave not my full term of years, when I must bear such blame as this. The wrong of this rumour touches me not in one point alone, but has the largest scope, if I am to be called a traitor in the city, a traitor too by thee and by my friends.

Ch. Nay, but this taunt came under stress, perchance, of anger, rather than from the purpose of the heart.

Cr. And the saying was uttered, that *my* counsels won the seer to utter his falsehoods?

Ch. Such things were said—I know not with what meaning.

Cr. And was this charge laid against me with steady eyes and steady mind?

Ch. I know not; I see not what my masters do: but here comes our lord forth from the house.

OEDIPUS.

Sirrah, how camest thou here? Hast thou a front so bold that thou hast come to my house, who art the proved assassin of its master,—the palpable robber of my crown? Come, tell me, in the name of the gods, was it cowardice or folly that thou sawest in me, that thou didst plot to do this thing? Didst thou think that I would not note this deed of thine creeping on me by stealth, or, aware, would not ward it off? Now is not thine attempt foolish,—to seek, without followers or friends, a throne,—a prize which followers and wealth must win?

Cr. Mark me now,—in answer to thy words, hear a fair reply, and then judge for thyself on knowledge.

Oe. Thou art apt in speech, but I have a poor wit for thy lessons, since I have found thee my malignant foe.

Cr. Now first hear how I will explain this very thing—

Oe. Explain me not one thing—that thou art not false.

Cr. If thou deemest that stubbornness without sense is a good gift, thou art not wise.

Oe. If thou deemest that thou canst wrong a kinsman and escape the penalty, thou art not sane.

Cr. Justly said, I grant thee: but tell me what is the wrong that thou sayest thou hast suffered from me.

Oe. Didst thou advise, or didst thou not, that I should send for that reverend seer?

Cr. And now I am still of the same mind.

Oe. How long is it, then, since Laïus—

Cr. Since Laïus... ? I take not thy drift...

Oe. —was swept from men's sight by a deadly violence?

Cr. The count of years would run far into the past.

Oe. Was this seer, then, of the craft in those days?

Cr. Yea, skilled as now, and in equal honour.

Oe. Made he, then, any mention of me at that time?

Cr. Never, certainly, when I was within hearing.

Oe. But held ye not a search touching the murder?

Cr. Due search we held, of course—and learned nothing.

Oe. And how was it that this sage did not tell his story *then*?

Cr. I know not; where I lack light, 'tis my wont to be silent.

Oe. Thus much, at least, thou knowest, and couldst declare with light enough.

Cr. What is that? If I know it, I will not deny.

Oe. That, if he had not conferred with thee, he would never have named *my* slaying of Laïus.

Cr. If so he speaks, thou best knowest; but I claim to learn from thee as much as thou hast now from me.

Oe. Learn thy fill: I shall never be found guilty of the blood.

Cr. Say, then—thou hast married my sister?

Oe. The question allows not of denial.

Cr. And thou rulest the land as she doth, with like sway?

Oe. She obtains from me all her desire.

Cr. And rank not I as a third peer of you twain?

Oe. Aye, 'tis just therein that thou art seen a false friend.

Cr. Not so, if thou wouldst reason with thine own heart as I with mine. And first weigh this,—whether thou thinkest that any one would choose to rule amid terrors rather than in unruffled peace,—granting that he is to have the same powers. Now I, for one, have no yearning in my nature to be a king rather than to do kingly deeds, no, nor hath any man who knows how to keep a sober mind. For now I win all boons from thee without fear; but, were I ruler myself, I should be doing much e'en against mine own pleasure.

How, then, could royalty be sweeter for me to have than painless rule and influence? Not yet am I so misguided as to desire other honours than those which profit. Now, all wish me joy; now, every man has a greeting for me; now, those who have a suit to thee crave speech with me, since therein is all their hope of success. Then why should I resign these things, and take those? No mind will become false, while it is wise. Nay, I am no lover of such policy, and, if another put it into deed, never could I bear to act with him.

And, in proof of this, first, go to Pytho, and ask if I brought thee true word of the oracle; then next, if thou find that I have planned aught in concert with the soothsayer, take and slay me, by the sentence not of one mouth, but of twain—by mine own, no less than thine. But make me not guilty in a corner, on unproved surmise. It is not right to adjudge bad men good at random, or good men bad. I count it a like thing for a man to cast off a true friend as to cast away the life in his own bosom, which most he loves. Nay, thou wilt learn these things with sureness in time, for time alone shows a just man; but thou couldst discern a knave even in one day.

Ch. Well hath he spoken, O king, for one who giveth heed not to fall: the quick in counsel are not sure.

Oe. When the stealthy plotter is moving on me in quick sort, I, too, must be quick with my counterplot. If I await him in repose, his ends will have been gained, and mine missed.

Cr. What wouldst thou, then? Cast me out of the land?

Oe. Not so: I desire thy death—not thy banishment—that thou mayest show forth what manner of thing is envy.

Cr. Thou speakest as resolved not to yield or to believe?

[Oe. No; for thou persuadest me not that thou art worthy of belief.]

Cr. No, for I find thee not sane. Oe. Sane, at least, in mine own interest.

Cr. Nay, thou shouldst be so in mine also. Oe. Nay, thou art false.

Cr. But if thou understandest nought? Oe. Yet must I rule.

Cr. Not if thou rule ill. Oe. Hear him, O Thebes!

Cr. Thebes is for me also—not for thee alone.

Ch. Cease, princes; and in good time for you I see Iocasta coming yonder from the house, with whose help ye should compose your present feud.

IOCASTA.

Misguided men, why have ye raised such foolish strife of tongues? Are ye not ashamed, while the land is thus sick, to stir up troubles of your own? Come, go thou into the house,—and thou, Creon, to thy home,—and forbear to make much of a petty grief.

Cr. Kinswoman, Oedipus thy lord claims to do dread things unto me, even one or other of two ills,—to thrust me from the land of my fathers, or to slay me amain.

Oe. Yea; for I have caught him, lady, working evil, by ill arts, against my person.

Cr. Now may I see no good, but perish accursed, if I have done aught to thee of that wherewith thou chargest me!

Io. O, for the gods' love, believe it, Oedipus—first, for the awful sake of this oath unto the gods,—then for my sake and for theirs who stand before thee?

str. 1.Ch. Consent, reflect, hearken, O my king, I pray thee!

Oe. What grace, then, wouldest thou have me grant thee?

Ch. Respect him who aforetime was not foolish, and who now is strong in his oath.

Oe. Now dost thou know what thou cravest?

Ch. Yea.

Oe. Declare, then, what thou meanest.

Ch. That thou shouldest never use an unproved rumour to cast a dishonouring charge on the friend who has bound himself with a curse.

Oe. Then be very sure that, when thou seekest this, for me thou art seeking destruction, or exile from this land.

str. 2.Ch. No, by him who stands in the front of all the heavenly host, no, by the Sun! Unblest, unfriended, may I die by the uttermost doom, if I have that thought! But my unhappy soul is worn by the withering of the land, and again by the thought that our old sorrows should be crowned by sorrows springing from you twain.

Oe. Then let him go, though I am surely doomed to death, or to be thrust dishonoured from the land. Thy lips, not his, move my compassion by their plaint; but he, where'er he be, shall be hated.

Cr. Sullen in yielding art thou seen, even as vehement in the excesses of thy wrath; but such natures are justly sorest for themselves to bear.

Oe. Then wilt thou not leave me in peace, and get thee gone?

Cr. I will go my way; I have found thee undiscerning, but in the sight of these I am just. [*Exit.*

ant. 1.Ch. Lady, why dost thou delay to take yon man into the house?

Io. I will do so, when I have learned what hath chanced.

Ch. Blind suspicion, bred of talk, arose; and, on the other part, injustice wounds.

Io. It was on both sides?

Ch. Aye.

Io. And what was the story?

Ch. Enough, methinks, enough—when our land is already vexed—that the matter should rest where it ceased.

Oe. Seest thou to what thou hast come, for all thy honest purpose, in seeking to slack and blunt my zeal?

ant. 2.Ch. King, I have said it not once alone—be sure that I should have been shown a madman, bankrupt in sane counsel, if I put thee away—thee, who gavest a true course to my beloved country when distraught by troubles—thee, who now also art like to prove our prospering guide.

Io. In the name of the gods, tell me also, O king, on what account thou hast conceived this steadfast wrath.

Oe. That will I; for I honour thee, lady, above yonder men:—the cause is Creon, and the plots that he hath laid against me.

Io. Speak on—if thou canst tell clearly how the feud began.

Oe. He says that I stand guilty of the blood of Laïus.

Io. As on his own knowledge? Or on hearsay from another?

Oe. Nay, he hath made a rascal seer his mouthpiece; as for himself, he keeps his lips wholly pure.

Io. Then absolve thyself of the things whereof thou speakest; hearken to me, and learn for thy comfort that nought of mortal birth is a sharer in the science of the seer. I will give thee pithy proof of that.

An oracle came to Laïus once—I will not say from Phoebus himself, but from his ministers—that the doom should overtake him to die by the hand of his child, who should spring from him and me.

Now Laïus,—as, at least, the rumour saith,—was murdered one day by foreign robbers at a place where three highways meet. And the child's birth was not three days past, when Laïus pinned its ankles together, and had it thrown, by others' hands, on a trackless mountain.

So, in that case, Apollo brought it not to pass that the babe should become the slayer of his sire, or that Laïus should die—the dread thing which he feared—by his child's hand. Thus did the messages of seer-craft map out the future. Regard them, thou, not at all. Whatsoever needful things the god seeks, he himself will easily bring to light.

Oe. What restlessness of soul, lady, what tumult of the mind hath just come upon me since I heard thee speak!

Io. What anxiety hath startled thee, that thou sayest this?

Oe. Methought I heard this from thee,—that Laïus was slain where three highways meet.

Io. Yea, that was the story; nor hath it ceased yet.

Oe. And where is the place where this befell?

Io. The land is called Phocis; and branching roads lead to the same spot from Delphi and from Daulia.

Oe. And what is the time that hath passed since these things were?

Io. The news was published to the town shortly before thou wast first seen in power over this land.

Oe. O Zeus, what hast thou decreed to do unto me?

Io. And wherefore, Oedipus, doth this thing weigh upon thy soul?

Oe. Ask me not yet; but say what was the stature of Laïus, and how ripe his manhood.

Io. He was tall,—the silver just lightly strewn among his hair; and his form was not greatly unlike to thine.

Oe. Unhappy that I am! Methinks I have been laying myself even now under a dread curse, and knew it not.

Io. How sayest thou? I tremble when I look on thee, my king.

Oe. Dread misgivings have I that the seer can see. But thou wilt show better if thou wilt tell me one thing more.

Io. Indeed—though I tremble—I will answer all thou askest, when I hear it.

Oe. Went he in small force, or with many armed followers, like a chieftain?

Io. Five they were in all,—a herald one of them; and there was one carriage, which bore Laïus.

Oe. Alas! 'Tis now clear indeed.—Who was he who gave you these tidings, lady?

Io. A servant—the sole survivor who came home.

Oe. Is he haply at hand in the house now?

Io. No, truly; so soon as he came thence, and found thee reigning in the stead of Laïus, he supplicated me, with hand laid on mine, that I would send him to the fields, to the pastures of the flocks, that he might be far from the sight of this town. And I sent him; he was worthy, for a slave, to win e'en a larger boon than that.

Oe. Would, then, that he could return to us without delay!

Io. It is easy: but wherefore dost thou enjoin this?

Oe. I fear, lady, that mine own lips have been unguarded; and therefore am I fain to behold him.

Io. Nay, he shall come. But I too, methinks, have a claim to learn what lies heavy on thy heart, my king.

Oe. Yea, and it shall not be kept from thee, now that my forebodings have advanced so far. Who, indeed, is more to me than thou, to whom I should speak in passing through such a fortune as this?

My father was Polybus of Corinth,—my mother, the Dorian Meropè; and I was held the first of all the folk in that town, until a chance befell me, worthy, indeed, of wonder, though not worthy of mine own heat concerning it. At a banquet, a man full of wine cast it at me in his cups that I was not the true son of my sire. And I, vexed, restrained myself for that day as best I might; but on the next I went to my mother and father, and questioned them; and they were wroth for the taunt with him who had let that word fly. So on their part I had comfort; yet was this thing ever rankling in my heart; for it still crept abroad with strong rumour. And, unknown to mother or father, I went to Delphi; and Phoebus sent me forth disappointed of that knowledge for which I came, but in his response set forth other things, full of sorrow and terror and woe; even that I was fated to defile my mother's bed; and that I should show unto men a brood which they could not endure to behold; and that I should be the slayer of the sire who begat me.

And I, when I had listened to this, turned to flight from the land of Corinth, thenceforth wotting of its region by the stars alone, to some spot where I should never see fulfilment of the infamies foretold in mine evil doom. And on my way I came to the regions in which thou sayest that this prince perished. Now, lady, I will tell thee the truth. When in my journey I was near to those three roads, there met me a herald, and a man seated in a carriage drawn by colts, as thou hast described; and he who was in front, and the old man himself, were for thrusting me rudely from the path. Then, in anger, I struck him who pushed me aside—the driver; and the old man, seeing it, watched the moment when I was passing, and, from the carriage, brought his goad with two teeth down full upon my head. Yet was he paid with interest; by one swift blow from the staff in this hand he was rolled right out of the carriage, on his back; and I slew every man of them.

But if this stranger had any tie of kinship with Laïus, who is now more wretched than the man before thee? What mortal could prove more hated of heaven? Whom no stranger, no citizen, is allowed to receive in his house; whom it is unlawful that any one accost; whom all must repel from their homes! And this—this curse—was laid on me by no mouth but mine own! And I pollute the bed of the slain man with the hands by which he perished. Say, am I vile? Oh, am I not utterly unclean?—seeing that I must be banished, and in banishment see not mine own people, nor set foot in mine own land, or else be joined in wedlock to my mother, and slay my sire, even Polybus, who begat and reared me.

Then would not he speak aright of Oedipus, who judged these things sent by some cruel power above man? Forbid, forbid, ye pure and awful gods, that I should see that day! No, may I be swept from among men, ere I behold myself visited with the brand of such a doom!

Ch. To us, indeed, these things, O king, are fraught with fear; yet have hope, until at least thou hast gained full knowledge from him who saw the deed.

Oe. Hope, in truth, rests with me thus far alone; I can await the man summoned from the pastures.

Io. And when he has appeared—what wouldst thou have of him?

Oe. I will tell thee. If his story be found to tally with thine, I, at least, shall stand clear of disaster.

Io. And what of special note didst thou hear from me?

Oe. Thou wast saying that he spoke of Laïus as slain by robbers. If, then, he still speaks, as before, of several, I was not the slayer: a solitary man could not be held the same with that band. But if he names one lonely wayfarer, then beyond doubt this guilt leans to me.

Io. Nay, be assured that thus, at least, the tale was first told; he cannot revoke that, for the city heard it, not I alone. But even if he should diverge somewhat from his former story, never, king, can he show that the murder of Laïus, at least, is truly square to prophecy; of whom Loxias plainly said that he must die by the hand of my child. Howbeit that poor innocent never slew him, but perished first itself. So henceforth, for what touches divination, I would not look to my right hand or my left.

Oe. Thou judgest well. But nevertheless send some one to fetch the peasant, and neglect not this matter.

Io. I will send without delay. But let us come into the house: nothing will I do save at thy good pleasure.

str. 1.Ch. May destiny still find me winning the praise of reverent purity in all words and deeds sanctioned by those laws of range sublime, called into life throughout the high clear heaven, whose father is Olympus alone; their parent was no race of mortal men, no, nor shall oblivion ever lay them to sleep; the god is mighty in them, and he grows not old.

ant. 1.Insolence breeds the tyrant; Insolence, once vainly surfeited on wealth that is not meet nor good for it, when it hath scaled the topmost ramparts, is hurled to a dire doom, wherein no service of the feet can serve. But I pray that the god never quell such rivalry as benefits the State; the god will I ever hold for our protector.

str. 2.But if any man walks haughtily in deed or word, with no fear of Justice, no reverence for the images of gods, may an evil doom seize him for his ill-starred pride, if he will not win his vantage fairly, nor keep him from unholy deeds, but must lay profaning hands on sanctities.

Where such things are, what mortal shall boast any more that he can ward the arrows of the gods from his life? Nay, if such deeds are in honour, wherefore should we join in the sacred dance?

ant. 2.No more will I go reverently to earth's central and inviolate shrine, no more to Abae's temple or Olympia, if these oracles fit not the issue, so that all men shall point at them with the finger. Nay, king,—if thou art rightly called,—Zeus all-ruling, may it not escape thee and thine ever-deathless power!

The old prophecies concerning Laïus are fading; already men are setting them at nought, and nowhere is Apollo glorified with honours; the worship of the gods is perishing.

Io. Princes of the land, the thought has come to me to visit the shrines of the gods, with this wreathed branch in my hands, and these gifts of incense. For Oedipus excites his soul overmuch with all manner of alarms, nor, like a man of sense, judges the new things by the old, but is at the will of the speaker, if he speak terrors.

Since, then, by counsel I can do no good, to thee, Lycean Apollo, for thou art nearest, I have come, a suppliant with these symbols of prayer, that thou mayest find us some riddance from uncleanness. For now we are all afraid, seeing *him* affrighted, even as they who see fear in the helmsman of their ship.

MESSENGER.

Might I learn from you, strangers, where is the house of the king Oedipus? Or, better still, tell me where he himself is—if ye know.

Ch. This is his dwelling, and he himself, stranger, is within; and this lady is the mother of his children.

Me. Then may she be ever happy in a happy home, since she is his heaven-blest queen.

Io. Happiness to thee also, stranger! 'tis the due of thy fair greeting.—But say what thou hast come to seek or to tell.

Me. Good tidings, lady, for thy house and for thy husband.

Io. What are they? And from whom hast thou come?

Me. From Corinth: and at the message which I will speak anon thou wilt rejoice—doubtless; yet haply grieve.

Io. And what is it? How hath it thus a double potency?

Me. The people will make him king of the Isthmian land, as 'twas said there.

Io. How then? Is the aged Polybus no more in power?

Me. No, verily: for death holds him in the tomb.

Io. How sayest thou? Is Polybus dead, old man?

Me. If I speak not the truth, I am content to die.

Io. O handmaid, away with all speed, and tell this to thy master! O ye oracles of the gods, where stand ye now! This is the man whom Oedipus long feared and shunned, lest he should slay him; and now this man hath died in the course of destiny, not by his hand. [*Enter*Oedipus.

Oe. Iocasta, dearest wife, why hast thou summoned me forth from these doors?

Io. Hear this man, and judge, as thou listenest, to what the awful oracles of the gods have come.

Oe. And he—who may he be, and what news hath he for me?

Io. He is from Corinth, to tell that thy father Polybus lives no longer, but hath perished.

Oe. How, stranger? Let me have it from thine own mouth.

Me. If I must first make these tidings plain, know indeed that he is dead and gone.

Oe. By treachery, or by visit of disease?

Me. A light thing in the scale brings the aged to their rest.

Oe. Ah, he died, it seems, of sickness?

Me. Yea, and of the long years that he had told.

Oe. Alas, alas! Why, indeed, my wife, should one look to the hearth of the Pythian seer, or to the birds that scream above our heads, on whose showing I was doomed to slay my sire? But he is dead, and hid already beneath the earth; and here am I, who have not put hand to spear.—Unless, perchance, he was killed by longing for me: thus, indeed, I should be the cause of his death. But the oracles as they stand, at least, Polybus hath swept with him to his rest in Hades: they are worth nought.

Io. Nay, did I not so foretell to thee long since?

Oe. Thou didst: but I was misled by my fear.

Io. Now no more lay aught of those things to heart.

Oe. But surely I must needs fear my mother's bed?

Io. Nay, what should mortal fear, for whom the decrees of Fortune are supreme, and who hath clear foresight of nothing? 'Tis best to live at random, as one may. But fear not thou touching wedlock with thy mother. Many men ere now have so fared in dreams also: but he to whom these things are as nought bears his life most easily.

Oe. All these bold words of thine would have been well, were not my mother living; but as it is, since she lives, I must needs fear—though thou sayest well.

Io. Howbeit thy father's death is a great sign to cheer us.

Oe. Great, I know; but my fear is of her who lives.

Me. And who is the woman about whom ye fear?

Oe. Meropè, old man, the consort of Polybus.

Me. And what is it in her that moves your fear?

Oe. A heaven-sent oracle of dread import, stranger.

Me. Lawful, or unlawful, for another to know?

Oe. Lawful, surely. Loxias once said that I was doomed to espouse mine own mother, and to shed with mine own hands my father's blood. Wherefore my home in Corinth was long kept by me afar; with happy event, indeed,—yet still 'tis sweet to see the face of parents.

Me. Was it indeed for fear of this that thou wast an exile from that city?

Oe. And because I wished not, old man, to be the slayer of my sire.

Me. Then why have I not freed thee, king, from this fear, seeing that I came with friendly purpose?

Oe. Indeed thou shouldst have guerdon due from me.

Me. Indeed 'twas chiefly for this that I came—that, on thy return home, I might reap some good.

Oe. Nay, I will never go near my parents.

Me. Ah my son, 'tis plain enough that thou knowest not what thou doest.

Oe. How, old man? For the gods' love, tell me.

Me. If for these reasons thou shrinkest from going home.

Oe. Aye, I dread lest Phoebus prove himself true for me.

Me. Thou dreadest to be stained with guilt through thy parents?

Oe. Even so, old man—this it is that ever affrights me.

Me. Dost thou know, then, that thy fears are wholly vain?

Oe. How so, if I was born of those parents?

Me. Because Polybus was nothing to thee in blood.

Oe. What sayest thou? Was Polybus not my sire?

Me. No more than he who speaks to thee, but just so much.

Oe. And how can my sire be level with him who is as nought to me?

Me. Nay, he begat thee not, any more than I.

Oe. Nay, wherefore, then, called he me his son?

Me. Know that he had received thee as a gift from my hands of yore.

Oe. And yet he loved me so dearly, who came from another's hand?

Me. Yea, his former childlessness won him thereto.

Oe. And thou—hadst thou bought me or found me by chance, when thou gavest me to him?

Me. Found thee in Cithaeron's winding glens.

Oe. And wherefore wast thou roaming in those regions?

Me. I was there in charge of mountain flocks.

Oe. What, thou wast a shepherd—a vagrant hireling?

Me. But thy preserver, my son, in that hour.

Oe. And what pain was mine when thou didst take me in thine arms?

Me. The ankles of thy feet might witness.

Oe. Ah me, why dost thou speak of that old trouble?

Me. I freed thee when thou hadst thine ankles pinned together.

Oe. Aye, 'twas a dread brand of shame that I took from my cradle.

Me. Such, that from that fortune thou wast called by the name which still is thine.

Oe. Oh, for the gods' love—was the deed my mother's or father's? Speak!

Me. I know not; he who gave thee to me wots better of that than I.

Oe. What, thou hadst me from another? Thou didst not light on me thyself?

Me. No: another shepherd gave thee up to me.

Oe. Who was he? Art thou in case to tell clearly?

Me. I think he was called one of the household of Laïus.

Oe. The king who ruled this country long ago?

Me. The same: 'twas in his service that the man was a herd.

Oe. Is he still alive, that I might see him?

Me. Nay, ye folk of the country should know best.

Oe. Is there any of you here present that knows the herd of whom he speaks— that hath seen him in the pastures or the town? Answer! The hour hath come that these things should be finally revealed.

Ch. Methinks he speaks of no other than the peasant whom thou wast already fain to see; but our lady Iocasta might best tell that.

Oe. Lady, wottest thou of him whom we lately summoned? Is it of him that this man speaks?

Io. Why ask of whom he spoke? Regard it not... waste not a thought on what he said...'twere idle.

Oe. It must not be that, with such clues in my grasp, I should fail to bring my birth to light.

Io. For the gods' sake, if thou hast any care for thine own life, forbear this search! My anguish is enough.

Oe. Be of good courage; though I be found the son of servile mother,—aye, a slave by three descents,—*thou* wilt not be proved base-born.

Io. Yet hear me, I implore thee: do not thus.

Oe. I must not hear of not discovering the whole truth.

Io. Yet I wish thee well—I counsel thee for the best.

Oe. These best counsels, then, vex my patience.

Io. Ill-fated one! Mayst thou never come to know who thou art!

Oe. Go, some one, fetch me the herdsman hither,— and leave yon woman to glory in her princely stock.

Io. Alas, alas, miserable!—that word alone can I say unto thee, and no other word henceforth for ever.

[*She rushes into the palace.*

36

Ch. Why hath the lady gone, Oedipus, in a transport of wild grief? I misdoubt, a storm of sorrow will break forth from this silence.

Oe. Break forth what will! Be my race never so lowly, I must crave to learn it. Yon woman, perchance,—for she is proud with more than a woman's pride—thinks shame of my base source. But I, who hold myself son of Fortune that gives good, will not be dishonoured. She is the mother from whom I spring; and the months, my kinsmen, have marked me sometimes lowly, sometimes great. Such being my lineage, never more can I prove false to it, or spare to search out the secret of my birth.

*str.*Ch. If I am a seer or wise of heart, O Cithaeron, thou shalt not fail—by yon heaven, thou shalt not!— to know at tomorrow's full moon that Oedipus honours thee as native to him, as his nurse, and his mother, and that thou art celebrated in our dance and song, because thou art well-pleasing to our prince. O Phoebus to whom we cry, may these things find favour in thy sight!

*ant.*Who was it, my son, who of the race whose years are many that bore thee in wedlock with Pan, the mountain-roaming father? Or was it a bride of Loxias that bore thee? For dear to him are all the upland pastures. Or perchance 'twas Cyllene's lord, or the Bacchants' god, dweller on the hill-tops, that received thee, a new-born joy, from one of the Nymphs of Helicon, with whom he most doth sport.

Oe. Elders, if 'tis for me to guess, who have never met with him, I think I see the herdsman of whom we have long been in quest; for in his venerable age he tallies with yon stranger's years, and withal I know those who bring him, methinks, as servants of mine own. But perchance thou mayest have the advantage of me in knowledge, if thou hast seen the herdsman before.

Ch. Aye, I know him, be sure; he was in the service of Laïus—trusty as any man, in his shepherd's place.

[*The herdsman is brought in.*]

Oe. I ask thee first, Corinthian stranger, is this he whom thou meanest?

Me. This man whom thou beholdest.

Oe. Ho thou, old man—I would have thee look this way, and answer all that I ask thee.—Thou wast once in the service of Laïus?

HERDSMAN.

I was—a slave not bought, but reared in his house.

Oe. Employed in what labour, or what way of life?

He. For the best part of my life I tended flocks.

Oe. And what the regions that thou didst chiefly haunt?

He. Sometimes it was Cithaeron, sometimes the neighbouring ground.

Oe. Then wottest thou of having noted yon man in these parts—

He. Doing what?...What man dost thou mean?...

Oe. This man here—or of having ever met him before?

He. Not so that I could speak at once from memory.

Me. And no wonder, master. But I will bring clear recollection to his ignorance. I am sure that he well wots of the time when we abode in the region of Cithaeron,— he with two flocks, I, his comrade, with one,—three full half-years, from spring to Arcturus; and then for the winter I used to drive my flock to mine own fold, and he took his to the fold of Laïus. Did aught of this happen as I tell, or did it not?

He. Thou speakest the truth—though 'tis long ago.

Me. Come, tell me now—wottest thou of having given me a boy in those days, to be reared as mine own foster-son?

He. What now? Why dost thou ask the question?

Me. Yonder man, my friend, is he who then was young.

He. Plague seize thee—be silent once for all!

Oe. Ha! chide him not, old man—thy words need chiding more than his.

He. And wherein, most noble master, do I offend?

Oe. In not telling of the boy concerning whom he asks.

He. He speaks without knowledge—he is busy to no purpose.

Oe. Thou wilt not speak with a good grace, but thou shalt on pain.

He. Nay, for the gods' love, misuse not an old man!

Oe. Ho, some one—pinion him this instant!

He. Alas, wherefore? what more wouldst thou learn?

Oe. Didst thou give this man the child of whom he asks?

He. I did,—and would I had perished that day!

Oe. Well, thou wilt come to that, unless thou tell the honest truth.

He. Nay, much more am I lost, if I speak.

Oe. The fellow is bent, methinks, on more delays...

He. No, no!—I said before that I gave it to him.

Oe. Whence hadst thou got it? In thine own house, or from another?

He. Mine own it was not—I had received it from a man.

Oe. From whom of the citizens here? from what home?

He. Forbear, for the gods' love, master, forbear to ask more!

Oe. Thou art lost if I have to question thee again.

He. It was a child, then, of the house of Laïus.

Oe. A slave? or one born of his own race?

He. Ah me—I am on the dreaded brink of speech.

Oe. And I of hearing; yet must I hear.

He. Thou must know, then, that 'twas said to be his own child—but thy lady within could best say how these things are.

Oe. How? She gave it to thee?

He. Yea, O King.

Oe. For what end?

He. That I should make away with it.

Oe. Her own child, the wretch?

He. Aye, from fear of evil prophecies.

Oe. What were they?

He. The tale ran that he must slay his sire.

Oe. Why, then, didst thou give him up to this old man?

He. Through pity, master, as deeming that he would bear him away to another land, whence he himself came; but he saved him for the direst woe. For if thou art what this man saith, know that thou wast born to misery.

Oe. Oh, oh! All brought to pass—all true! Thou light, may I now look my last on thee—I who have been found accursed in birth, accursed in wedlock, accursed in the shedding of blood!

[He rushes into the palace.

38

str. 1.Ch. Alas, ye generations of men, how mere a shadow do I count your life! Where, where is the mortal who wins more of happiness than just the seeming, and, after the semblance, a falling away? Thine is a fate that warns me,—thine, thine, unhappy Oedipus—to call no earthly creature blest.

ant. 1.For he, O Zeus, sped his shaft with peerless skill, and won the prize of an all-prosperous fortune; he slew the maiden with crooked talons who sang darkly; he arose for our land as a tower against death. And from that time, Oedipus, thou hast been called our king, and hast been honoured supremely, bearing sway in great Thebes.

str. 2.But now whose story is more grievous in men's ears? Who is a more wretched captive to fierce plagues and troubles, with all his life reversed?

Alas, renowned Oedipus! The same bounteous place of rest sufficed thee, as child and sire also, that thou shouldst make thereon thy nuptial couch. Oh, how can the soil wherein thy father sowed, unhappy one, have suffered thee in silence so long?

ant. 2.Time the all-seeing hath found thee out in thy despite: he judgeth the monstrous marriage wherein begetter and begotten have long been one.

Alas, thou child of Laïus, would, would that I had never seen thee! I wail as one who pours a dirge from his lips; sooth to speak, 'twas thou that gavest me new life, and through thee darkness hath fallen upon mine eyes.

SECOND MESSENGER (*FROM THE HOUSE*).

2 Me. Ye who are ever most honoured in this land, what deeds shall ye hear, what deeds behold, what burden of sorrow shall be yours, if, true to your race, ye still care for the house of Labdacus! For I ween that not Ister nor Phasis could wash this house clean, so many are the ills that it shrouds, or will soon bring to light,—ills wrought not unwittingly, but of purpose. And those griefs smart most which are seen to be of our own choice.

Ch. Indeed those which we knew before fall not short of claiming sore lamentation: besides them, what dost thou announce?

2 Me. This is the shortest tale to tell and to hear: our royal lady Iocasta is dead.

Ch. Alas, hapless one! From what cause?

2 Me. By her own hand. The worst pain in what hath chanced is not for you, for yours it is not to behold. Nevertheless, so far as mine own memory serves, ye shall learn that unhappy woman's fate.

When, frantic, she had passed within the vestibule, she rushed straight towards her nuptial couch, clutching her hair with the fingers of both hands; once within the chamber, she dashed the doors together at her back; then called on the name of Laïus, long since a corpse, mindful of that son, begotten long ago, by whom the sire was slain, leaving the mother to breed accursed offspring with his own.

And she bewailed the wedlock wherein, wretched, she had borne a twofold brood, husband by husband, children by her child. And how thereafter she perished, is more than I know. For with a shriek Oedipus burst in, and suffered us not to watch her woe unto the end; on him, as he rushed around, our eyes were set. To and fro he went, asking us to give him a sword,—asking where he should find the wife who was no wife, but a mother whose womb had borne alike himself and his children. And, in his frenzy, a power above man was his guide; for 'twas none of us mortals who were nigh. And with a dread shriek, as though some one beckoned him on, he sprang at the double doors, and from their sockets forced the bending bolts, and rushed into the room.

There beheld we the woman hanging by the neck in a twisted noose of swinging cords. But he, when he saw her, with a dread, deep cry of misery, loosed the halter whereby she hung. And when the hapless woman was stretched upon the ground, then was the sequel dread to see. For he tore from her raiment the golden brooches wherewith she was decked, and lifted them, and smote full on his own eye-balls, uttering words like these: 'No more shall ye behold such horrors as I was suffering and working! long enough have ye looked on those whom ye ought never to have seen, failed in knowledge of those whom I yearned to know—henceforth ye shall be dark!'

To such dire refrain, not once alone but oft struck he his eyes with lifted hand; and at each blow the ensanguined eye-balls bedewed his beard, nor sent forth sluggish drops of gore, but all at once a dark shower of blood came down like hail.

From the deeds of twain such ills have broken forth, not on one alone, but with mingled woe for man and wife. The old happiness of their ancestral fortune was aforetime happiness indeed; but to-day—lamentation, ruin, death, shame, all earthly ills that can be named—all, all are theirs.

Ch. And hath the sufferer now any respite from pain?

2 Me. He cries for some one to unbar the gates and show to all the Cadmeans his father's slayer, his mother's—the unholy word must not pass my lips,— as purposing to cast himself out of the land, and abide no more, to make the house accursed under his own curse. Howbeit he lacks strength, and one to guide his steps; for the anguish is more than man may bear. And he will show this to thee also; for lo, the bars of the gates are withdrawn, and soon thou shalt behold a sight which even he who abhors it must pity.

ENTER OEDIPUS.

Ch. O dread fate for men to see, O most dreadful of all that have met mine eyes! Unhappy one, what madness hath come on thee? Who is the unearthly foe that, with a bound of more than mortal range, hath made thine ill-starred life his prey?

Alas, alas, thou hapless one! Nay, I cannot e'en look on thee, though there is much that I would fain ask, fain lèarn, much that draws my wistful gaze,—with such a shuddering dost thou fill me!

Oe. Woe is me! Alas, alas, wretched that I am! Whither, whither am I borne in my misery? How is my voice swept abroad on the wings of the air? Oh my Fate, how far hast thou sprung!

Ch. To a dread place, dire in men's ears, dire in their sight.

str. 1.Oe. O thou horror of darkness that enfoldest me, visitant unspeakable, resistless, sped by a wind too fair!

Ay me! and once again, ay me!

How is my soul pierced by the stab of these goads, and withal by the memory of sorrows!

Ch. Yea, amid woes so many a twofold pain may well be thine to mourn and to bear.

ant. 1.Oe. Ah, friend, thou still art steadfast in thy tendance of me,—thou still hast patience to care for the blind man! Ah me! Thy presence is not hid from me—no, dark though I am, yet know I thy voice full well.

Ch. Man of dread deeds, how couldst thou in such wise quench thy vision? What more than human power urged thee?

str. 2.Oe. Apollo, friends, Apollo was he that brought these my woes to pass, these my sore, sore woes: but the hand that struck the eyes was none save mine, wretched that I am! Why was I to see, when sight could show me nothing sweet?

Ch. These things were even as thou sayest.

Oe. Say, friends, what can I more behold, what can I love, what greeting can touch mine ear with joy? Haste, lead me from the land, friends, lead me hence. the utterly lost, the thrice accursed, yea, the mortal most abhorred of heaven!

Ch. Wretched alike for thy fortune and for thy sense thereof, would that I had never so much as known thee!

ant. 2.Oe. Perish the man, whoe'er he was, that freed me in the pastures from the cruel shackle on my feet, and saved me from death, and gave me back to life,—a thankless deed! Had I died then, to my friends and to mine own soul I had not been so sore a grief.

Ch. I also would have had it thus.

Oe. So had I not come to shed my father's blood, nor been called among men the spouse of her from whom I sprang: but now am I forsaken of the gods, son of a defiled mother, successor to his bed who gave me mine own wretched being: and if there be yet a woe surpassing woes, it hath become the portion of Oedipus.

Ch. I know not how I can say that thou hast counselled well: for thou wert better dead than living and blind.

Oe. Show me not at large that these things are not best done thus: give me counsel no more. For, had I sight, I know not with what eyes I could e'en have looked on my father, when I came to the place of the dead, aye, or on my miserable mother, since against both I have sinned such sins as strangling could not punish. But deem ye that the sight of children, born as mine were born, was lovely for me to look upon? No, no, not lovely to mine eyes for ever! No, nor was this town with its towered walls, nor the sacred statues of the gods, since I, thrice wretched that I am,—I, noblest of the sons of Thebes,—have doomed myself to know these no more, by mine own command that all should thrust away the impious one,—even him whom gods have shown to be unholy—and of the race of Laïus!

After bearing such a stain upon me, was I to look with steady eyes on this folk? No, verily: no, were there yet a way to choke the fount of hearing, I had not spared to make a fast prison of this wretched frame, that so I should have known nor sight nor sound; for 'tis sweet that our thought should dwell beyond the sphere of griefs.

Alas, Cithaeron, why hadst thou a shelter for me? When I was given to thee, why didst thou not slay me straightway, that so I might never have revealed my source to men? Ah, Polybus,—ah, Corinth, and thou that wast called the ancient house of my fathers, how seeming-fair was I your nurseling, and what ills were festering beneath! For now I am found evil, and of evil birth. O ye three roads, and thou secret glen,—thou coppice, and narrow way where three paths met—ye who drank from my hands that father's blood which was mine own,—remember ye, perchance, what deeds I wrought for you to see,—and then, when I came hither, what fresh deeds I went on to do?

O marriage-rites, ye gave me birth, and when ye had brought me forth, again ye bore children to your child, ye created an incestuous kinship of fathers, brothers, sons,—brides, wives, mothers,—yea, all the foulest shame that is wrought among men! Nay, but 'tis unmeet to name what 'tis unmeet to do:—haste ye, for the gods' love, hide me somewhere beyond the land, or slay me, or cast me into the sea, where ye shall never behold me more! Approach,—deign to lay your hands on a wretched man;—hearken, fear not,—my plague can rest on no mortal beside.

Ch. Nay, here is Creon, in meet season for thy requests, crave they act or counsel; for he alone is left to guard the land in thy stead.

Oe. Ah me, how indeed shall I accost him? What claim to credence can be shown on my part? For in the past I have been found wholly false to him.

CREON.

I have not come in mockery, Oedipus, nor to reproach thee with any bygone fault.—(*To the attendants.*) But ye, if ye respect the children of men no more, revere at least the all-nurturing flame of our lord the Sun,—spare to show thus nakedly a pollution such as this,—one which neither earth can welcome, nor the holy rain, nor the light. Nay, take him into the house as quickly as ye may; for it best accords with piety that kinsfolk alone should see and hear a kinsman's woes.

Oe. For the gods' love—since thou hast done a gentle violence to my presage, who hast come in a spirit so noble to me, a man most vile—grant me a boon:—for thy good I will speak, not for mine own.

Cr. And what wish art thou so fain to have of me?

Oe. Cast me out of this land with all speed, to a place where no mortal shall be found to greet me more.

Cr. This would I have done, be thou sure, but that I craved first to learn all my duty from the god.

Oe. Nay, his behest hath been set forth in full,—to let me perish, the parricide, the unholy one, that I am.

Cr. Such was the purport; yet, seeing to what a pass we have come, 'tis better to learn clearly what should be done.

Oe. Will ye, then, seek a response on behalf of such a wretch as I am?

Cr. Aye, for thou thyself wilt now surely put faith in the god.

Oe. Yea; and on thee lay I this charge, to thee will I make this entreaty:—give to her who is within such burial as thou thyself wouldest; for thou wilt meetly render the last rites to thine own. But for me—never let this city of my sire be condemned to have me dwelling therein, while I live: no, suffer me to abide on the hills, where yonder is Cithaeron, famed as mine,—which my mother and sire, while they lived, set for my appointed tomb,—that so I may die by their decree who sought to slay me. Howbeit of thus much am I sure,—that neither sickness nor aught else can destroy me; for never had I been snatched from death, but in reserve for some strange doom.

Nay, let *my* fate go whither it will: but as touching my children,—I pray thee, Creon, take no care on thee for my sons; they are men, so that, be they where they may, they can never lack the means to live. But my two girls, poor hapless ones,—who never knew my table spread apart, or lacked their father's presence, but ever in all things shared my daily bread,—I pray thee, care for *them;* and—if thou canst—suffer me to touch them with my hands, and to indulge my grief. Grant it, prince, grant it, thou noble heart! Ah, could I but once touch them with my hands, I should think that they were with me, even as when I had sight...

[Creon's *attendants lead in the children* Antigone *and* Ismene.

Ha? O ye gods, can it be my loved ones that I hear sobbing,—can Creon have taken pity on me and sent me my children—my darlings? Am I right?

Cr. Yea: 'tis of my contriving, for I knew thy joy in them of old,—the joy that now is thine.

Oe. Then blessed be thou, and, for guerdon of this errand, may heaven prove to thee a kinder guardian than it hath to me! My children, where are ye? Come hither,—hither to the hands of him whose mother was your own, the hands whose offices have wrought that your sire's once bright eyes should be such orbs as these,—his, who seeing nought, knowing nought, became your father by her from whom he sprang! For you also do I weep—behold you I cannot—when I think of the bitter life in days to come which men will make you live. To what company of the citizens will ye go, to what festival, from which ye shall not return home in tears, instead of sharing in the holiday? But when ye are now come to years ripe for marriage, who shall he be, who shall be the man, my daughters, that will hazard taking unto him such reproaches as must be baneful alike to my offspring and to yours? For what misery is wanting? Your sire slew his sire, he had seed of her who bare him, and begat you at the sources of his own being! Such are the taunts that will be cast at you; and who then will wed? The man lives not, no, it cannot be, my children, but ye must wither in barren maidenhood.

Ah, son of Menoeceus, hear me—since thou art the only father left to them, for we, their parents, are lost, both of us,—allow them not to wander poor and unwed, who are thy kinswomen, nor abase them to the level of my woes. Nay, pity them, when thou seest them at this tender age so utterly forlorn, save for thee. Signify thy promise, generous man, by the touch of thy hand! To you, my children, I would have given much counsel, were your minds mature; but now I would have this to be your prayer—that ye live where occasion suffers, and that the life which is your portion may be happier than your sire's.

Cr. Thy grief hath had large scope enough: nay, pass into the house.

Oe. I must obey, though 'tis in no wise sweet.

Cr. Yea: for it is in season that all things are good.

Oe. Knowest thou, then, on what conditions I will go? Cr. Thou shalt name them; so shall I know them when I hear.

Oe. See that thou send me to dwell beyond this land. Cr. Thou askest me for what the god must give.

Oe. Nay, to the gods I have become most hateful. Cr. Then shalt thou have thy wish anon.

Oe. So thou consentest? Cr. 'Tis not my wont to speak idly what I do not mean.

Oe. Then 'tis time to lead me hence. Cr. Come, then,—but let thy children go.

Oe. Nay, take not these from me! Cr. Crave not to be master in all things: for the mastery which thou didst win hath not followed thee through life.

43

Ch. Dwellers in our native Thebes, behold, this is Oedipus, who knew the famed riddle, and was a man most mighty; on whose fortunes what citizen did not gaze with envy? Behold into what a stormy sea of dread trouble he hath come!

Therefore, while our eyes wait to see the destined final day, we must call no one happy who is of mortal race, until he hath crossed life's border, free from pain.

OEDIPUS AT COLONUS

PERSONS OF THE DRAMA.

Oedipus.
Antigone} *his daughters.*
Ismene
A Man of Colonus.
Theseus,*King of Athens.*
Creon,*of Thebes.*
Polyneices,*the elder son of Oedipus.*
A Messenger.
Chorus of Elders of Colonus.

Scene: At Colonus, about a mile and a quarter N.W. of Athens, in front of a grove sacred to the Erinyes or Furies,—there worshipped under the propitiatory name of the Eumenides, or Kindly Powers.

Many years have passed since the events set forth in Oedipus the King. For some time after his fall, Oedipus had remained at Thebes: but at last the Thebans, moved by Creon, decided to expel him; and his sons did nothing in arrest of that sentence. His daughter Antigone went forth from Thebes with her blind father, his sole attendant: Ismene stayed at Thebes, but was watchful there in her father's interests, and on one occasion brought him secret intelligence. After his expulsion, his sons were at first disposed to resign all claim to royal power in favour of their uncle Creon. But afterwards they fell to striving with each other for the throne; and Eteocles, the younger brother, gained it. Polyneices was driven out of Thebes. He went to Argos, and there married the daughter of King Adrastus; with whose support he is now preparing to march against Thebes.

Meanwhile an oracle has come from Delphi to Thebes. If Thebes is to prosper, the grave of Oedipus must be in Theban soil. If that grave be in Attica, Athens will prevail against Thebes. Thus the wanderer, old, blind, and destitute, carries with him a mysterious blessing of the gods on the place where he shall find rest.

OEDIPUS.

Daughter of the blind old man, to what region have we come, Antigone, or what city of men? Who will entertain the wandering Oedipus to-day with scanty gifts? Little crave I, and win yet less than that little, and therewith am content; for patience is the lesson of suffering, and of the years in our long fellowship, and lastly of a noble mind.—My child, if thou seest any resting-place, whether on profane ground or by groves of the gods, stay me and set me down, that we may inquire where we are: for we stand in need to learn as strangers of denizens, and to perform their bidding.

ANTIGONE.

Father, toil-worn Oedipus, the towers that guard the city, to judge by sight, are far off; and this place is sacred, to all seeming,—thick-set with laurel, olive, vine; and in its heart a feathered choir of nightingales makes music. So sit thee here on this unhewn stone; thou hast travelled a long way for an old man.

Oe. Seat me, then, and watch over the blind.

An. If time can teach, I need not to learn that.

Oe. Canst thou tell me, now, where we have arrived?

An. Athens I know, but not this place.

Oe. Aye, so much every wayfarer told us.

An. Well, shall I go and learn how the spot is called?

Oe. Yes, child,—if indeed 'tis habitable.

An. Nay, inhabited it surely is;—but I think there is no need;—yonder I see a man near us.

Oe. Hitherward moving and setting forth?

An. Nay, he is at our side already. Speak as the moment prompts thee, for the man is here.

Enter Stranger (a man of Colonus).

Oe. Stranger, hearing from this maiden, who hath sight for herself and for me, that thou hast drawn nigh with timely quest for the solving of our doubts—

St. Now, ere thou question me at large, quit this seat; for thou art on ground which 'tis not lawful to tread.

Oe. And what is this ground? To what deity sacred?

St. Ground inviolable, whereon none may dwell: for the dread goddesses hold it, the daughters of Earth and Darkness.

Oe. Who may they be, whose awful name I am to hear and invoke?

St. The all-seeing Eumenides the folk here would call them: but other names please otherwhere.

Oe. Then graciously may they receive their suppliant! for nevermore will I depart from my rest in this land.

St. What means this? Oe. 'Tis the watchword of my fate.

St. Nay, for my part, I dare not remove thee without warrant from the city, ere I report what I am doing.

Oe. Now for the gods' love, stranger, refuse me not, hapless wanderer that I am, the knowledge for which I sue to thee.

St. Speak, and from me thou shalt find no refusal.

Oe. What, then, is the place that we have entered?

St. All that *I* know, thou shalt learn from my mouth. This whole place is sacred; awful Poseidon holds it, and therein is the fire-fraught god, the Titan Prometheus; but as for the spot whereon thou treadest, 'tis called the Brazen Threshold of this land, the stay of Athens; and the neighbouring fields claim yon knight Colonus for their primal lord, and all the people bear his name in common for their own. Such, thou mayest know, stranger, are these haunts, not honoured in story, but rather in the life that loves them.

Oe. Are there indeed dwellers in this region?

St. Yea, surely, the namesakes of yonder god.

Oe. Have they a king? Or doth speech rest with the folk?

St. These parts are ruled by the king in the city.

Oe. And who is thus sovereign in counsel and in might?

St. Theseus he is called, son of Aegeus who was before him.

Oe. Could a messenger go for him from among you?

St. With what aim to speak, or to prepare his coming?

Oe. That by small service he may find a great gain.

St. And what help can be from one who sees not?

Oe. In all that I speak there shall be sight.

St. Mark me now, friend—I would not have thee come to harm,—for thou art noble, if one may judge by thy looks, leaving thy fortune aside;—stay here, e'en where I found thee, till I go and tell these things to the folk on this spot,—not in the town: they will decide for thee whether thou shalt abide or retire. [*Exit.*

Oe. My child, say, is the stranger gone?

An. He is gone, and so thou canst utter what thou wilt, father, in quietness, as knowing that I alone am near.

Oe. Queens of dread aspect, since your seat is the first in this land whereat I have bent the knee, show not yourselves ungracious to Phoebus or to myself; who, when he proclaimed that doom of many woes, spake of *this* as a rest for me after long years,—on reaching my goal in a land where I should find a seat of the Awful Goddesses, and a hospitable shelter,—even that there I should close my weary life, with benefits, through my having dwelt therein, for mine hosts, but ruin for those who sent me forth—who drove me away. And he went on to warn me that signs of these things should come, in earthquake, or in thunder, haply, or in the lightning of Zeus.

Now I perceive that in this journey some faithful omen from you hath surely led me home to this grove: never else could I have met with you, first of all, in my wanderings,—I, the austere, with you who delight not in wine,—or taken this solemn seat not shaped by man.

Then, goddesses, according to the word of Apollo, give me at last some way to accomplish and close my course,—unless, perchance, I seem beneath your grace, thrall that I am evermore to woes the sorest on the earth. Hear, sweet daughters of primeval Darkness! Hear, thou that art called the city of great Pallas,—Athens, of all cities most honoured! Pity this poor wraith of Oedipus,—for verily 'tis the man of old no more.

An. Hush! Here come some aged men, I wot, to spy out thy resting-place.

Oe. I will be mute,—and do thou hide me in the grove, apart from the road, till I learn how these men will speak; for in knowledge is the safeguard of our course. [*Exeunt.*

*The*Chorus (elders of Colonus) *enter the orchestra, from the right of the spectators, as if in eager search.*

CHORUS.

str. 1.Give heed—who was he, then? Where lodges he?—whither hath he rushed from this place, insolent, he, above all who live? Scan the ground, look well, urge the quest in every part.

A wanderer that old man must have been,—a wanderer, not a dweller in the land; else never would he have advanced into this untrodden grove of the maidens with whom none may strive, whose name we tremble to speak, by whom we pass with eyes turned away, moving our lips, without sound or word, in still devotion.

But now 'tis rumoured that one hath come who in no wise reveres them; and him I cannot yet discern, though I look round all the holy place, nor wot I where to find his lodging.

syst. 1.Oedipus (*stepping forward, with*Antigone,*from his place of concealment in the grove*). Behold the man whom ye seek! for in sound is my sight, as the saying hath it.

Ch. O! O!

Dread to see, and dread to hear!

Oe. Regard me not, I entreat you, as a lawless one.

Ch. Zeus defend us! who may the old man be?

Oe. Not wholly of the best fortune, that ye should envy him, O guardians of this land!—'Tis plain: else would I not be walking thus by the eyes of others, and buoying my strength upon weakness.

ant. 1.Ch. Alas! wast thou sightless e'en from thy birth? Evil have been thy days, and many, to all seeming; but at least, if I can help, thou shalt not add this curse to thy doom. Too far thou goest—too far! But, lest thy rash steps intrude on the sward of yonder voiceless glade, where the bowl of water blends its stream with the flow of honied offerings, (be thou well ware of such trespass, unhappy stranger,)— retire,—withdraw!—A wide space parts us: hearest thou, toil-worn wanderer? If thou hast aught to say in converse with us, leave forbidden ground, and speak where 'tis lawful for all; but, till then, refrain.

syst. 2.Oe. Daughter, to what counsel shall we incline?

An. My father, we must conform us to the customs of the land, yielding, where 'tis meet, and hearkening.

Oe. Then give me thy hand.

An. 'Tis laid in thine.

Oe. Strangers, oh let me not suffer wrong when I have trusted in you, and have passed from my refuge!

str. 2.Ch. Never, old man, never shall any one remove thee from this place of rest against thy will.

[Oedipus*now begins to move forward.*

Oe. (*pausing in his gradual advance*). Further, then?

Ch. Come still further.

Oe. (*having advanced another step*). Further?

Ch. Lead him onward, maiden, for thou understandest.

[A verse for Antigone, a verse for Oedipus, and then another verse for Antigone, seem to have been lost here.]

An. * * * Come, follow me this way with thy dark steps, father, as I lead thee.

[Here has been lost a verse for Oe.]

Ch. A stranger in a strange land, ah, hapless one, incline thy heart to abhor that which the city holds in settled hate, and to reverence what she loves!

syst. 3.Oe. Lead me thou, then, child, to a spot where I may speak and listen within piety's domain, and let us not wage war with necessity.

[*Moving forward, he now sets foot on a platform of rock at the verge of the grove.*

ant. 2.Ch. There!—bend not thy steps beyond that floor of native rock.

Oe. Thus far?

Ch. Enough, I tell thee.

Oe. Shall I sit down?

Ch. Yea, move sideways and crouch low on the edge of the rock.

An. Father, this is my task: to quiet step (Oe. Ah me! ah me!) knit step, and lean thy aged frame upon my loving arm.

Oe. Woe for the doom of a dark soul!

[*Antigone seats him on the rock.*

Ch. Ah, hapless one, since now thou hast ease, speak,—whence art thou sprung? In what name art thou led on thy weary way? What is the fatherland whereof thou hast to tell us?

Oe. Strangers, I am an exile—but forbear......

Ch. What is this that thou forbiddest, old man?

Oe. — forbear, forbear to ask me who I am;—seek—probe—no further!

Ch. What means this? Oe. Dread the birth...

Ch. Speak!

Oe. (*to Antigone*). My child—alas!—what shall I say?

Ch. What is thy lineage, stranger,—speak!—and who thy sire?

Oe. Woe is me!—What will become of me, my child?

An. Speak,—for thou art driven to the verge.

Oe. Then speak I will—I have no way to hide it.

Ch. Ye twain make a long delay—come, haste thee!

Oe. Know ye a son of Laïus...O!...(*The Chorus utter a cry*)...and the race of the Labdacidae?...(Ch. O Zeus!)...the hapless Oedipus?...

Ch. Thou art he?

Oe. Have no fear of any words that I speak—

(*The Chorus drown his voice with a great shout of execration, half turning away, and holding their mantles before their eyes.*)

Oe. Unhappy that I am!...(*The clamour of the Chorus continues*)...Daughter, what is about to befall?

Ch. Out with you! forth from the land!

Oe. And thy promise—to what fulfilment wilt thou bring it?

Ch. No man is visited by fate if he requites deeds which were first done to himself; deceit on the one part matches deceits on the other, and gives pain, instead of benefit, for reward. And thou—back with thee! out from these seats! avaunt! away from my land with all speed, lest thou fasten some heavier burden on my city!

An. Strangers of reverent soul, since ye have not borne with mine aged father,—knowing, as ye do, the rumour of his unpurposed deeds,—pity, at least, my hapless self, I implore you, who supplicate you for my sire alone,—supplicate you with eyes that can still look on your own, even as though I were sprung from your own blood, that the sufferer may find compassion.

On you, as on a god, we depend in our misery. Nay, hear us! grant the boon for which we scarce dare hope! By everything sprung from you that ye hold dear, I implore you, yea, by child—by wife, or treasure, or god! Look well, and thou wilt not find the mortal who, if a god should lead him on, could escape.

Ch. Nay, be thou sure, daughter of Oedipus, we pity thee and him alike for your fortune; but, dreading the judgment of the gods, we could not say aught beyond what hath now been said to thee.

Oe. What good comes, then, of repute or fair fame, if it ends in idle breath; seeing that Athens, as men say, has the perfect fear of Heaven, and the power, above all cities, to shelter the vexed stranger, and the power, above all, to succour him?

And where find I these things, when, after making me rise up from these rocky seats, ye then drive me from the land, afraid of my name alone? Not, surely, afraid of my person or of mine acts; since mine acts, at least, have been in suffering rather than doing—were it seemly that I should tell you the story of my mother or my sire, by reason whereof ye dread me—that know I full well.

And yet in *nature* how was I evil? I, who was but requiting a wrong, so that, had I been acting with knowledge, even then I could not be accounted wicked; but, as it was, all unknowing went I—whither I went—while they who wronged me knowingly sought my ruin.

Wherefore, strangers, I beseech you by the gods, even as ye made me leave my seat, so protect me, and do not, while ye honour the gods, refuse to give those gods their due; but rather deem that they look on the god-fearing among men, and on the godless, and that never yet hath escape been found for an impious mortal on the earth.

With the help of those gods, spare to cloud the bright fame of Athens by ministering to unholy deeds; but, as ye have received the suppliant under your pledge, rescue me and guard me to the end; nor scorn me when ye look on this face unlovely to behold: for I have come to you as one sacred, and pious, and fraught with comfort for this people. But when the master is come, whosoever he be that is your chief, then shall ye hear and know all; meanwhile in no wise show yourself false.

Ch. The thoughts urged on thy part, old man, must needs move awe; they have been set forth in words not light; but I am content that the rulers of our country should judge in this cause.

Oe. And where, strangers, is the lord of this realm?

Ch. He is at the city of his father in our land; and the messenger who sent us hither hath gone to fetch him.

Oe. Think ye that he will have any regard or care for the blind man, so as to come hither himself?

Ch. Yea, surely, so soon as he learns thy name.

Oe. Who is there to bring him that message?

Ch. The way is long, and many rumours from wayfarers are wont to go abroad; when he hears them, he will soon be with us, fear not. For thy name, old man, hath been mightily noised through all lands; so that, even if he is taking his ease, and slow to move, when he hears of *thee* he will arrive with speed.

Oe. Well, may he come with a blessing to his own city, as to me!—What good man is not his own friend?

An. O Zeus! what shall I say, what shall I think, my father?

Oe. What is it, Antigone, my child?

An. I see a woman coming towards us, mounted on a colt of Etna; she wears a Thessalian bonnet to screen her face from the sun. What shall I say? Is it she, or is it not? Doth fancy cheat me? Yes—no—I cannot tell—ah me! It is no other—yes!— she greets me with bright glances as she draws nigh, and shows that Ismene, and no other, is before me.

Oe. What sayest thou, my child?

An. That I see thy daughter and my sister;—thou canst know her straightway by her voice.

50

ISMENE.

Father and sister, names most sweet to me! How hardly have I found you! and now I scarce can see you for my tears.

Oe. My child, thou hast come? Is. Ah, father, sad is thy fate to see!

Oe. Thou art with us, my child! Is. And it hath cost me toil.

Oe. Touch me, my daughter! Is. I give a hand to each.

Oe. Ah, children—ah, ye sisters! Is. Alas, twice-wretched life!

Oe. Her life and mine? Is. And mine, hapless, with you twain.

Oe. Child, and why hast thou come? Is. Through care, father, for thee.

Oe. Through longing to see me? Is. Yes, and to bring thee tidings by mine own mouth,—with the only faithful servant that I had.

Oe. And where are the young men thy brothers at our need?

Is. They are—where they are: 'tis their dark hour.

Oe. O, true image of the ways of Egypt that they show in their spirit and their life! For there the men sit weaving in the house, but the wives go forth to win the daily bread. And in your case, my daughters, those to whom these toils belonged keep the house at home like girls, while ye, in their stead, bear your hapless father's burdens.

One, from the time when her tender age was past and she came to a woman's strength, hath ever been the old man's guide in weary wanderings, oft roaming, hungry and bare-foot, through the wild wood, oft sorevexed by rains and scorching heat,—but regarding not the comforts of home, if so her father should have tendance.

And thou, my child, in former days camest forth, bringing thy father, unknown of the Cadmeans, all the oracles that had been given touching Oedipus; and thou didst take on thee the office of a faithful watcher in my behalf, when I was being driven from the land. And now what new tidings hast thou brought thy father, Ismene? On what mission hast thou set forth from home? For thou comest not empty-handed, well I wot, or without some word of fear for me.

Is. The sufferings that I bore, father, in seeking where thou wast living, I will pass by; I would not renew the pain in the recital. But the ills that now beset thine ill-fated sons,—'tis of these that I have come to tell thee.

At first it was their desire that the throne should be left to Creon, and the city spared pollution, when they thought calmly on the blight of the race from of old, and how it hath clung to thine ill-starred house. But now, moved by some god and by a sinful mind, an evil rivalry hath seized them, thrice infatuate!—to grasp at rule and kingly power.

And the hot-brained youth, the younger born, hath deprived the elder, Polyneices, of the throne, and hath driven him from his father-land. But he, as the general rumour saith among us, hath gone, an exile, to the hillgirt Argos, and is taking unto him a new kinship, and warriors for his friends,—as deeming that Argos shall soon possess the Cadmean land in honour, or lift that land's praise to the stars.

These are no vain words, my father, but deeds terrible; and where the gods will have pity on thy griefs, I cannot tell.

Oe. What, hadst thou come to hope that the gods would ever look on me for my deliverance?

Is. Yea, mine is that hope, father, from the present oracles.

Oe. What are they? What hath been prophesied, my child?

Is. That thou shalt yet be desired, alive and dead, by the men of that land, for their welfare's sake.

Oe. And who could have good of such an one as I?

Is. Their power, 'tis said, comes to be in *thy* hand.

Oe. When I am nought, in that hour, then, I am a man?

Is. Yea, for the gods lift thee now, but before they were working thy ruin.

Oe. 'Tis little to lift age, when youth was ruined.

Is. Well, know, at least, that Creon will come to thee in this cause—and rather soon than late.

Oe. With what purpose, daughter? expound to me.

Is. To plant thee near the Cadmean land, so that they may have thee in their grasp, but thou mayest not set foot on their borders.

Oe. And how can I advantage them while I rest beyond their gates?

Is. Thy tomb hath a curse for them, if all be not well with it.

Oe. It needs no god to help our wit so far.

Is. Well, therefore they would fain acquire thee as a neighbour, in a place where thou shalt not be thine own master.

Oe. Will they also shroud me in Theban dust?

Is. Nay, the guilt of a kinsman's blood debars thee, father.

Oe. Then never shall they become my masters.

Is. Some day, then, this shall be a grief for the Cadmeans.

Oe. In what conjuncture of events, my child?

Is. By force of thy wrath, when they take their stand at thy tomb.

Oe. And who hath told thee what thou tellest, my child?

Is. Sacred envoys, from the Delphian hearth.

Oe. And Phoebus hath indeed spoken thus concerning me?

Is. So say the men who have come back to Thebes.

Oe. Hath either of my sons, then, heard this?

Is. Yea, both have heard, and know it well.

Oe. And then those base ones, aware of this, held the kingship dearer than the wish to recall me?

Is. It grieves me to hear that,—but I must bear it.

Oe. Then may the gods quench not their fated strife, and may it become mine to decide this warfare whereto they are now setting their hands, spear against spear! For then neither should he abide who now holds the sceptre and the throne, nor should the banished one ever return; seeing that when I, their sire, was being thrust so shamefully from my country, they hindered not, nor defended me; no, they saw me sent forth homeless, they heard my doom of exile cried aloud.

Thou wilt say that it was mine own wish then, and that the city meetly granted me that boon. No, verily: for in that first day, when my soul was seething, and my darling wish was for death, aye, death by stoning, no one was found to help me in that desire: but after a time, when all my anguish was now assuaged, and when I began to feel that my wrath had run too far in punishing those past errors,—then it was that the city, on her part, went about to drive me perforce from the land—after all that time; and my sons, when they might have brought help—the sons to the sire—would not do it: no—for lack of one little word from them, I was left to wander, an outcast and a beggar evermore.

'Tis to these sisters, girls as they are, that, so far as nature enables them, I owe my daily food, and a shelter in the land, and the offices of kinship; the brothers have bartered their sire for a throne, and sceptred sway, and rule of the realm. Nay, never shall they win Oedipus for an ally, nor shall good ever come to them from this reign at Thebes; that know I, when I hear this maiden's oracles, and meditate on the old prophecies stored in mine own mind, which Phoebus hath fulfilled for me at last.

Therefore let them send Creon to seek me, and whoso beside is mighty in Thebes. For if ye, strangers,—with the championship of the dread goddesses who dwell among your folk,—are willing to succour, ye shall procure a great deliverer for this State, and troubles for my foes.

Ch. Right worthy art thou of compassion, Oedipus, thou, and these maidens; and since to this plea thou addest thy power to save our land, I fain would advise thee for thy weal.

Oe. Kind sir, be sure, then, that I will obey in all,—stand thou my friend.

Ch. Now make atonement to these deities, to whom thou hast first come, and on whose ground thou hast trespassed.

Oe. With what rites? instruct me, strangers.

Ch. First, from a perennial spring fetch holy drink-offerings, borne in clean hands.

Oe. And when I have gotten this pure draught?

Ch. Bowls there are, the work of a cunning craftsman: crown their edges and the handles at either brim.

Oe. With branches, or woollen cloths, or in what wise?

Ch. Take the freshly-shorn wool of an ewe-lamb.

Oe. Good; and then,—to what last rite shall I proceed?

Ch. Pour thy drink-offerings, with thy face to the dawn.

Oe. With these vessels whereof thou speakest shall I pour them?

Ch. Yea, in three streams; but empty the last vessel wholly.

Oe. Wherewith shall I fill this, ere I set it? Tell me this also.

Ch. With water and honey; but bring no wine thereto.

Oe. And when the ground under the dark shade hath drunk of these?

Ch. Lay on it thrice nine sprays of olive with both thine hands, and make this prayer the while.

Oe. The prayer I fain would hear—'tis of chief moment.

Ch. That, as we call them Benign Powers, with hearts benign they may receive the suppliant for saving: be this the prayer,—thine own, or his who prays for thee; speak inaudibly, and lift not up thy voice; then retire, without looking behind. Thus do, and I would be bold to stand by thee; but otherwise, stranger, I would fear for thee.

Oe. Daughters, hear ye these strangers, who dwell near?

An. We have listened; and do thou bid us what to do.

Oe. I cannot go; for I am disabled by lack of strength and lack of sight, evils twain. But let one of you two go and do these things. For I think that one soul suffices to pay this debt for ten thousand, if it come with good will to the shrine. Act, then, with speed; yet leave me not solitary; for the strength would fail me to move without help or guiding hand.

Is. Then I will go to perform the rite; but where I am to find the spot—this I fain would learn.

Ch. On the further side of this grove, maiden. And if thou hast need of aught, there is a guardian of the place, who will direct thee.

Is. So to my task:—but thou, Antigone, watch our father here. In parents' cause, if toil there be, we must not reck of toil. [*Exit.*

str. 1.Ch. Dread is it, stranger, to arouse the old grief that hath so long been laid to rest: and yet I yearn to hear......

Oe. What now?......

Ch. —of that grievous anguish, found cureless, wherewith thou hast wrestled.

Oe. By thy kindness for a guest, bare not the shame that I have suffered!

Ch. Seeing, in sooth, that the tale is wide-spread, and in no wise wanes, I am fain, friend, to hear it aright.

Oe. Woe is me!

Ch. Be content, I pray thee!

Oe. Alas, alas!

Ch. Grant my wish, as I have granted thine in its fulness.

ant. 1.Oe. I have suffered misery, strangers,—suffered it through unwitting deeds, and of those acts—be Heaven my witness!—no part was of mine own choice.

Ch. But in what regard?

Oe. By an evil wedlock, Thebes bound me, all unknowing, to the bride that was my curse......

Ch. Can it be, as I hear, that thou madest thy mother the partner of thy bed, for its infamy?

Oe. Woe is me! Cruel as death, strangers, are these words in mine ears;—but those maidens, begotten of me—

Ch. What wilt thou say?—

Oe. —two daughters—two curses—

Ch. O Zeus!

Oe. —sprang from the travail of the womb that bore me.

str. 2.Ch. These, then, are at once thine offspring, and......

Oe. —yea, very sisters of their sire.

Ch. Oh, horror! Oe. Horror indeed—yea, horrors untold sweep back upon my soul!

Ch. Thou hast suffered— Oe. Suffered woes dread to bear.—

Ch. Thou hast sinned— Oe. No wilful sin—

Ch. How?— Oe. A gift was given to me—O, broken-hearted that I am, would I had never won from Thebes that meed for having served her!

ant. 2Ch. Wretch! How then?...thine hand shed blood?...

Oe. Wherefore this? What wouldst thou learn?

Ch. A father's blood? Oe. Oh! oh! a second stab—wound on wound!

Ch. Slayer! Oe. Aye, slayer—yet have I a plea— Ch. What canst thou plead?— Oe. —a plea in justice.... Ch. What?...

Oe. Ye shall hear it; they whom I slew would have taken mine own life: stainless before the law, void of malice, have I come unto this pass!

Ch. Lo, yonder cometh our prince, Theseus son of Aegeus, at thy voice, to do the part whereunto he was summoned.

Enter Theseus, *on spectators' right.*

Th. Hearing from many in time past concerning the cruel marring of thy sight, I have recognised thee, son of Laïus; and now, through hearsay in this my coming, I have the fuller certainty. For thy garb, and that hapless face, alike assure me of thy name; and in all compassion would I ask thee, ill-fated Oedipus, what is thy suit to Athens or to me that thou hast taken thy place here, thou and the hapless maiden at thy side. Declare it; dire indeed must be the fortune told by thee, from which I should stand aloof; who know that I myself also was reared in exile, like to thine, and in strange lands wrestled with perils to my life, as no man beside. Never, then, would I turn aside from a stranger, such as thou art now, or refuse to aid in his deliverance; for well know I that I am a man, and that in the morrow my portion is no greater than thine.

Oe. Theseus, thy nobleness hath in brief words shown such grace that for me there is need to say but little. Thou hast rightly said who I am, from what sire I spring, from what land I have come; and so nought else remains for me but to speak my desire,—and the tale is told.

Th. Even so—speak that—I fain would hear.

Oe. I come to offer thee my woe-worn body as a gift,—not goodly to look upon; but the gains from it are better than beauty.

Th. And what gain dost thou claim to have brought?

Oe. Hereafter thou shalt learn; not yet, I think.

Th. At what time, then, will thy benefit be shown?

Oe. When I am dead, and thou hast given me burial.

Th. Thou cravest life's last boon; for all between thou hast no memory,—or no care.

Oe. Yea, for by that boon I reap all the rest.

Th. Nay, then, this grace which thou cravest from me hath small compass.

Oe. Yet give heed; this issue is no light one,—no, verily.

Th. Meanest thou, as between thy sons and me?

Oe. King, they would fain convey me to Thebes.

Th. But if to thy content, then for thee exile is not seemly.

Oe. Nay, when *I* was willing, *they* refused.

Th. But, foolish man, temper in misfortune is not meet.

Oe. When thou hast heard my story, chide; till then, forbear.

Th. Say on: I must not pronounce without knowledge.

Oe. I have suffered, Theseus, cruel wrong on wrong.

Th. Wilt thou speak of the ancient trouble of thy race?

Oe. No, verily: *that* is noised throughout Hellas.

Th. What, then, is thy grief that passeth the griefs of man?

Oe. Thus it is with me. From my country I have been driven by mine own offspring; and my doom is to return no more, as guilty of a father's blood.

Th. How, then, should they fetch thee to them, if ye must dwell apart?

Oe. The mouth of the god will constrain them.

Th. In fear of what woe foreshown?

Oe. That they must be smitten in this land.

Th. And how should bitterness come between them and me?

Oe. Kind son of Aegeus, to the gods alone comes never old age or death, but all else is confounded by all-mastering time. Earth's strength decays, and the strength of the body; faith dies, distrust is born; and the same spirit is never steadfast among friends, or betwixt city and city; for, be it soon or be it late, men find sweet turn to bitter, and then once more to love.

And if now all is sunshine between Thebes and thee, yet time, in his untold course, gives birth to days and nights untold, wherein for a small cause they shall sunder with the spear that plighted concord of to-day; when my slumbering and buried corpse, cold in death, shall one day drink their warm blood, if Zeus is still Zeus, and Phoebus, the son of Zeus, speaks true.

But, since I would not break silence touching mysteries, suffer me to cease where I began; only make thine own word good, and never shalt thou say that in vain didst thou welcome Oedipus to dwell in this realm,—unless the gods cheat my hope.

Ch. King, from the first yon man hath shown the mind to perform these promises, or the like, for our land.

Th. Who, then, would reject the friendship of such an one?—to whom, first, the hearth of an ally is ever open, by mutual right, among us; and then he hath come as a suppliant to our gods, fraught with no light recompense for this land and for me. In reverence for these claims, I will never spurn his grace, but will establish him as a citizen in the land. And if it is the stranger's pleasure to abide here, I will charge you to guard him; or if to come with me be more pleasing,—this choice, or that, Oedipus, thou canst take; thy will shall be mine.

Oe. O Zeus, mayest thou be good unto such men!

Th. What wouldst thou, then? wouldst thou come to my house?

Oe. Yea, were it lawful;—but *this* is the place—

Th. What art thou to do here? I will not thwart thee...

Oe. —where I shall vanquish those who cast me forth.

Th. Great were this promised boon from thy presence.

Oe. It shall be—if thy pledge is kept with me indeed.

Th. Fear not touching me; never will I fail thee.

Oe. I will not bind thee with an oath, as one untrue.

Th. Well, thou wouldst win nought more than by my word.

Oe. How wilt thou act, then? Th. What may be thy fear?

Oe. Men will come— Th. Nay, these will look to that.

Oe. Beware lest, if thou leave me— Th. Teach me not my part.

Oe. Fear constrains— Th. My heart feels not fear.

Oe. Thou knowest not the threats— Th. I know that none shall take thee hence in my despite. Oft have threats blustered, in men's wrath, with threatenings loud and vain; but when the mind is lord of himself once more, the threats are gone. And for yon men, haply,—aye, though they have waxed bold to speak dread things of bringing thee back,—the sundering waters will prove wide, and hard to sail. Now I would have thee be of a good courage, apart from any resolve of mine, if indeed Phoebus hath sent thee on thy way; still, though I be not here, my name, I wot, will shield thee from harm.

str. 1.Ch. Stranger, in this land of goodly steeds thou hast come to earth's fairest home, even to our white Colonus; where the nightingale, a constant guest, trills her clear note in the covert of green glades, dwelling amid the wine-dark ivy and the god's inviolate bowers, rich in berries and fruit, unvisited by sun, unvexed by wind of any storm; where the reveller Dionysus ever walks the ground, companion of the nymphs that nursed him.

ant. 1.And, fed of heavenly dew, the narcissus blooms morn by morn with fair clusters, crown of the Great Goddesses from of yore; and the crocus blooms with golden beam. Nor fail the sleepless founts whence the waters of Cephisus wander, but each day with stainless tide he moveth over the plains of the land's swelling bosom, for the giving of quick increase; nor hath the Muses' quire abhorred this place, nor Aphrodite of the golden rein.

str. 2.And a thing there is such as I know not by fame on Asian ground, or as ever born in the great Dorian isle of Pelops,—a growth unconquered, self-renewing, a terror to the spears of the foemen, a growth which mightily flourishes in this land,— the gray-leafed olive, nurturer of children. Youth shall not mar it by the ravage of his hand, nor any who dwells with old age; for the sleepless eye of the Morian Zeus beholds it, and the gray-eyed Athena.

ant. 2.And another praise have I to tell for this the city our mother, the gift of a great god, a glory of the land most high; the might of horses, the might of young horses, the might of the sea.

For thou, son of Cronus, our lord Poscidon, hast throned her in this pride, since in these roads first thou didst show forth the curb that cures the rage of steeds. And the shapely oar, apt to men's hands, hath a wondrous speed on the brine, following the hundred-footed Nereids.

An. O land that art praised above all lands, now is it for thee to make those bright praises seen in deeds!

Oe. What new thing hath chanced, my daughter?

An. Yonder Creon draws near us,—not without followers, father.

Oe. Ah, kind elders, now give me, I pray you, the final proof of my safety!

Ch. Fear not—it shall be thine. If *I* am aged, this country's strength hath not grown old.

Enter Creon, *with attendants.*

Cr. Sirs, noble dwellers in this land, I see that a sudden fear hath troubled your eyes at my coming; but shrink not from me, and let no ungentle word escape you.

I am here with no thought of force;—I am old, and I know that the city whereunto I have come is mighty, if any in Hellas hath might;—no,—I have been sent, in these my years, to plead with yonder man that he return with me to the land of Cadmus;—not one man's envoy am I, but with charge from our people all; since 'twas mine, by kinship, to mourn his woes as no Theban beside.

Nay, unhappy Oedipus, hear us, and come home! Rightfully art thou called by all the Cadmean folk, and in chief by me, even as I—unless I am the basest of all men born—chiefly sorrow for thine ills, old man, when I see thee, hapless one, a stranger and a wanderer evermore, roaming in beggary, with one handmaid for thy stay. Alas, I had not thought that she could fall to such a depth of misery as that whereunto she hath fallen—yon hapless girl!—while she ever tends thy dark life amid penury,—in ripe youth, but unwed,—a prize for the first rude hand.

Is it not a cruel reproach—alas!—that I have cast at thee, and me, and all our race? But indeed an open shame cannot be hid; then—in the name of thy fathers' gods, hearken to me, Oedipus!—hide it *thou*, by consenting to return to the city and the house of thy fathers, after a kindly farewell to this State,—for she is worthy: yet thine own hath the first claim on thy piety, since 'twas she that nurtured thee of old.

Oe. All-daring, who from any plea of right wouldst draw a crafty device, why dost thou attempt me thus, and seek once more to take me in the toils where capture would be sorest? In the old days—when, distempered by my self-wrought woes, I yearned to be cast out of the land—thy will went not with mine to grant the boon. But when my fierce grief had spent its force, and the seclusion of the house was sweet, *then* wast thou for thrusting me from the house and from the land—nor had this kinship any dearness for thee then: and now, again—when thou seest that I have kindly welcome from this city and from all her sons, thou seekest to pluck me away, wrapping hard thoughts in soft words. And yet what joy is there here,—in kindness shown to us against our will? As if a man should give thee no gift, bring thee no aid, when thou wast fain of the boon; but after thy soul's desire was sated, should grant it then, when the grace could be gracious no more: wouldst thou not find that pleasure vain? Yet such are thine own offers unto me,—good in name, but in their substance evil.

And I will declare it to these also, that I may show thee false. Thou hast come to fetch me, not that thou mayest take me home, but that thou mayest plant me near thy borders, and so thy city may escape unscathed by troubles from this land. *That* portion is not for thee, but *this*,—my curse upon the country, ever abiding therein;—and for my sons, this heritage—room enough in my realm wherein—to die.

Am I not wiser than thou in the fortunes of Thebes? Yea, wiser far, as truer are the sources of my knowledge, even Phoebus, and his father, Zeus most high. But thou hast come hither with fraud on thy lips, yea, with a tongue keener than the edge of the sword; yet by thy pleading thou art like to reap more woe than weal. Howbeit, I know that I persuade thee not of this,—go!—and suffer us to live here; for even in this plight our life would not be evil, so were we content therewith.

Cr. Which, thinkest thou, most suffers in this parley,—I by thy course, or thou by thine own?

Oe. For me, 'tis enough if thy pleading fails, as with me, so with yon men who are nigh.

Cr. Unhappy man, shall it be seen that not even thy years have brought thee wit? Must thou live to be the reproach of age?

Oe. Thou hast a ready tongue, but I know not the honest man who hath fair words for every cause.

Cr. Words may be many, and yet may miss their aim.

Oe. As if thine, forsooth, were few, but aimed aright.

Cr. No, truly, for one whose wit is such as thine.

Oe. Depart—for I will say it in the name of yon men also!—and beset me not with jealous watch in the place where I am destined to abide.

Cr. These men—not thee—call I to witness: but, as for the strain of thine answer to thy kindred, if ever I take thee—

Oe. And who could take me in despite of these allies?

Cr. I promise thee, thou soon shalt smart without that.

Oe. Where is the deed which warrants that blustering word?

Cr. One of thy two daughters hath just been seized by me, and sent hence,—the other I will remove forthwith.

Oe. Woe is me! Cr. More woeful thou wilt find it soon.

Oe. Thou hast my child? Cr. And will have this one ere long.

Oe. Alas! friends, what will ye do? Will ye forsake me? will ye not drive the godless man from this land?

Ch. Hence, stranger, hence—begone! Unrighteous is thy present deed— unrighteous the deed which thou hast done.

Cr. (*to his attendants*). 'Twere time for you to lead off yon girl perforce, if she will not go of her free will.

An. Wretched that I am! whither shall I fly?—where find help from gods or men?

Ch. (*threateningly, to*Creon). What wouldst thou, stranger?

Cr. I will not touch yon man, but her who is mine.

Oe. O, elders of the land! Ch. Stranger,—thy deed is not just.

Cr. 'Tis just. Ch. How just? Cr. I take mine own. [*He lays his hand on Antigone.*

*str.*Oe. Hear, O Athens!

Ch. What wouldst thou, stranger? Release her! Thy strength, and ours, will soon be proved.

[*They approach him with threatening gestures.*

Cr. Stand back! Ch. Not from thee, while this is thy purpose.

Cr. Nay, 'twill be war with Thebes for thee, if thou harm me.

Oe. Said I not so? Ch. Unhand the maid at once!

Cr. Command not where thou art not master.

Ch. Leave hold, I tell thee! Cr. (*to one of his guards, who at a signal seizes Antigone*). And I tell thee—begone!

Ch. To the rescue, men of Colonus—to the rescue! Athens—yea, Athens—is outraged with the strong hand! Hither, hither to our help!

An. They drag me hence—ah me!—friends, friends!

Oe. Where art thou, my child? (*blindly seeking for her*). An. I am taken by force—

Oe. Thy hands, my child!— An. Nay, I am helpless.

Cr. (*to his guards*). Away with you! Oe. Ah me, ah me! [*Exeunt guards with*Antigone.

Cr. So *those* two crutches shall never more prop thy steps. But since 'tis thy will to worst thy country and thy friends—whose mandate, though a prince, I here discharge—then be that victory thine. For hereafter, I wot, thou wilt come to know all this,—that now, as in time past, thou hast done thyself no good, when, in despite of friends, thou hast indulged anger, which is ever thy bane. [*He turns to follow his guards.*

Ch. Hold, stranger! Cr. Hands off, I say!

Ch. I will not let thee go, unless thou give back the maidens.

Cr. Then wilt thou soon give Thebes a still dearer prize:—I will seize more than those two girls.

Ch. What—whither wilt thou turn?Cr. Yon man shall be my captive.

Ch. A valiant threat! Cr. 'Twill forthwith be a deed.

Ch. Aye, unless the ruler of this realm hinder thee.

Oe. Shameless voice! Wilt thou indeed touch me?

Cr. Be silent! Oe. Nay, may the powers of this place suffer me to utter yet this curse! Wretch, who, when these eyes were dark, hast reft from me by force the helpless one who was mine eyesight! Therefore to thee and to thy race may the Sun-god, the god who sees all things, yet grant an old age such as mine!

Cr. See ye this, people of the land?

Oe. They see both me and thee; they know that my wrongs are deeds, and my revenge—but breath.

Cr. I will not curb my wrath—nay, alone though I am, and slow with age, I'll take yon man by force.

[*He approaches* Oedipus *as if to seize him.*

ant. Oe. Woe is me!

Ch. 'Tis a bold spirit that thou hast brought with thee, stranger, if thou thinkest to achieve this.

Cr. I do. Ch. Then will I deem Athens a city no more.

Cr. In a just cause the weak vanquishes the strong.

Oe. Hear ye his words? Ch. Yea, words which he shall not turn to deeds, Zeus knows! Cr. Zeus haply knows—thou dost not.

Ch. Insolence! Cr. Insolence which thou must bear.

Ch. What ho, people, rulers of the land, ho, hither with all speed, hither! These men are on their way to cross our borders!

Enter Theseus.

Th. What means this shout? What is the trouble? What fear can have moved you to stay my sacrifice at the altar unto the sea-god, the lord of your Colonus? Speak, that I may know all, since therefore have I sped hither with more than easeful speed of foot.

Oe. Ah, friend,—I know thy voice,—yon man, but now, hath done me foul wrong.

Th. What is that wrong? And who hath wrought it? Speak!

Oe. Creon, whom thou seest there, hath torn away from me my two children,—mine all.

Th. What dost thou tell me? Oe. Thou hast heard my wrong.

Th. (*to his attendants*). Haste, one of you, to the altars yonder,—constrain the folk to leave the sacrifice, and to speed—footmen,—horsemen all, with slack rein,—to the region where the two highways meet, lest the maidens pass, and I become a mockery to this stranger, as one spoiled by force. Away, I tell thee—quick!—(*Turning towards* Creon.) As for yon man—if my wrath went as far as he deserves—I would not have suffered him to go scatheless from my hand. But now such law as he himself hath brought, and no other, shall be the rule for his correction.—(*Addressing* Creon.) Thou shalt not quit this land until thou bring those maidens, and produce them in my sight; for thy deed is a disgrace to me, and to thine own race, and to thy country. Thou hast come unto a city that observes justice, and sanctions nothing without law,—yet thou hast put her lawful powers aside,—thou hast made this rude inroad,—thou art taking captives at thy pleasure, and snatching prizes by violence, as in the belief that my city was void of men, or manned by slaves, and I—a thing of nought.

Yet 'tis not by Theban training that thou art base; Thebes is not wont to rear unrighteous sons; nor would she praise thee, if she learned that thou art spoiling me,—yea, spoiling the gods, when by force thou leadest off their hapless suppliants. Now, were my foot upon thy soil, never would I wrest or plunder, without licence from the ruler of the land, whoso he might be—no, though my claim were of all claims most just: I should know how an alien ought to live among citizens. But thou art shaming a city that deserves it not, even thine own; and the fulness of thy years brings thee an old age bereft of wit.

I have said, then, and I say it once again—let the maidens be brought hither with all speed, unless thou wouldst sojourn in this land by no free choice;—and this I tell thee from my soul, as with my lips.

Ch. Seest thou thy plight, O stranger? Thou art deemed to come of a just race; but thy deeds are found evil.

Cr. Not counting this city void of manhood, son of Aegeus, nor of counsel,—as thou sayest,—have I wrought this deed; but because I judged that its folk could never be so enamoured of my kinsfolk as to foster them against my will. And I knew that this people would not receive a parricide,—a polluted man,—a man with whom had been found the unholy bride of her son. Such the wisdom, I knew, that dwells on the Mount of Ares in their land; which suffers not such wanderers to dwell within this realm. In that faith, I sought to take this prize. Nor had I done so, but that he was calling down bitter curses on me, and on my race; when, being so wronged, I deemed that I had warrant for this requital. For anger knows no old age, till death come; the dead alone feel no smart.

Therefore thou shalt act as seems to thee good; for, though my cause is just, the lack of aid makes me weak: yet, old though I am, I will endeavour to meet deed with deed

Oe. O shameless soul, where, thinkest thou, falls this thy taunt,—on my age, or on thine own? Bloodshed—incest—misery—all this thy lips have launched against me,—all this that I have borne, woe is me! by no choice of mine: for such was the pleasure of the gods, wroth, haply, with the race from of old. Take me alone, and thou couldst find no sin to upbraid me withal, in quittance whereof I was driven to sin thus against myself and against my kin. Tell me, now,—if, by voice of oracle, some divine doom was coming on my sire, that he should die by a son's hand, how couldst thou justly reproach me therewith, who was then unborn,—whom no sire had yet begotten, no mother's womb conceived? And if, when born to woe—as I was born—I met my sire in strife, and slew him, all ignorant what I was doing, and to whom,—how couldst thou justly blame the unknowing deed?

And my mother—wretch, hast thou no shame in forcing me to speak of her nuptials, when she was thy sister, and they such as I will now tell—for verily I will not be silent, when thou hast gone so far in impious speech. Yea, she was my mother,—oh, misery!—my mother,—I knew it not, nor she—and, for her shame, bare children to the son whom she had borne. But one thing, at least, I know,—that thy will consents thus to revile her and me; but not of my free will did I wed her, and not of free will do I speak now.

Nay, not in this marriage shall I be called guilty, nor in that slaying of my sire which thou ever urgest against me with bitter reviling. Answer me but one thing that I ask thee. If, here and now, one should come up and seek to slay thee—thee, the righteous—wouldst thou ask if the murderer was thy father, or wouldst thou reckon with him straightway? I think, as thou lovest thy life, thou wouldst requite the culprit, nor look around thee for thy warrant. But such the plight into which I came, led by

61

gods; and in this, could my sire come back to life, methinks he would not gainsay me.

Yet *thou*,—for thou art not a just man, but one who holds all things meet to utter, knowing no barrier betwixt speech and silence—*thou* tauntest me in such wise, before yon men. And thou findest it timely to flatter the renowned Theseus, and Athens, saying how well her state hath been ordered: yet, while giving such large praise, thou forgettest this,—that if any land knows how to worship the gods with due rites, this land excels therein; whence thou hadst planned to steal me, the suppliant, the old man, and didst seek to seize me, and hast already carried off my daughters. Wherefore I now call on yon goddesses, I supplicate them, I adjure them with prayers, to bring me help and to fight in my cause, that thou mayest learn well by what manner of men this realm is guarded.

Ch. The stranger is a good man, O king; his fate hath been accurst; but 'tis worthy of our succour.

Th. Enough of words:—the doers of the deed are in flight, while we, the sufferers, stand still.

Cr. What, then, wouldst thou have a helpless man to do?

Th. Show the way in their track,—while I escort thee,—that, if in these regions thou hast the maidens of our quest, thou thyself mayest discover them to me; but if thy men are fleeing with the spoil in their grasp, we may spare our trouble; the chase is for others, from whom they will never escape out of this land, to thank their gods.

Come,—forward! The spoiler hath been spoiled, I tell thee—Fate hath taken the hunter in the toils; gains got by wrongful arts are soon lost. And thou shalt have no ally in thine aim, for well wot I that not without accomplice or resource hast thou gone to such a length of violence in the daring mood which hath inspired thee here: no,—there was some one in whom thou wast trusting when thou didst essay these deeds. And to this I must look, nor make this city weaker than one man. Dost thou take my drift? Or seem these words as vain as seemed the warnings when thy deed was still a-planning?

Cr. Say what thou wilt while thou art here,—I will not cavil: but at home I, too, will know how to act.

Th. For the present, threaten, but go forward.—Do thou, Oedipus, stay here in peace, I pray thee,—with my pledge that, unless I die before, I will not cease till I put thee in possession of thy children.

Oe. Heaven reward thee, Theseus, for thy nobleness, and thy loyal care in my behalf!

[*Exeunt* Theseus *and attendants, with* Creon, *on spectators' left.*

str. 1.Ch. Oh to be where the foeman, turned to bay, will soon join in the brazen clangour of battle, haply by the shores loved of Apollo, haply by that torch-lit strand where the Great Goddesses cherish dread rites for mortals, on whose lips the ministrant Eumolpidae have laid the precious seal of silence; where, methinks, the war-waking Theseus and the captives twain, the sister maids, will soon meet within our borders, amid a war-cry of men strong to save!

ant. 1.Or perchance they will soon draw nigh to the pastures on the west of Oea's snowy rock, borne on horses in their flight, or in chariots racing at speed.

Creon will be worsted! Terrible are the warriors of Colonus, and the followers of Theseus are terrible in their might. Yea, the steel of every bridle flashes,—with slack bridle-rein all the knighthood rides apace that worships our Queen of Chivalry, Athena, and the earth-girdling Sea-god, the son of Rhea's love.

str. 2.Is the battle now, or yet to be? For somehow my soul woos me to the hope that soon I shall be face to face with the maidens thus sorely tried, thus sorely visited by the hand of a kinsman.

To-day, to-day, Zeus will work some great thing: I have presage of victory in the strife. O to be a dove with swift strength as of the storm, that I might reach an airy cloud, with gaze lifted above the fray!

ant. 2.Hear, all-ruling lord of heaven, all-seeing Zeus! Enable the guardians of this land, in might triumphant, to achieve the capture that gives the prize to their hands! So grant thy daughter also, our dread Lady, Pallas Athena! And Apollo, the hunter, and his sister, who follows the dappled, swift-footed deer—fain am I that they should come, a twofold strength, to this land and to her people.

Ah, wanderer friend, thou wilt not have to tax thy watcher with false augury,—for yonder I see the maidens drawing near with an escort.

Oe. Where—where? How? What sayest thou?

*Enter*Antigone*and*Ismene,*with*Theseus*and his attendants, on the spectators' left.*

An. O father, father, that some god would suffer thine eyes to see this noble man, who hath brought us here to thee!

Oe. My child!—ye are here indeed?

An. Yea, for these strong arms have saved us—Theseus, and his trusty followers.

Oe. Come ye hither, my child,—let me embrace you—restored beyond all hope!

An. Thy wish shall be granted—we crave what we bestow.

Oe. Where, then, where are ye? An. Here approaching thee together.

Oe. My darlings! An. A father loves his own.

Oe. Props of mine age! An. And sharers of thy sorrow.

Oe. I hold my dear ones; and now, should I die, I were not wholly wretched, since ye have come to me. Press close to me on either side, children, cleave to your sire, and repose from this late roaming, so forlorn, so grievous! And tell me what hath passed as shortly as ye may; brief speech sufficeth for young maidens.

An. Here is our deliverer: from him thou shouldst hear the story, father, since his is the deed; so shall my part be brief.

Oe. Sir, marvel not, if with such yearning I prolong my words unto my children, found again beyond my hope. For well I wot that this joy in respect of them hath come to me from thee, and thee alone: thou hast rescued them, and no man beside. And may the gods deal with thee after my wish,—with thee, and with this land; for among you, above all human kind, have I found the fear of heaven, and the spirit of fairness, and the lips that lie not. I know these things, which with these words I requite; for what I have, I have through thee, and no man else.

Stretch forth thy right hand, O king, I pray thee, that I may touch it, and, if 'tis lawful, kiss thy cheek.— But what am I saying? Unhappy as I have become, how could I wish thee to touch one with whom all stain of sin hath made its dwelling? No, not I,—nor allow thee, if thou wouldst. They alone can share this burden, to whom it hath come home.—Receive my greeting where thou standest; and in the future still give me thy loyal care, as thou hast given it to this hour.

Th. No marvel is it to me, if thou hast shown some mind to large discourse, for joy in these thy children, and if thy first care hath been for their words, rather than for me; indeed, there is nought to vex me in that. Not in words so much as deeds would I make the lustre of my life. Thou hast the proof; I have failed in nothing of my sworn faith to thee, old man; here am I, with the maidens living,—yea, scatheless of those threats. And how the fight was won, what need that I should idly boast, when thou wilt learn it from these maidens in converse?

But there is a matter that hath newly chanced to me, as I came hither; lend me thy counsel thereon, for, small though it be, 'tis food for wonder; and mortal man should deem nothing beneath his care.

Oe. What is it, son of Aegeus? Tell me;—I myself know nought of that whereof thou askest.

Th. A man, they say,—not thy countryman, yet thy kinsman,—hath somehow cast himself, a suppliant, at our altar of Poseidon, where I was sacrificing when I first set out hither.

Oe. Of what land is he? What craves he by the supplication?

Th. I know one thing only; they say, he asks brief speech with thee, which shall not irk thee much.

Oe. On what theme? That suppliant posture is not trivial.

Th. He asks, they say, no more than that he may confer with thee, and return unharmed from his journey hither.

Oe. Who can he be who thus implores the god?

Th. Look if ye have any kinsman at Argos, who might crave this boon of thee.

Oe. O friend! Say no word more! Th. What ails thee?

Oe. Ask it not of me— Th. Ask what?—Speak!

Oe. By those words I know who is the suppliant.

Th. And who can he be, against whom I should have a grief?

Oe. My son, O king,—the hated son whose words would vex mine ear as the words of no man beside.

Th. What? Canst thou not listen, without doing what thou wouldst not? Why should it pain thee to hear him?

Oe. Most hateful, king, hath that voice become to his sire:—lay me not under constraint to yield in this.

Th. But think whether his suppliant state constrains thee: what if thou hast a duty of respect for the god?

An. Father, hearken to me, though I be young who counsel. Allow the king to gratify his own heart, and to gratify the god as he wishes; and, for thy daughter's sake, allow our brother to come. For he will not pluck thee perforce from thy resolve,— never fear,—by such words as shall not be spoken for thy good. But to hear him speak,—what harm can be in that? Ill-devised deeds, thou knowest, are bewrayed by speech. Thou art his sire; so that, e'en if he were to wrong thee with the most impious of foul wrongs, my father, it is not lawful for thee to wrong him again.

Oh, let him come: other men, also, have evil off-spring, and are swift to wrath; but they hear advice, and are charmed from their mood by the gentle spells of friends.

Look thou to the past, not to the present,—think on all that thou hast borne through sire and mother; and if thou considerest those things, well I wot, thou wilt discern how evil is the end that waits on evil wrath; not slight are thy reasons to think thereon, bereft, as thou art, of the sight that returns no more.

Nay, yield to us! It is not seemly for just suitors to sue long; it is not seemly that a man should receive good, and thereafter lack the mind to requite it.

Oe. My child, 'tis sore for me, this pleasure that ye win from me by your pleading;—but be it as ye will. Only, if that man is to come hither,—friend, let no one ever become master of my life!

Th. I need not to hear such words more than once, old man:—I would not boast; but be sure that thy life is safe, while any god saves mine.

[*Exit* Theseus, *to the right of the spectators.*

str. Ch. Whoso craves the ampler length of life, not content to desire a modest span, him will I judge with no uncertain voice; he cleaves to folly.

For the long days lay up full many things nearer unto grief than joy; but as for thy delights, their place shall know them no more, when a man's life hath lapsed beyond the fitting term; and the Deliverer comes at the last to all alike,—when the doom of Hades is suddenly revealed, without marriage-song, or lyre, or dance,—even Death at the last.

ant. Not to be born is, past all prizing, best; but, when a man hath seen the light, this is next best by far, that with all speed he should go thither, whence he hath come.

For when he hath seen youth go by, with its light follies, what troublous affliction is strange to his lot, what suffering is not therein?—envy, factions, strife, battles and slaughters; and, last of all, age claims him for her own,—age, dispraised, infirm, unsociable, unfriended, with whom all woe of woe abides.

ep. In such years is yon hapless one, not I alone: and as some cape that fronts the North is lashed on every side by the waves of winter, so he also is fiercely lashed evermore by the dread troubles that break on him like billows, some from the setting of the sun, some from the rising, some in the region of the noon-tide beam, some from the gloom-wrapped hills of the North.

An. Lo, yonder, methinks, I see the stranger coming hither,—yea, without attendants, my father,—the tears streaming from his eyes.

Oe. Who is he?

An. The same who was in our thoughts from the first;—Polyneices hath come to us.

Enter Polyneices, *on the spectators' left.*

Po. Ah me, what shall I do? Whether shall I weep first for mine own sorrows, sisters, or for mine aged sire's, as I see them yonder? Whom I have found in a strange land, an exile here with you twain, clad in such raiment, whereof the foul squalor hath dwelt with that aged form so long, a very blight upon his flesh,—while above the sightless eyes the unkempt hair flutters in the breeze; and matching with these things, meseems, is the food that he carries, hapless one, against hunger's pinch.

Wretch that I am! I learn all this too late: and I bear witness that I am proved the vilest of men in all that touches care for thee:—from mine own lips hear what I am. But, seeing that Zeus himself, in all that he doeth, hath Mercy for the sharer of his throne, may she come to thy side also, my father; for the faults can be healed, but can never more be made worse.

[*A pause.*

Why art thou silent?......Speak, father:—turn not away from me. Hast thou not even an answer for me? Wilt thou dismiss me in mute scorn, without telling wherefore thou art wroth?

O ye, his daughters, sisters mine, strive ye, at least, to move our sire's implacable, inexorable silence, that he send me not away dishonoured,—who am the suppliant of the god,—in such wise as this, with no word of response.

An. Tell him thyself, unhappy one, what thou hast come to seek. As words flow, perchance they touch to joy, perchance they glow with anger, or with tenderness, and so they somehow give a voice to the dumb.

Po. Then will I speak boldly,—for thou dost admonish me well,—first claiming the help of the god himself, from whose altar the king of this land raised me, that I might come hither, with warranty to speak and hear, and go my way unharmed. And I will crave, strangers, that these pledges be kept with me by you, and by my sisters here, and by my sire.—But now I would fain tell thee, father, why I came.

I have been driven, an exile, from my fatherland, because, as eldest-born, I claimed to sit in thy sovereign seat. Wherefore Eteocles, though the younger, thrust me from the land, when he had neither worsted me in argument, nor come to trial of might and deed,—no, but won the city over. And of this I deem it most likely that the curse on thy house is the cause; then from soothsayers also I so hear. For when I came to Dorian Argos, I took the daughter of Adrastus to wife; and I bound to me by oath all of the Apian land who are foremost in renown of war, that with them I might levy the sevenfold host of spearmen against Thebes, and die in my just cause, or cast the doers of this wrong from the realm.

Well, and wherefore have I come hither now? With suppliant prayers, my father, unto thee—mine own, and the prayers of mine allies, who now, with seven hosts behind their seven spears, have set their leaguer round the plain of Thebes; of whom is swift-speared Amphiaraus, matchless warrior, matchless augur; then the son of Oeneus, Aetolian Tydeus; Eteoclus third, of Argive birth; the fourth, Hippomedon, sent by Talaos, his sire; while Capaneus, the fifth, vaunts that he will burn Thebes with fire, unto the ground; and sixth, Arcadian Parthenopaeus rushes to the war, named from that virgin of other days whose marriage in after-time gave him birth, trusty son of Atalanta. Last, I, thy son,—or if not thine, but offspring of an evil fate, yet thine at least in name,—lead the fearless host of Argos unto Thebes.

And we, by these thy children and by thy life, my father, implore thee all, praying thee to remit thy stern wrath against me, as I go forth to chastise my brother, who hath thrust me out and robbed me of my fatherland. For if aught of truth is told by oracles, they said that victory should be with those whom thou shouldst join.

Then, by our fountains and by the gods of our race, I ask thee to hearken and to yield; a beggar and an exile am I, an exile thou; by court to others we have a home, both thou and I, sharers of one doom; while *he,* king in the house—woe is me!— mocks in his pride at thee and me alike. But, if thou assist my purpose, small toil or time, and I will scatter his strength to the winds: and so will I bring thee and stablish thee in thine own house, and stablish myself, when I have cast him out by force. Be thy will with me, and that boast may be mine: without thee, I cannot e'en return alive.

Ch. For his sake who hath sent him, Oedipus, speak, as seems thee good, ere thou send the man away.

Oe. Nay, then, my friends, guardians of this land, were not Theseus he who had sent him hither to me, desiring that he should have my response, never should he have heard this voice. But now he shall be graced with it, ere he go,—yea, and hear from me such words as shall never gladden his life:—villain, who when thou hadst the sceptre and the throne, which now thy brother hath in Thebes, dravest me, thine own father, into exile, and madest me citiless, and madest me to wear this garb which now thou weepest to behold, when thou hast come unto the same stress of misery as I. The time for tears is past: no, I must bear this burden while I live, ever thinking of thee as of a murderer; for 'tis thou that hast brought my days to this anguish, 'tis thou that hast thrust me out; to thee I owe it that I wander, begging my daily bread from strangers. And, had these daughters not been born to be my comfort, verily I had been dead, for aught of help from thee. Now, these girls preserve me, these my nurses, these who are men, not women, in true service: but ye are aliens, and no sons of mine.

Therefore the eyes of Fate look upon thee—not yet as they will look anon, if indeed those hosts are moving against Thebes. Never canst thou overthrow that city; no, first shalt thou fall stained with bloodshed, and thy brother likewise. Such the curses that my soul sent forth before against you twain, and such do I now invoke to fight for me, that ye may deem it meet to revere parents, nor scorn your father utterly, because he is sightless who begat such sons; for these maidens did not thus. So my curses have control of thy 'supplication' and thy 'throne,'—if indeed Justice, revealed from of old, sits with Zeus in the might of the eternal laws.

And thou—begone, abhorred of me, and unfathered!—begone, thou vilest of the vile, and with thee take these my curses which I call down on thee—never to vanquish the land of thy race, no, nor ever return to hill-girt Argos, but by a kindred hand to die, and slay him by whom thou hast been driven out. Such is my prayer; and I call the paternal darkness of dread Tartarus to take thee unto another home,— I call the spirits of this place,—I call the Destroying God, who hath set that dreadful hatred in you twain. Go, with these words in thine ears—go, and publish it to the Cadmeans all, yea, and to thine own staunch allies, that Oedipus hath divided such honours to his sons.

Ch. Polyneices, in thy past goings I take no joy; and now go thy way with speed.

Po. Alas, for my journey and my baffled hope: alas, for my comrades! What an end was that march to have, whereon we sallied forth from Argos: woe is me!—aye, such an end, that I may not even utter it to any of my companions, or turn them back, but must go in silence to meet this doom.

Ah ye, his daughters and my sisters,—since ye hear these hard prayers of your sire,—if this father's curses be fulfilled, and some way of return to Thebes be found for you, oh, as ye fear the gods, do not, for your part, dishonour me,—nay, give me burial, and due funeral rites. And so the praise which ye now win from yonder man, for your service, shall be increased by another praise not less, by reason of the office wrought for me.

An. Polyneices, I entreat thee, hear me in one thing!

Po. What is it, dearest Antigone? Speak!

An. Turn thy host back to Argos,—aye, with all speed,—and destroy not thyself and Thebes.

Po. Nay, it cannot be: for how again could I lead the same host, when once I had blenched?

An. But why, my brother, should thine anger rise again? What gain is promised thee in destroying thy native city?

Po. 'Tis shame to be an exile, and, eldest born as I am, to be thus mocked on my brother's part.

An. Seest thou, then, to what sure fulfilment thou art bringing his prophecies, who bodes mutual slaying for you twain?

Po. Aye, for he wishes it:—but I must not yield.

An. Ah me unhappy!—But who will dare to follow thee, hearing what prophecies yon man hath uttered?

Po. I will not e'en report ill tidings: 'tis a good leader's part to tell the better news, and not the worse.

An. Brother! Thy resolve, then, is thus fixed?

Po. Yea,—and detain me not. For mine it now shall be to tread yon path, with evil doom and omen from this my sire and from his Furies; but for you twain, may Zeus make your path bright, if ye do my wishes when I am dead,—since in my life ye can do them no more.—(*He gently disengages himself from their embrace.*) Now, release me,—and farewell; for nevermore shall ye behold me living.

An. Woe is me! Po. Mourn not for me. An. And who would not bewail thee, brother, who thus art hurrying to death foreseen?

Po. If 'tis fate, I must die. An. Nay, nay,—hear my pleading!

Po. Plead not amiss. An. Then woe is me, indeed, if I must lose thee! Po. Nay, that rests with Fortune,—that end or another.—For you twain, at least, I pray the gods that ye never meet with ill; for in all men's eyes ye are unworthy to suffer. [*Exit, on spectators' left.*

Kommos str. 1.Ch. Behold, new ills have newly come, in our hearing, from the sightless stranger,—ills fraught with a heavy doom; unless, perchance, Fate is finding its goal. For 'tis not mine to say that a decree of Heaven is ever vain: watchful, aye watchful of those decrees is Time, overthrowing some fortunes, and on the morrow lifting others, again, to honour.—Hark that sound in the sky!—Zeus defend us! [*Thunder is heard.*

Oe. My children, my children! If there be any man to send, would that some one would fetch hither the peerless Theseus!

An. And what, father, is the aim of thy summons?

Oe. This winged thunder of Zeus will lead me anon to Hades: nay, send, and tarry not.

[*A second peal is heard.*

ant. 1.Ch. Hark! With louder noise it crashes down, unutterable, hurled by Zeus! The hair of my head stands up for fear, my soul is sore dismayed; for again the lightning flashes in the sky. Oh, to what event will it give birth? I am afraid, for never in vain doth it rush forth, or without grave issue. O thou dread sky! O Zeus!

Oe. Daughters, his destined end hath come upon your sire; he can turn his face from it no more.

An. How knowest thou? What sign hath told thee this?

Oe. I know it well.—But let some one go, I pray you, with all speed, and bring hither the lord of this realm. [*Another peal.*

str. 2.Ch. Ha! Listen! Once again that piercing thundervoice is around us! Be merciful, O thou god, be merciful, if thou art bringing aught of gloom for the land our mother! Gracious may I find thee, nor, because I have looked on a man accurst, have some meed, not of blessing for my portion! O Zeus our lord, to thee I cry!

Oe. Is the man near? Will he find me still alive, children, and master of my mind?

An. And what is the pledge which thou wouldst have fixed in thy mind?

Oe. In return for his benefits, I would duly give him the requital promised when I received them.

ant. 2.Ch. What ho, my son, hither, come hither! Or if in the glade's inmost recess, for the honour of the seagod Poseidon, thou art hallowing his altar with sacrifice,—come thence! Worthy art thou in the stranger's sight, worthy are thy city and thy folk, that he should render a just recompense for benefits. Haste, come quickly, O king!

Enter Theseus, *on the spectators' right.*

Th. Wherefore once more rings forth a summons from you all,—from my people as clearly as from our guest? Can a thunderbolt from Zeus be the cause, or rushing hail in its fierce onset? All forebodings may find place, when the god sends such a storm.

Oe. King, welcome is thy presence; and 'tis some god that hath made for thee the good fortune of this coming.

Th. And what new thing hath now befallen, son of Laïus?

Oe. My life hangs in the scale: and I fain would die guiltless of bad faith to thee and to this city, in respect of my pledges.

Th. And what sign of thy fate holds thee in suspense?

Oe. The gods, their own heralds, bring me the tidings, with no failure in the signs appointed of old.

Th. What sayest thou are the signs of these things, old man?

Oe. The thunder, peal on peal,—the lightning, flash on flash, hurled from the unconquered hand.

Th. Thou winnest my belief, for in much I find thee a prophet whose voice is not false;—then speak what must be done.

Oe. Son of Aegeus, I will unfold that which shall be a treasure for this thy city, such as age can never mar. Anon, unaided, and with no hand to guide me, I will show the way to the place where I must die. But that place reveal thou never unto mortal man,—tell not where it is hidden, nor in what region it lies; that so it may ever make for thee a defence, better than many shields, better than the succouring spear of neighbours.

But, for mysteries which speech may not profane, thou shalt mark them for thyself, when thou comest to that place alone: since neither to any of this people can I utter them, nor to mine own children, dear though they are. No, guard them thou alone; and when thou art coming to the end of life, disclose them to thy heir alone; let him teach his heir; and so thenceforth.

And thus shalt thou hold this city unscathed from the side of the Dragon's brood;—full many States lightly enter on offence, e'en though their neighbour lives aright. For the gods are slow, though they are sure, in visitation, when men scorn godliness, and turn to frenzy. Not such be thy fate, son of Aegeus.—Nay, thou knowest such things, without my precepts.

But to that place—for the divine summons urges me—let us now set forth, and hesitate no more.—(*As if suddenly inspired, he moves with slow but firm steps towards the left of the scene, beckoning the others onward.*) My children, follow me,—thus,—for I now have in strange wise been made your guide, as ye were your sire's. On,—touch me not,—

69

nay, suffer me unaided to find out that sacred tomb where 'tis my portion to be buried in this land.

This way,—hither,—this way!—for this way doth Guiding Hermes lead me, and the goddess of the dead!

O light,—no light to me,—mine once thou wast, I ween,—but now my body feels thee for the last time! For now go I to hide the close of my life with Hades.— Truest of friends! blessed be thou, and this land, and thy lieges; and, when your days are blest, think on me the dead, for your welfare evermore.

[*He passes from the stage on the spectators' left,—followed by his daughters,*Theseus,*and attendants.*

*str.*Ch. If with prayer I may adore the Unseen Goddess, and thee, lord of the children of night, O hear me, Aïdoneus, Aïdoneus! Not in pain, not by a doom that wakes sore lament, may the stranger pass to the fields of the dead below, the all-enshrouding, and to the Stygian house. Many were the sorrows that came to him without cause; but in requital a just god will lift him up.

*ant.*Goddesses Infernal! And thou, dread form of the unconquered hound, thou who hast thy lair in those gates of many guests, thou untameable Watcher of Hell, gnarling from the cavern's jaws, as rumour from the beginning tells of thee!

Hear me, O Death, son of Earth and Tartarus! May that Watcher leave a clear path for the stranger on his way to the nether fields of the dead! To thee I call, giver of the eternal sleep.

MESSENGER.

Countrymen, my tidings might most shortly be summed thus: Oedipus is gone. But the story of the hap may not be told in brief words, as the deeds yonder were not briefly done.

Ch. He is gone, hapless one? Me. Be sure that he hath passed from life.

Ch. Ah, how? by a god-sent doom, and painless?

Me. There thou touchest on what is indeed worthy of wonder. How he moved hence, thou thyself must know, since thou wast here,—with no friend to show the way, but guide himself unto us all.

Now, when he had come to the sheer Threshold, bound by brazen steps to earth's deep roots, he paused in one of many branching paths, near the basin in the rock, where the inviolate covenant of Theseus and Peirithous hath its memorial. He stood midway between that basin and the Thorician stone,—the hollow pear-tree and the marble tomb; then sate him down, and loosed his sordid raiment.

And then he called his daughters, and bade them fetch water from some fount, that he should wash, and make a drink-offering. And they went to the hill which was in view, Demeter's hill who guards the tender plants, and in short space brought that which their father had enjoined; then they ministered to him with washing, and dressed him, as use ordains.

But when he had content of doing all, and no part of his desire was now unheeded, then was thunder from the Zeus of the Shades: and the maidens shuddered as they heard; they fell at their father's knees, and wept, nor ceased from beating the breast, and wailing very sore.

70

And when he heard their sudden bitter cry, he put his arms around them, and said: 'My children, this day ends your father's life. For now all hath perished that was mine, and no more shall ye bear the burden of tending me,—no light one, well I know, my children; yet one little word makes all those toils as nought; *love* had ye from me, as from none beside; and now ye shall have me with you no more, through all your days to come.'

On such wise, close-clinging to each other, sire and daughters sobbed and wept. But when they had made an end of wailing, and the sound went up no more, there was a stillness; and suddenly a voice of one who cried aloud to him, so that the hair of all stood up on their heads for sudden fear, and they were afraid. For the god called him with many callings and manifold: '*Oedipus, Oedipus, why delay we to go? Thou tarriest too long.*'

But when he perceived that he was called of the god, he craved that the king Theseus should draw near; and when he came near, said: 'O my friend, give, I pray thee, the solemn pledge of thy right hand to my children, and ye, daughters, to him; and promise thou never to forsake them of thy free will, but to do all things for their good, as thy friendship and the time may prompt.' And he, like a man of noble spirit, without making lament, sware to keep that promise to his friend.

But when Theseus had so promised, straightway Oedipus felt for his children with blind hands, and said: 'O my children, ye must be nobly brave of heart, and depart from this place, nor ask to behold unlawful sights, or to hear such speech as may not be heard. Nay, go with all haste; only let Theseus be present, as is his right, a witness of those things which are to be.'

So spake he, and we all heard; and with streaming tears and with lamentation we followed the maidens away. But when we had gone apart, after no long time we looked back, and Oedipus we saw nowhere any more, but the king alone, holding his hand before his face to screen his eyes, as if some dread sight had been seen, and such as none might endure to behold. And then, after a short space, we saw him salute the earth and the home of the gods above, both at once, in one prayer.

But by what doom Oedipus perished, no man can tell, save Theseus alone. No fiery thunderbolt of the god removed him in that hour, nor any rising of storm from the sea; but either a messenger from the gods, or the world of the dead, the nether adamant, riven for him in love, without pain; for the passing of the man was not with lamentation, or in sickness and suffering, but, above mortal's, wonderful. And if to any I seem to speak folly, I would not woo their belief, who count me foolish.

Ch. And where are the maidens, and their escort?

Me. Not far hence; for the sounds of mourning tell plainly that they approach.

str. 1.An. Woe, woe! Now, indeed, is it for us, unhappy sisters, in all fulness to bewail the curse on the blood that is ours from our sire! For him, while he lived, we bore that long pain without pause; and at the last a sight and a loss that baffle thought are ours to tell.

Ch. And how is it with you? An. We can but conjecture, friends.

Ch. He is gone? An. Even as thou mightest wish: yea, surely, when death met him not in war, or on the deep, but he was snatched to the viewless fields by some swift, strange doom. Ah me! and a night as of death hath come on the eyes of us twain: for how shall we find our bitter livelihood, roaming to some far land, or on the waves of the sea?

Is. I know not. Oh that deadly Hades would join me in death unto mine aged sire! Woe is me! I cannot live the life that must be mine.

Ch. Best of daughters, sisters twain, Heaven's doom must be borne: be no more fired with too much grief: ye have so fared that ye should not repine.

ant. 1.An. Ah, so care past can seem lost joy! For that which was no way sweet had sweetness, while therewith I held *him* in mine embrace. Ah, father, dear one, ah thou who hast put on the darkness of the under-world for ever, not even there shalt thou ever lack our love,—her love and mine.

Ch. He hath fared— An. He hath fared as he would.

Ch. In what wise? An. On foreign ground, the ground of his choice, he hath died; in the shadow of the grave he hath his bed for ever; and he hath left mourning behind him, not barren of tears. For with these streaming eyes, father, I bewail thee; nor know I, ah me, how to quell my sorrow for thee, my sorrow that is so great.—Ah me! 'twas thy wish to die in a strange land; but now thou hast died without gifts at my hand.

Is. Woe is me! What new fate, think'st thou, awaits thee and me, my sister, thus orphaned of our sire?

Ch. Nay, since he hath found a blessed end, my children, cease from this lament; no mortal is hard for evil fortune to capture.

str. 2.An. Sister, let us hasten back. Is. Unto what deed?

An. A longing fills my soul. Is. Whereof?

An. To see the dark home— Is. Of whom?

An. Ah me! of our sire. Is. And how can this thing be lawful? Hast thou no understanding?

An. Why this reproof? Is. And knowest thou not this also— An. What wouldst thou tell me more?— Is. That he was perishing without tomb, apart from all?

An. Lead me thither, and then slay me also.

Is. Ah me unhappy! Friendless and helpless, where am I now to live my hapless life?

ant. 2.Ch. My children, fear not. An. But whither am I to flee?

Ch. Already a refuge hath been found— An. How meanest thou?—

Ch. —for your fortunes, that no harm should touch them.

An. I know it well. Ch. What, then, is thy thought?

An. How we are to go home, I cannot tell. Ch. And do not seek to go.

An. Trouble besets us. Ch. And erstwhile bore hardly on you.

An. Desperate then, and now more cruel than despair.

Ch. Great, verily, is the sea of your troubles.

An. Alas, alas! O Zeus, whither shall we turn? To what last hope doth fate now urge us?

Enter Theseus, *on the spectators' right.*

syst. Th. Weep no more, maidens; for where the kindness of the Dark Powers is an abiding grace to the quick and to the dead, there is no room for mourning; divine anger would follow.

An. Son of Aegeus, we supplicate thee!

Th. For the obtaining of what desire, my children?

An. We fain would look with our own eyes upon our father's tomb.

Th. Nay, it is not lawful.

An. How sayest thou, king, lord of Athens?

Th. My children, he gave me charge that no one should draw nigh unto that place, or greet with voice the sacred tomb wherein he sleeps. And he said that, while I duly kept that word, I should always hold the land unharmed. These pledges, therefore, were heard from my lips by the god, and by the all-seeing Watcher of oaths, the servant of Zeus.

An. Nay, then, if this is pleasing to the dead, with this we must content us. But send us to Thebes the ancient, if haply we may hinder the bloodshed that is threatened to our brothers.

Th. So will I do; and if in aught beside I can profit you, and pleasure the dead who hath lately gone from us, I am bound to spare no pains.

Ch. Come, cease lamentation, lift it up no more; for verily these things stand fast.

ANTIGONE

PERSONS OF THE DRAMA.

Antigone} *daughters of Oedipus.*
Ismene
Creon,*King of Thebes.*
Eurydice,*his wife.*
Haemon,*his son.*
Teiresias,*the blind prophet.*
Guard,*set to watch the corpse of Polyneices.*
First Messenger.
Second Messenger,*from the house.*
Chorus of Theban Elders.
Scene: Before the Royal Palace at Thebes.

Polyneices, supported by an Argive army, had marched against Thebes, in order to wrest the sovereignty from his brother Eteocles. The day before that on which the drama opens had been disastrous for the invaders. At six of the city's seven gates, a Theban champion slew his Argive opponent: at the seventh, Eteocles met Polyneices, and each fell by the other's hand. The Argive army fled in the night. Creon, now King of Thebes, has just issued an edict, proclaiming that Eteocles shall be interred with public honours, but that the corpse of Polyneices shall be left unburied.

ANTIGONE.

Ismene, sister, mine own dear sister, knowest thou what ill there is, of all bequeathed by Oedipus, that Zeus fulfils not for us twain while we live? Nothing painful is there, nothing fraught with ruin, no shame, no dishonour, that I have not seen in thy woes and mine.

And now what new edict is this of which they tell, that our Captain hath just published to all Thebes? Knowest thou aught? Hast thou heard? Or is it hidden from thee that our friends are threatened with the doom of our foes?10

ISMENE.

No word of friends, Antigone, gladsome or painful, hath come to me, since we two sisters were bereft of brothers twain, killed in one day by a twofold blow; and since in this last night the Argive host hath fled, I know no more, whether my fortune be brighter, or more grievous.

An. I knew it well, and therefore sought to bring thee beyond the gates of the court, that thou mightest hear alone.

Is. What is it? 'Tis plain that thou art brooding20 on some dark tidings.

An. What, hath not Creon destined our brothers, the one to honoured burial, the other to unburied shame? Eteocles, they say, with due observance of right and custom, he hath laid in the earth, for his honour among the dead below. But the hapless corpse of Polyneices—as rumour saith, it hath been published to the town that none shall entomb him or mourn, but leave unwept, unsepulchred,30 a welcome store for the birds, as they espy him, to feast on at will.

74

Such, 'tis said, is the edict that the good Creon hath set forth for thee and for me,—yes, for *me*,—and is coming hither to proclaim it clearly to those who know it not; nor counts the matter light, but, whoso disobeys in aught, his doom is death by stoning before all the folk. Thou knowest it now; and thou wilt soon show whether thou art nobly bred, or the base daughter of a noble line.

Is. Poor sister,—and if things stand thus, what40 could I help to do or undo?

An. Consider if thou wilt share the toil and the deed.

Is. In what venture? What can be thy meaning?

An. Wilt thou aid this hand to lift the dead?

Is. Thou wouldst bury him,—when 'tis forbidden to Thebes?

An. I will do my part,—and thine, if thou wilt not,—to a brother. False to him will I never be found.

Is. Ah, over-bold! when Creon hath forbidden?

An. Nay, he hath no right to keep me from mine own.

Is.50 Ah me! think, sister, how our father perished, amid hate and scorn, when sins bared by his own search had moved him to strike both eyes with self-blinding hand; then the mother wife, two names in one, with twisted noose did despite unto her life; and last, our two brothers in one day,—each shedding, hapless one, a kinsman's blood,—wrought out with mutual hands their common doom. And now *we* in turn—we two left all alone—think how we shall perish, more miserably than all the rest, if, in defiance of the law, we brave60 a king's decree or his powers. Nay, we must remember, first, that we were born women, as who should not strive with men; next, that we are ruled of the stronger, so that we must obey in these things, and in things yet sorer. I, therefore, asking the Spirits Infernal to pardon, seeing that force is put on me herein, will hearken to our rulers; for 'tis witless to be over busy.

An. I will not urge thee,—no, nor, if thou yet shouldst have the mind, wouldst thou be welcome as70 a worker with *me*. Nay, be what thou wilt; but I will bury him: well for me to die in doing that. I shall rest, a loved one with him whom I have loved, sinless in my crime; for I owe a longer allegiance to the dead than to the living: in that world I shall abide for ever. But if *thou* wilt, be guilty of dishonouring laws which the gods have stablished in honour.

Is. I do them no dishonour; but to defy the State,—I have no strength for that.

An. Such be thy plea:—I, then, will go to heap the80 earth above the brother whom I love.

Is. Alas, unhappy one! How I fear for thee!

An. Fear not for me: guide thine own fate aright.

Is. At least, then, disclose this plan to none, but hide it closely,—and so, too, will I.

An. Oh, denounce it! Thou wilt be far more hateful for thy silence, if thou proclaim not these things to all.

Is. Thou hast a hot heart for chilling deeds.

An. I know that I please where I am most bound to please.

Is.90 Aye, if thou canst; but thou wouldst what thou canst not.

An. Why, then, when my strength fails, I shall have done.

Is. A hopeless quest should not be made at all.

An. If thus thou speakest, thou wilt have hatred from me, and will justly be subject to the lasting hatred of the dead. But leave me, and the folly that is mine

75

alone, to suffer this dread thing; for I shall not suffer aught so dreadful as an ignoble death.

Is. Go, then, if thou must; and of this be sure,—that, though thine errand is foolish, to thy dear ones thou art truly dear.

[*Exit*Antigone*on the spectators' left.*Ismene*retires into the palace by one of the two side-doors.*

CHORUS.

str. 1.Beam of the sun, fairest light that ever dawned on Thebè of the seven gates, thou hast shone forth at last, eye of golden day, arisen above Dircè's streams! The warrior of the white shield, who came from Argos in his panoply, hath been stirred by thee to headlong flight, in swifter career;

syst. 1.who set forth against our land by reason of the vexed claims of Polyneices; and, like shrill-screaming eagle, he flew over into our land, in snow-white pinion sheathed, with an armèd throng, and with plumage of helms.

ant. 1.He paused above our dwellings; he ravened around our sevenfold portals with spears athirst for blood; but he went hence, or ever his jaws were glutted with our gore, or the Fire-god's pine-fed flame had seized our crown of towers. So fierce was the noise of battle raised behind him, a thing too hard for him to conquer, as he wrestled with his dragon foe.

syst. 2.For Zeus utterly abhors the boasts of a proud tongue; and when he beheld them coming on in a great stream, in the haughty pride of clanging gold, he smote with brandished fire one who was now hasting to shout victory at his goal upon our ramparts.

str. 2.Swung down, he fell on the earth with a crash, torch in hand, he who so lately, in the frenzy of the mad onset, was raging against us with the blasts of his tempestuous hate. But those threats fared not as he hoped; and to other foes the mighty War-god dispensed their several dooms, dealing havoc around, a mighty helper at our need.

syst. 3.For seven captains at seven gates, matched against seven, left the tribute of their panoplies to Zeus who turns the battle; save those two of cruel fate, who, born of one sire and one mother, set against each other their twain conquering spears, and are sharers in a common death.

ant. 2.But since Victory of glorious name hath come to us, with joy responsive to the joy of Thebè whose chariots are many, let us enjoy forgetfulness after the late wars, and visit all the temples of the gods with night-long dance and song; and may Bacchus be our leader, whose dancing shakes the land of Thebè.

syst. 4.But lo, the king of the land comes yonder, Creon, son of Menoeceus, our new ruler by the new fortunes that the gods have given; what counsel is he pondering, that he hath proposed this special conference of elders, summoned by his general mandate?

*Enter*Creon,*from the central doors of the palace, in the garb of king; with two attendants.*

Cr. Sirs, the vessel of our State, after being tossed on wild waves, hath once more been safely steadied by the gods: and ye, out of all the folk, have been called apart by my summons, because I knew, first of all, how true and constant was your reverence for the royal power of Laïus; how, again, when Oedipus was ruler of our land, and when he had perished, your steadfast loyalty still upheld their children. Since, then, his sons have fallen in one day by a twofold doom,—each smitten by the other, each stained with a brother's blood,—I now possess the throne and all its powers, by nearness of kinship to the dead.

No man can be fully known, in soul and spirit and mind, until he hath been seen versed in rule and lawgiving. For if any, being supreme guide of the State, cleaves not to the best counsels, but, through some fear, keeps his lips locked, I hold, and have ever held, him most base; and if any makes a friend of more account than his fatherland, that man hath no place in my regard. For I—be Zeus my witness, who sees all things always—would not be silent if I saw ruin, instead of safety, coming to the citizens; nor would I ever deem the country's foe a friend to myself; remembering this, that our country is the ship that bears us safe, and that only while she prospers in our voyage can we make true friends.

Such are the rules by which I guard this city's greatness. And in accord with them is the edict which I have now published to the folk touching the sons of Oedipus;— that Eteocles, who hath fallen fighting for our city, in all renown of arms, shall be entombed, and crowned with every rite that follows the noblest dead to their rest. But for his brother, Polyneices,—who came back from exile, and sought to consume utterly with fire the city of his fathers and the shrines of his fathers' gods,—sought to taste of kindred blood, and to lead the remnant into slavery;—touching this man, it hath been proclaimed to our people that none shall grace him with sepulture or lament, but leave him unburied, a corpse for birds and dogs to eat, a ghastly sight of shame.

Such the spirit of my dealing; and never, by deed of mine, shall the wicked stand in honour before the just; but whoso hath good will to Thebes, he shall be honoured of me, in his life and in his death.

Ch. Such is thy pleasure, Creon, son of Menoeceus, touching this city's foe, and its friend; and thou hast power, I ween, to take what order thou wilt, both for the dead, and for all us who live.

Cr. See, then, that ye be guardians of the mandate.

Ch. Lay the burden of this task on some younger man.

Cr. Nay, watchers of the corpse have been found.

Ch. What, then, is this further charge that thou wouldst give?

Cr. That ye side not with the breakers of these commands.

Ch. No man is so foolish that he is enamoured of death.

Cr. In sooth, that is the meed; yet lucre hath oft ruined men through their hopes. *Enter* Guard.

Gu. My liege, I will not say that I come breathless from speed, or that I have plied a nimble foot; for often did my thoughts make me pause, and wheel round in my path, to return. My mind was holding large discourse with me; 'Fool, why goest thou to thy certain doom?' 'Wretch, tarrying again? And if Creon hears this from another, must not thou smart for it?' So debating, I went on my way with lagging steps, and thus a short road was made long. At last, however, it carried the day that I should come hither—to thee; and, though my tale be nought, yet will I tell it; for I come with a good grip on one hope,—that I can suffer nothing but what is my fate.

Cr. And what is it that disquiets thee thus?

Gu. I wish to tell thee first about myself—I did not do the deed—I did not see the doer—it were not right that I should come to any harm.

Cr. Thou hast a shrewd eye for thy mark; well dost thou fence thyself round against the blame:—clearly thou hast some strange thing to tell.

Gu. Aye, truly; dread news makes one pause long.

Cr. Then tell it, wilt thou, and so get thee gone?

Gu. Well, this is it.—The corpse—some one hath just given it burial, and gone away,—after sprinkling thirsty dust on the flesh, with such other rites as piety enjoins.

Cr. What sayest thou? What living man hath dared this deed?

Gu. I know not; no stroke of pickaxe was seen there, no earth thrown up by mattock; the ground was hard and dry, unbroken, without track of wheels; the doer was one who had left no trace. And when the first day-watchman showed it to us, sore wonder fell on all. The dead man was veiled from us; not shut within a tomb, but lightly strewn with dust, as by the hand of one who shunned a curse. And no sign met the eye as though any beast of prey or any dog had come nigh to him, or torn him.

Then evil words flew fast and loud among us, guard accusing guard; and it would e'en have come to blows at last, nor was there any to hinder. Every man was the culprit, and no one was convicted, but all disclaimed knowledge of the deed. And we were ready to take red-hot iron in our hands;—to walk through fire;—to make oath by the gods that we had not done the deed,—that we were not privy to the planning or the doing.

At last, when all our searching was fruitless, one spake, who made us all bend our faces on the earth in fear; for we saw not how we could gainsay him, or escape mischance if we obeyed. His counsel was that this deed must be reported to thee, and not hidden. And this seemed best; and the lot doomed my hapless self to win this prize. So here I stand,—as unwelcome as unwilling, well I wot; for no man delights in the bearer of bad news.

Ch. O king, my thoughts have long been whispering, can this deed, perchance, be e'en the work of gods?

Cr. Cease, ere thy words fill me utterly with wrath, lest thou be found at once an old man and foolish. For thou sayest what is not to be borne, in saying that the gods have care for this corpse. Was it for high reward of trusty service that they sought to hide his nakedness, who came to burn their pillared shrines and sacred treasures, to burn their land, and scatter its laws to the winds? Or dost thou behold the gods honouring the wicked? It cannot be. No! From the first there were certain in the town that muttered against me, chafing at this edict, wagging their heads in secret; and kept not their necks duly under the yoke, like men contented with my sway.

'Tis by them, well I know, that these have been beguiled and bribed to do this deed. Nothing so evil as money ever grew to be current among men. This lays cities low, this drives men from their homes, this trains and warps honest souls till they set themselves to works of shame; this still teaches folk to practise villanies, and to know every godless deed.

But all the men who wrought this thing for hire have made it sure that, soon or late, they shall pay the price. Now, as Zeus still hath my reverence, know this—I tell it thee on my oath:—If ye find not the very author of this burial, and produce him before mine eyes, death alone shall not be enough for you, till first, hung up alive, ye have revealed this outrage,—that henceforth ye may thieve with better knowledge whence lucre should be won, and learn that it is not well to love gain from every source. For thou wilt find that ill-gotten pelf brings more men to ruin than to weal.

Gu. May I speak? Or shall I just turn and go?

Cr. Knowest thou not that even now thy voice offends?

Gu. Is thy smart in the ears, or in the soul?

Cr. And why wouldst thou define the seat of my pain?

Gu. The doer vexes thy mind, but I, thine ears.

Cr. Ah, thou art a born babbler, 'tis well seen.

Gu. May be, but never the doer of this deed.

Cr. Yea, and more,—the seller of thy life for silver.

Gu. Alas! 'Tis sad, truly, that he who judges should misjudge.

Cr. Let thy fancy play with 'judgment' as it will;—but, if ye show me not the doers of these things, ye shall avow that dastardly gains work sorrows. [*Exit.*

Gu. Well, may he be found! so 'twere best. But, be he caught or be he not—fortune must settle that—truly thou wilt not see me here again. Saved, even now, beyond hope and thought, I owe the gods great thanks. [*Exit.*

CHORUS.

str. 1.Wonders are many, and none is more wonderful than man; the power that crosses the white sea, driven by the stormy south-wind, making a path under surges that threaten to engulf him; and Earth, the eldest of the gods, the immortal, the unwearied, doth he wear, turning the soil with the offspring of horses, as the ploughs go to and fro from year to year.

ant. 1.And the light-hearted race of birds, and the tribes of savage beasts, and the sea-brood of the deep, he snares in the meshes of his woven toils, he leads captive, man excellent in wit. And he masters by his arts the beast whose lair is in the wilds, who roams the hills; he tames the horse of shaggy mane, he puts the yoke upon its neck, he tames the tireless mountain bull.

str. 2.And speech, and wind-swift thought, and all the moods that mould a state, hath he taught himself; and how to flee the arrows of the frost, when 'tis hard lodging under the clear sky, and the arrows of the rushing rain; yea, he hath resource for all; without resource he meets nothing that must come: only against Death shall he call for aid in vain; but from baffling maladies he hath devised escapes.

ant. 2.Cunning beyond fancy's dream is the fertile skill which brings him, now to evil, now to good. When he honours the laws of the land, and that justice which he hath sworn by the gods to uphold, proudly stands his city: no city hath he who, for his rashness, dwells with sin. Never may he share my hearth, never think my thoughts, who doth these things!

Enter the Guard on the spectators' left, leading in Antigone.

What portent from the gods is this?—my soul is amazed. I know her—how can I deny that yon maiden is Antigone?

O hapless, and child of hapless sire,—of Oedipus! What means this? Thou brought a prisoner?—thou, disloyal to the king's laws, and taken in folly?

GUARD.

Here she is, the doer of the deed:—we caught this girl burying him:—but where is Creon?

Ch. Lo, he comes forth again from the house, at our need.

Cr. What is it? What hath chanced, that makes my coming timely?

Gu. O king, against nothing should men pledge their word; for the after-thought belies the first intent. I could have vowed that I should not soon be here again,—scared by thy threats, with which I had just been lashed: but,—since the joy that surprises and transcends our hopes is like in fulness to no other pleasure,—I have come, though 'tis in breach of my sworn oath, bringing this maid; who was taken showing grace to the dead. This time there was no casting of lots; no, this luck hath fallen to me, and to none else. And now, sire, take her thyself, question her, examine her, as thou wilt; but I have a right to free and final quittance of this trouble.

Cr. And thy prisoner here—how and whence hast thou taken her?

Gu. She was burying the man; thou knowest all.

Cr. Dost thou mean what thou sayest? Dost thou speak aright?

Gu. I saw her burying the corpse that thou hadst forbidden to bury. Is that plain and clear?

Cr. And how was she seen? how taken in the act?

Gu. It befell on this wise. When we had come to the place,—with those dread menaces of thine upon us,—we swept away all the dust that covered the corpse, and bared the dank body well; and then sat us down on the brow of the hill, to windward, heedful that the smell from him should not strike us; every man was wide awake, and kept his neighbour alert with torrents of threats, if any one should be careless of this task.

So went it, until the sun's bright orb stood in mid heaven, and the heat began to burn: and then suddenly a whirlwind lifted from the earth a storm of dust, a trouble in the sky, and filled the plain, marring all the leafage of its woods; and the wide air was choked therewith: we closed our eyes, and bore the plague from the gods.

And when, after a long while, this storm had passed, the maid was seen; and she cried aloud with the sharp cry of a bird in its bitterness,—even as when, within the empty nest, it sees the bed stripped of its nestlings. So she also, when she saw the corpse bare, lifted up a voice of wailing, and called down curses on the doers of that deed. And straightway she brought thirsty dust in her hands; and from a shapely ewer of bronze, held high, with thrice-poured drink-offering she crowned the dead.

We rushed forward when we saw it, and at once closed upon our quarry, who was in no wise dismayed. Then we taxed her with her past and present doings; and she stood not on denial of aught,—at once to my joy and to my pain. To have escaped from ills one's self is a great joy; but 'tis painful to brng friends to ill. Howbeit, all such things are of less account to me than mine own safety.

Cr. Thou—thou whose face is bent to earth—dost thou avow, or disavow, this deed?

An. I avow it; I make no denial.

Cr. (To Guard.) Thou canst betake thee whither thou wilt, free and clear of a grave charge. [Exit Guard.

(*To* Antigone.) Now, tell me thou—not in many words, but briefly—knewest thou that an edict had forbidden this?

An. I knew it: could I help it? It was public.

Cr. And thou didst indeed dare to transgress that law?

An. Yes; for it was not Zeus that had published me that edict; not such are the laws set among men by the Justice who dwells with the gods below; nor deemed I that thy decrees were of such force, that a mortal could override the unwritten and unfailing statutes of heaven. For their life is not of to-day or yesterday, but from all time, and no man knows when they were first put forth.

Not through dread of any human pride could I answer to the gods for breaking *these*. Die I must,—I knew that well (how should I not?)—even without thy edicts. But if I am to die before my time, I count that a gain: for when any one lives, as I do, compassed about with evils, can such an one find aught but gain in death?

So for me to meet this doom is trifling grief; but if I had suffered my mother's son to lie in death an unburied corpse, that would have grieved me; for this, I am not grieved. And if my present deeds are foolish in thy sight, it may be that a foolish judge arraigns my folly.

Ch. The maid shows herself passionate child of passionate sire, and knows not how to bend before troubles.

Cr. Yet I would have thee know that o'er-stubborn spirits are most often humbled; 'tis the stiffest iron, baked to hardness in the fire, that thou shalt oftenest see snapped and shivered; and I have known horses that show temper brought to order by a little curb; there is no room for pride, when thou art thy neighbour's slave.—This girl was already versed in insolence when she transgressed the laws that had been set forth; and, that done, lo, a second insult,—to vaunt of this, and exult in her deed.

Now verily I am no man, she is the man, if this victory shall rest with her, and bring no penalty. No! be she sister's child, or nearer to me in blood than any that worships Zeus at the altar of our house,—she and her kinsfolk shall not avoid a doom most dire; for indeed I charge that other with a like share in the plotting of this burial.

And summon her—for I saw her e'en now within,—raving, and not mistress of her wits. So oft, before the deed, the mind stands self-convicted in its treason, when folks are plotting mischief in the dark. But verily this, too, is hateful,—when one who hath been caught in wickedness then seeks to make the crime a glory.

An. Wouldst thou do more than take and slay me?

Cr. No more, indeed; having that, I have all.

An. Why then dost thou delay? In thy discourse there is nought that pleases me,—never may there be!—and so my words must needs be unpleasing to thee. And yet, for glory—whence could I have won a nobler, than by giving burial to mine own brother? All here would own that they thought it well, were not their lips sealed by fear. But royalty, blest in so much besides, hath the power to do and say what it will.

Cr. Thou differest from all these Thebans in that view.

An. These also share it; but they curb their tongues for thee.

Cr. And art thou not ashamed to act apart from them?

An. No; there is nothing shameful in piety to a brother.

Cr. Was it not a brother, too, that died in the opposite cause?

An. Brother by the same mother and the same sire.

Cr. Why, then, dost thou render a grace that is impious in his sight?

An. The dead man will not say that he so deems it.

Cr. Yea, if thou makest him but equal in honour with the wicked.

An. It was his brother, not his slave, that perished.

Cr. Wasting this land; while *he* fell as its champion.

An. Nevertheless, Hades desires these rites.

Cr. But the good desires not a like portion with the evil.

An. Who knows but this seems blameless in the world below?

Cr. A foe is never a friend—not even in death.

An. 'Tis not my nature to join in hating, but in loving.

Cr. Pass, then, to the world of the dead, and, if thou must needs love, love them. While I live, no woman shall rule me.

Enter Ismene *from the house, led in by two attendants.*

Ch. Lo, yonder Ismene comes forth, shedding such tears as fond sisters weep; a cloud upon her brow casts its shadow over her darkly-flushing face, and breaks in rain on her fair cheek.

Cr. And thou, who, lurking like a viper in my house, wast secretly draining my life-blood, while I knew not that I was nurturing two pests, to rise against my throne—come, tell me now, wilt thou also confess thy part in this burial, or wilt thou forswear all knowledge of it?

Is. I have done the deed,—if she allows my claim,—and share the burden of the charge.

An. Nay, justice will not suffer thee to do that: thou didst not consent to the deed, nor did I give thee part in it.

Is. But, now that ills beset thee, I am not ashamed to sail the sea of trouble at thy side.

An. Whose was the deed, Hades and the dead are witnesses: a friend in words is not the friend that I love.

Is. Nay, sister, reject me not, but let me die with thee, and duly honour the dead.

An. Share not thou my death, nor claim deeds to which thou hast not put thy hand: my death will suffice.

Is. And what life is dear to me, bereft of thee?

An. Ask Creon; all thy care is for him.

Is. Why vex me thus, when it avails thee nought?

An. Indeed, if I mock, 'tis with pain that I mock thee.

Is. Tell me,—how can I serve thee, even now?

An. Save thyself: I grudge not thy escape.

Is. Ah, woe is me! And shall I have no share in thy fate?

An. Thy choice was to live; mine, to die.

Is. At least thy choice was not made without my protest.

An. One world approved thy wisdom; another, mine.

Is. Howbeit, the offence is the same for both of us.

An. Be of good cheer; thou livest; but my life hath long been given to death, that so I might serve the dead.

Cr. Lo, one of these maidens hath newly shown herself foolish, as the other hath been since her life began.

Is. Yea, O king, such reason as nature may have given abides not with the unfortunate, but goes astray.

Cr. Thine did, when thou chosest vile deeds with the vile.

Is. What life could I endure, without her presence?

Cr. Nay, speak not of her 'presence'; she lives no more.

Is. But wilt thou slay the betrothed of thine own son?

Cr. Nay, there are other fields for him to plough

Is. But there can never be such love as bound him to her.

Cr. I like not an evil wife for my son.

An. Haemon, beloved! How thy father wrongs thee!

Cr. Enough, enough of thee and of thy marriage!

Ch. Wilt thou indeed rob thy son of this maiden?

Cr. 'Tis Death that shall stay these bridals for me.

Ch. 'Tis determined, it seems, that she shall die.

Cr. Determined, yes, for thee and for me.—(*To the two attendants.*) No more delay—servants, take them within! Henceforth they must be women, and not range at large; for verily even the bold seek to fly, when they see Death now closing on their life.

[*Exeunt attendants, guarding*Antigone*and*Ismene.—Creon*remains.*

Ch. Blest are they whose days have not tasted of evil. For when a house hath once been shaken from heaven, there the curse fails nevermore, passing from life to life of the race; even as, when the surge is driven over the darkness of the deep by the fierce breath of Thracian sea-winds, it rolls up the black sand from the depths, and there is a sullen roar from wind-vexed headlands that front the blows of the storm.

I see that from olden time the sorrows in the house of the Labdacidae are heaped upon the sorrows of the dead; and generation is not freed by generation, but some god strikes them down, and the race hath no deliverance.

For now that hope of which the light had been spread above the last root of the house of Oedipus—that hope, in turn, is brought low—by the blood-stained dust due to the gods infernal, and by folly in speech, and frenzy at the heart.

Thy power, O Zeus, what human trespass can limit? That power which neither Sleep, the all-ensnaring, nor the untiring months of the gods can master; but thou, a ruler to whom time brings not old age, dwellest in the dazzling splendour of Olympus.

And through the future, near and far, as through the past, shall this law hold good: Nothing that is vast enters into the life of mortals without a curse.

For that hope whose wanderings are so wide is to many men a comfort, but to many a false lure of giddy desires; and the disappointment comes on one who knoweth nought till he burn his foot against the hot fire.

For with wisdom hath some one given forth the famous saying, that evil seems good, soon or late, to him whose mind the god draws to mischief; and but for the briefest space doth he fare free of woe.

But lo, Haemon, the last of thy sons;—comes he grieving for the doom of his promised bride, Antigone, and bitter for the baffled hope of his marriage?

*Enter*Haemon.

83

Cr. We shall know soon, better than seers could tell us.—My son, hearing the fixed doom of thy betrothed, art thou come in rage against thy father? Or have I thy good will, act how I may?

Hae. Father, I am thine; and thou, in thy wisdom, tracest for me rules which I shall follow. No marriage shall be deemed by me a greater gain than thy good guidance.

Cr. Yea, this, my son, should be thy heart's fixed law,—in all things to obey thy father's will. 'Tis for this that men pray to see dutiful children grow up around them in their homes,—that such may requite their father's foe with evil, and honour, as their father doth, his friend. But he who begets unprofitable children—what shall we say that he hath sown, but troubles for himself, and much triumph for his foes? Then do not thou, my son, at pleasure's beck, dethrone thy reason for a woman's sake; knowing that this is a joy that soon grows cold in clasping arms,—an evil woman to share thy bed and thy home. For what wound could strike deeper than a false friend? Nay, with loathing, and as if she were thine enemy, let this girl go to find a husband in the house of Hades. For since I have taken her, alone of all the city, in open disobedience, I will not make myself a liar to my people—I will slay her.

So let her appeal as she will to the majesty of kindred blood. If I am to nurture mine own kindred in naughtiness, needs must I bear with it in aliens. He who does his duty in his own household will be found righteous in the State also. But if any one transgresses, and does violence to the laws, or thinks to dictate to his rulers, such an one can win no praise from me. No, whomsoever the city may appoint, that man must be obeyed, in little things and great, in just things and unjust; and I should feel sure that one who thus obeys would be a good ruler no less than a good subject, and in the storm of spears would stand his ground where he was set, loyal and dauntless at his comrade's side.

But disobedience is the worst of evils. This it is that ruins cities; this makes homes desolate; by this, the ranks of allies are broken into headlong rout; but, of the lives whose course is fair, the greater part owes safety to obedience. Therefore we must support the cause of order, and in no wise suffer a woman to worst us. Better to fall from power, if we must, by a man's hand; then we should not be called weaker than a woman.

Ch. To us, unless our years have stolen our wit, thou seemest to say wisely what thou sayest.

Hae. Father, the gods implant reason in men, the highest of all things that we call our own. Not mine the skill—far from me be the quest!—to say wherein thou speakest not aright; and yet another man, too, might have some useful thought. At least, it is my natural office to watch, on thy behalf, all that men say, or do, or find to blame. For the dread of thy frown forbids the citizen to speak such words as would offend thine ear; but I can hear these murmurs in the dark, these moanings of the city for this maiden; 'no woman,' they say, 'ever merited her doom less,—none ever was to die so shamefully for deeds so glorious as hers; who, when her own brother had fallen in bloody strife, would not leave him unburied, to be devoured by carrion dogs, or by any bird:—deserves not *she* the meed of golden honour?'

Such is the darkling rumour that spreads in secret. For me, my father, no treasure is so precious as thy welfare. What, indeed, is a nobler ornament for children than a prospering sire's fair fame, or for sire than son's? Wear not, then, one mood only in thyself; think not that thy word, and thine alone, must be right. For if any man thinks that he alone is wise,—that in speech, or in mind, he hath no peer,—such a soul, when laid open, is ever found empty.

No, though a man be wise, 'tis no shame for him to learn many things, and to bend in season. Seest thou, beside the wintry torrent's course, how the trees that yield to it save every twig, while the stiff-necked perish root and branch? And even thus he who keeps the sheet of his sail taut, and never slackens it, upsets his boat, and finishes his voyage with keel uppermost.

Nay, forego thy wrath; permit thyself to change. For if I, a younger man, may offer my thought, it were far best, I ween, that men should be all-wise by nature; but, otherwise—and oft the scale inclines not so—'tis good also to learn from those who speak aright.

Ch. Sire, 'tis meet that thou shouldest profit by his words, if he speaks aught in season, and thou, Haemon, by thy father's; for on both parts there hath been wise speech.

Cr. Men of my age—are we indeed to be schooled, then, by men of his?

Hae. In nothing that is not right; but if I am young, thou shouldest look to my merits, not to my years.

Cr. Is it a merit to honour the unruly?

Hae. I could wish no one to show respect for evildoers.

Cr. Then is not she tainted with that malady?

Hae. Our Theban folk, with one voice, denies it.

Cr. Shall Thebes prescribe to me how I must rule?

Hae. See, there thou hast spoken like a youth indeed.

Cr. Am I to rule this land by other judgment than mine own?

Hae. That is no city, which belongs to one man.

Cr. Is not the city held to be the ruler's?

Hae. Thou wouldst make a good monarch of a desert.

Cr. This boy, it seems, is the woman's champion.

Hae. If thou art a woman; indeed, my care is for thee.

Cr. Shameless, at open feud with thy father!

Hae. Nay, I see thee offending against justice.

Cr. Do I offend, when I respect mine own prerogatives?

Hae. Thou dost not respect them, when thou tramplest on the gods' honours.

Cr. O dastard nature, yielding place to woman!

Hae. Thou wilt never find me yield to baseness.

Cr. All thy words, at least, plead for that girl.

Hae. And for thee, and for me, and for the gods below.

Cr. Thou canst never marry her, on this side the grave.

Hae. Then she must die, and in death destroy another.

Cr. How! doth thy boldness run to open threats?

Hae. What threat is it, to combat vain resolves?

Cr. Thou shalt rue thy witless teaching of wisdom.

Hae. Wert thou not my father, I would have called thee unwise.

Cr. Thou woman's slave, use not wheedling speech with me.

Hae. Thou wouldest speak, and then hear no reply?

Cr. Sayest thou so? Now, by the heaven above us—be sure of it—thou shalt smart for taunting me in this opprobrious strain. Bring forth that hated thing, that she may die forthwith in his presence—before his eyes—at her bridegroom's side!

Hae. No, not at my side—never think it—shall she perish; nor shalt thou ever set eyes more upon my face:—rave, then, with such friends as can endure thee.

[*Exit* Haemon.

Ch. The man is gone, O king, in angry haste; a youthful mind, when stung, is fierce.

Cr. Let him do, or dream, more than man—good speed to him!—But he shall not save these two girls from their doom.

Ch. Dost thou indeed purpose to slay both?

Cr. Not her whose hands are pure: thou sayest well.

Ch. And by what doom mean'st thou to slay the other?

Cr. I will take her where the path is loneliest, and hide her, living, in a rocky vault, with so much food set forth as piety prescribes, that the city may avoid a public stain. And there, praying to Hades, the only god whom she worships, perchance she will obtain release from death; or else will learn, at last, though late, that it is lost labour to revere the dead. [*Exit* Creon.

str. Ch. Love, unconquered in the fight, Love, who makest havoc of wealth, who keepest thy vigil on the soft cheek of a maiden; thou roamest over the sea, and among the homes of dwellers in the wilds; no immortal can escape thee, nor any among men whose life is for a day; and he to whom thou hast come is mad.

ant. The just themselves have their minds warped by thee to wrong, for their ruin: 'tis thou that hast stirred up this present strife of kinsmen; victorious is the love-kindling light from the eyes of the fair bride; it is a power enthroned in sway beside the eternal laws; for there the goddess Aphrodite is working her unconquerable will.

But now I also am carried beyond the bounds of loyalty, and can no more keep back the streaming tears, when I see Antigone thus passing to the bridal chamber where all are laid to rest.

str. 1. An. See me, citizens of my fatherland, setting forth on my last way, looking my last on the sunlight that is for me no more; no, Hades who gives sleep to all leads me living to Acheron's shore; who have had no portion in the chant that brings the bride, nor hath any song been mine for the crowning of bridals; whom the lord of the Dark Lake shall wed.

syst. 1. Ch. Glorious, therefore, and with praise, thou departest to that deep place of the dead: wasting sickness hath not smitten thee; thou hast not found the wages of the sword; no, mistress of thine own fate, and still alive, thou shalt pass to Hades, as no other of mortal kind hath passed.

ant. 1. An. I have heard in other days how dread a doom befell our Phrygian guest, the daughter of Tantalus, on the Sipylian heights; how, like clinging ivy, the growth of stone subdued her; and the rains fail not, as men tell, from her wasting form, nor fails the snow, while beneath her weeping lids the tears bedew her bosom; and most like to hers is the fate that brings me to my rest.

syst. 2. Ch. Yet she was a goddess, thou knowest, and born of gods; we are mortals, and of mortal race. But 'tis great renown for a woman who hath perished that she should have shared the doom of the godlike, in her life, and afterward in death.

str. 2.An. Ah, I am mocked! In the name of our fathers' gods, can ye not wait till I am gone,—must ye taunt me to my face, O my city, and ye, her wealthy sons? Ah, fount of Dircè, and thou holy ground of Thebè whose chariots are many; ye, at least, will bear me witness, in what sort, unwept of friends, and by what laws I pass to the rock-closed prison of my strange tomb, ah me unhappy! who have no home on the earth or in the shades, no home with the living or with the dead.

str. 3.Ch. Thou hast rushed forward to the utmost verge of daring; and against that throne where Justice sits on high thou hast fallen, my daughter, with a grievous fall. But in this ordeal thou art paying, haply, for thy father's sin.

ant. 2.An. Thou hast touched on my bitterest thought,—awaking the ever-new lament for my sire and for all the doom given to us, the famed house of Labdacus. Alas for the horrors of the mother's bed! alas for the wretched mother's slumber at the side of her own son,—and my sire! From what manner of parents did I take my miserable being! And to them I go thus, accursed, unwed, to share their home. Alas, my brother, illstarred in thy marriage, in thy death thou hast undone my life!

ant. 3.Ch. Reverent action claims a certain praise for reverence; but an offence against power cannot be brooked by him who hath power in his keeping. Thy self-willed temper hath wrought thy ruin.

*ep.*An. Unwept, unfriended, without marriage-song, I am led forth in my sorrow on this journey that can be delayed no more. No longer, hapless one, may I behold yon day-star's sacred eye; but for my fate no tear is shed, no friend makes moan.

Cr. Know ye not that songs and wailings before death would never cease, if it profited to utter them? Away with her—away! And when ye have enclosed her, according to my word, in her vaulted grave, leave her alone, forlorn—whether she wishes to die, or to live a buried life in such a home. Our hands are clean as touching this maiden. But this is certain—she shall be deprived of her sojourn in the light.

An. Tomb, bridal-chamber, eternal prison in the caverned rock, whither I go to find mine own, those many who have perished, and whom Persephone hath received among the dead! Last of all shall I pass thither, and far most miserably of all, before the term of my life is spent. But I cherish good hope that my coming will be welcome to my father, and pleasant to thee, my mother, and welcome, brother, to thee; for, when ye died, with mine own hands I washed and dressed you, and poured drink-offerings at your graves; and now, Polyneices, 'tis for tending thy corpse that I win such recompense as this.

[And yet I honoured thee, as the wise will deem, rightly. Never, had I been a mother of children, or if a husband had been mouldering in death, would I have taken this task upon me in the city's despite. What law, ye ask, is my warrant for that word? The husband lost, another might have been found, and child from another, to replace the first-born; but, father and mother hidden with Hades, no brother's life could ever bloom for me again. Such was the law whereby I held thee first in honour; but Creon deemed me guilty of error therein, and of outrage, ah brother mine! And now he leads me thus, a captive in his hands; no bridal bed, no bridal song hath been mine, no joy of marriage, no portion in the nurture of children; but thus, forlorn of friends, unhappy one, I go living to the vaults of death.]

And what law of heaven have I transgressed? Why, hapless one, should I look to the gods any more,—what ally should I invoke,—when by piety I have earned the name of impious? Nay, then, if these things are pleasing to the gods, when I have suffered my doom, I shall come to know my sin; but if the sin is with my judges, I could wish them no fuller measure of evil than they, on their part, mete wrongfully to me.

Ch. Still the same tempest of the soul vexes this maiden with the same fierce gusts.

Cr. Then for this shall her guards have cause to rue their slowness.

An. Ah me! that word hath come very near to death.

Cr. I can cheer thee with no hope that this doom is not thus to be fulfilled.

An. O city of my fathers in the land of Thebè! O ye gods, eldest of our race!—they lead me hence—now, now—they tarry not! Behold me, princes of Thebes, the last daughter of the house of your kings,—see what I suffer, and from whom, because I feared to cast away the fear of Heaven!

[Antigone *is led away by the guards.*

str. 1.Ch. Even thus endured Danaë in her beauty to change the light of day for brass-bound walls; and in that chamber, secret as the grave, she was held close prisoner; yet was she of a proud lineage, O my daughter, and charged with the keeping of the seed of Zeus, that fell in the golden rain.

But dreadful is the mysterious power of fate; there is no deliverance from it by wealth or by war, by fenced city, or dark, sea-beaten ships.

ant. 1.And bonds tamed the son of Dryas, swift to wrath, that king of the Edonians; so paid he for his frenzied taunts, when, by the will of Dionysus, he was pent in a rocky prison. There the fierce exuberance of his madness slowly passed away. That man learned to know the god, whom in his frenzy he had provoked with mockeries; for he had sought to quell the godpossessed women, and the Bacchanalian fire; and he angered the Muses that love the flute.

str. 2.And by the waters of the Dark Rocks, the waters of the twofold sea, are the shores of Bosporus, and Thracian Salmydessus; where Ares, neighbour to the city, saw the accurst, blinding wound dealt to the two sons of Phineus by his fierce wife,—the wound that brought darkness to those vengeance-craving orbs, smitten with her bloody hands, smitten with her shuttle for a dagger.

ant. 2.Pining in their misery, they bewailed their cruel doom, those sons of a mother hapless in her marriage; but she traced her descent from the ancient line of the Erechtheidae; and in far-distant caves she was nursed amid her father's storms, that child of Boreas, swift as a steed over the steep hills, a daughter of gods; yet upon her also the gray Fates bore hard, my daughter.

Enter Teiresias, *led by a Boy, on the spectators' right.*

Te. Princes of Thebes, we have come with linked steps, both served by the eyes of one; for thus, by a guide's help, the blind must walk.

Cr. And what, aged Teiresias, are thy tidings?

Te. I will tell thee; and do thou hearken to the seer.

Cr. Indeed, it has not been my wont to slight thy counsel.

Te. Therefore didst thou steer our city's course aright.

Cr. I have felt, and can attest, thy benefits.

Te. Mark that now, once more, thou standest on fate's fine edge.

Cr. What means this? How I shudder at thy message!

Te. Thou wilt learn, when thou hearest the warnings of mine art. As I took my place on mine old seat of augury, where all birds have been wont to gather within my ken, I heard a strange voice among them; they were screaming with dire, feverish rage, that drowned their language in a jargon; and I knew that they were rending each other with their talons, murderously; the whirr of wings told no doubtful tale.

Forthwith, in fear, I essayed burnt-sacrifice on a duly kindled altar: but from my offerings the Fire-god showed no flame; a dank moisture, oozing from the thigh-flesh, trickled forth upon the embers, and smoked, and sputtered; the gall was scattered to the air; and the streaming thighs lay bared of the fat that had been wrapped round them.

Such was the failure of the rites by which I vainly asked a sign, as from this boy I learned; for he is my guide, as I am guide to others. And 'tis thy counsel that hath brought this sickness on our State. For the altars of our city and of our hearths have been tainted, one and all, by birds and dogs, with carrion from the hapless corpse, the son of Oedipus: and therefore the gods no more accept prayer and sacrifice at our hands, or the flame of meat-offering; nor doth any bird give a clear sign by its shrill cry, for they have tasted the fatness of a slain man's blood.

Think, then, on these things, my son. All men are liable to err; but when an error hath been made, that man is no longer witless or unblest who heals the ill into which he hath fallen, and remains not stubborn.

Self-will, we know, incurs the charge of folly. Nay, allow the claim of the dead; stab not the fallen; what prowess is it to slay the slain anew? I have sought thy good, and for thy good I speak: and never is it sweeter to learn from a good counsellor than when he counsels for thine own gain.

Cr. Old man, ye all shoot your shafts at me, as archers at the butts;—ye must needs practise on me with seer-craft also;—aye, the seer-tribe hath long trafficked in me, and made me their merchandise. Gain your gains, drive your trade, if ye list, in the silver-gold of Sardis and the gold of India; but ye shall not hide that man in the grave,—no, though the eagles of Zeus should bear the carrion morsels to their Master's throne—no, not for dread of that defilement will I suffer his burial:—for well I know that no mortal can defile the gods.—But, aged Teiresias, the wisest fall with a shameful fall, when they clothe shameful thoughts in fair words, for lucre's sake.

Te. Alas! Doth any man know, doth any consider...
Cr. Whereof? What general truth dost thou announce?
Te. How precious, above all wealth, is good counsel.
Cr. As folly, I think, is the worst mischief.
Te. Yet thou art tainted with that distemper.
Cr. I would not answer the seer with a taunt.
Te. But thou dost, in saying that I prophesy falsely.
Cr. Well, the prophet-tribe was ever fond of money.
Te. And the race bred of tyrants loves base gain.
Cr. Knowest thou that thy speech is spoken of thy king?
Te. I know it; for through me thou hast saved Thebes.
Cr. Thou art a wise seer; but thou lovest evil deeds.
Te. Thou wilt rouse me to utter the dread secret in my soul.
Cr. Out with it!—Only speak it not for gain.
Te. Indeed, methinks, I shall not,—as touching thee.
Cr. Know that thou shalt not trade on my resolve.

Te. Then know thou—aye, know it well—that thou shalt not live through many more courses of the sun's swift chariot, ere one begotten of thine own loins shall have been given by thee, a corpse for corpses; because thou hast thrust children of the sunlight to the shades, and ruthlessly lodged a living soul in the grave; but keepest in this world one who belongs to the gods infernal, a corpse unburied, unhonoured, all unhallowed. In such thou hast no part, nor have the gods above, but this is a violence done to them by thee. Therefore the avenging destroyers lie in wait for thee, the Furies of Hades and of the gods, that thou mayest be taken in these same ills.

And mark well if I speak these things as a hireling. A time not long to be delayed shall awaken the wailing of men and of women in thy house. And a tumult of hatred against thee stirs all the cities whose mangled sons had the burial-rite from dogs, or from wild beasts, or from some winged bird that bore a polluting breath to each city that contains the hearths of the dead.

Such arrows for thy heart—since thou provokest me—have I launched at thee, archer-like, in my anger,—sure arrows, of which thou shalt not escape the smart.— Boy, lead me home, that he may spend his rage on younger men, and learn to keep a tongue more temperate, and to bear within his breast a better mind than now he bears. [*Exit*Teiresias.

Ch. The man hath gone, O king, with dread prophecies. And, since the hair on this head, once dark, hath been white, I know that he hath never been a false prophet to our city.

Cr. I, too, know it well, and am troubled in soul. 'Tis dire to yield; but, by resistance, to smite my pride with ruin—this, too, is a dire choice.

Ch. Son of Menoeceus, it behoves thee to take wise counsel.

Cr. What should I do, then? Speak, and I will obey.

Ch. Go thou, and free the maiden from her rocky chamber, and make a tomb for the unburied dead.

Cr. And this is thy counsel? Thou wouldst have me yield?

Ch. Yea, King, and with all speed; for swift harms from the gods cut short the folly of men.

Cr. Ah me, 'tis hard, but I resign my cherished resolve,—I obey. We must not wage a vain war with destiny.

Ch. Go, thou, and do these things; leave them not to others.

Cr. Even as I am I'll go:—on, on, my servants, each and all of you,—take axes in your hands, and hasten to the ground that ye see yonder! Since our judgment hath taken this turn, I will be present to unloose her, as I myself bound her. My heart misgives me, 'tis best to keep the established laws, even to life's end.

str. 1.Ch. O thou of many names, glory of the Cadmeian bride, offspring of loud-thundering Zeus! thou who watchest over famed Italia, and reignest, where all guests are welcomed, in the sheltered plain of Eleusinian Deô! O Bacchus, dweller in Thebè, mother-city of Bacchants, by the softly-gliding stream of Ismenus, on the soil where the fierce dragon's teeth were sown!

ant. 1.Thou hast been seen where torch-flames glare through smoke, above the crests of the twin peaks, where move the Corycian nymphs, thy votaries, hard by Castalia's stream.

Thou comest from the ivy-mantled slopes of Nysa's hills, and from the shore green with many-clustered vines, while thy name is lifted up on strains of more than mortal power, as thou visitest the ways of Thebè:

str. 2.Thebè, of all cities, thou holdest first in honour, thou, and thy mother whom the lightning smote; and now, when all our people is captive to a violent plague, come thou with healing feet over the Parnassian height, or over the moaning strait!

ant. 2.O thou with whom the stars rejoice as they move, the stars whose breath is fire; O master of the voices of the night; son begotten of Zeus; appear, O king, with thine attendant Thyiads, who in night-long frenzy dance before thee, the giver of good gifts, Iacchus!

*Enter*Messenger,*on the spectators' left hand.*

Me. Dwellers by the house of Cadmus and of Amphion, there is no estate of mortal life that I would ever praise or blame as settled. Fortune raises and Fortune humbles the lucky or unlucky from day to day, and no one can prophesy to men concerning those things which are established. For Creon was blest once, as I count bliss; he had saved this land of Cadmus from its foes; he was clothed with sole dominion in the land; he reigned, the glorious sire of princely children. And now all hath been lost. For when a man hath forfeited his pleasures, I count him not as living,—I hold him but a breathing corpse. Heap up riches in thy house, if thou wilt; live in kingly state; yet, if there be no gladness therewith, I would not give the shadow of a vapour for all the rest, compared with joy.

Ch. And what is this new grief that thou hast to tell for our princes?

Me. Death; and the living are guilty for the dead.

Ch. And who is the slayer? Who the stricken? Speak.

Me. Haemon hath perished; his blood hath been shed by no stranger.

Ch. By his father's hand, or by his own?

Me. By his own, in wrath with his sire for the murder.

Ch. O prophet, how true, then, hast thou proved thy word!

Me. These things stand thus; ye must consider of the rest.

Ch. Lo, I see the hapless Eurydicè, Creon's wife, approaching; she comes from the house by chance, haply,—or because she knows the tidings of her son.

*Enter*Eurydicè.

Eu. People of Thebes, I heard your words as I was going forth, to salute the goddess Pallas with my prayers. Even as I was loosing the fastenings of the gate, to open it, the message of a household woe smote on mine ear: I sank back, terror-stricken, into the arms of my handmaids, and my senses fled. But say again what the tidings were; I shall hear them as one who is no stranger to sorrow.

Me. Dear lady, I will witness of what I saw, and will leave no word of the truth untold. Why, indeed, should I soothe thee with words in which I must presently be found false? Truth is ever best.—I attended thy lord as his guide to the furthest part of the plain, where the body of Polyneices, torn by dogs, still lay unpitied. We prayed the goddess of the roads, and Pluto, in mercy to restrain their wrath; we washed the dead with holy washing; and with freshly-plucked boughs we solemnly burned such relics as there were. We raised a high mound of his native earth; and then we turned away to enter the maiden's nuptial chamber with rocky couch, the caverned mansion of the bride of Death. And, from afar off, one of us heard a voice of loud wailing at that bride's unhallowed bower; and came to tell our master Creon.

And as the king drew nearer, doubtful sounds of a bitter cry floated around him; he groaned, and said in accents of anguish, 'Wretched that I am, can my foreboding be true? Am I going on the wofullest way that ever I went? My son's voice greets me.—Go, my servants,—haste ye nearer, and when ye have reached the tomb, pass through the gap, where the stones have been wrenched away, to the cell's very mouth,—and look, and see if 'tis Haemon's voice that I know, or if mine ear is cheated by the gods.'

This search, at our despairing master's word, we went to make; and in the furthest part of the tomb we descried *her* hanging by the neck, slung by a thread-wrought halter of fine linen; while *he* was embracing her with arms thrown around her waist,— bewailing the loss of his bride who is with the dead, and his father's deeds, and his own ill-starred love.

But his father, when he saw him, cried aloud with a dread cry, and went in, and called to him with a voice of wailing:—'Unhappy, what a deed hast thou done! What thought hath come to thee? What manner of mischance hath marred thy reason? Come forth, my child! I pray thee—I implore!' But the boy glared at him with fierce eyes, spat in his face, and, without a word of answer, drew his cross-hilted sword:— as his father rushed forth in flight, he missed his aim;—then, hapless one, wroth with himself, he straightway leaned with all his weight against his sword, and drove it, half its length, into his side; and, while sense lingered, he clasped the maiden to his faint embrace, and, as he gasped, sent forth on her pale cheek the swift stream of the oozing blood.

Corpse enfolding corpse he lies; he hath won his nuptial rites, poor youth, not here, yet in the halls of Death; and he hath witnessed to mankind that, of all curses which cleave to man, ill counsel is the sovereign curse. [*Eurydicè retires into the house.*

Ch. What wouldst thou augur from this? The lady hath turned back, and is gone, without a word, good or evil.

Me. I, too, am startled; yet I nourish the hope that, at these sore tidings of her son, she cannot deign to give her sorrow public vent, but in the privacy of the house will set her handmaids to mourn the household grief. For she is not untaught of discretion, that she should err.

Ch. I know not; but to me, at least, a strained silence seems to portend peril, no less than vain abundance of lament.

Me. Well, I will enter the house, and learn whether indeed she is not hiding some repressed purpose in the depths of a passionate heart. Yea, thou sayest well: excess of silence, too, may have a perilous meaning.

[*Exit* Messenger.

Enter Creon, *on the spectators' left, with attendants, carrying the shrouded body of* Haemon *on a bier.*

Ch. Lo, yonder the king himself draws near, bearing that which tells too clear a tale,—the work of no stranger's madness,—if we may say it,—but of his own misdeeds.

str. 1. Cr. Woe for the sins of a darkened soul, stubborn sins, fraught with death! Ah, ye behold us, the sire who hath slain, the son who hath perished! Woe is me, for the wretched blindness of my counsels! Alas, my son, thou hast died in thy youth, by a timeless doom, woe is me!—thy spirit hath fled,—not by thy folly, but by mine own!

str. 2.Ch. Ah me, how all too late thou seemest to see the right!

Cr. Ah me, I have learned the bitter lesson! But then, methinks, oh then, some god smote me from above with crushing weight, and hurled me into ways of cruelty, woe is me,—overthrowing and trampling on my joy! Woe, woe, for the troublous toils of men!

*Enter*Messenger*from the house.*

Me. Sire, thou hast come, methinks, as one whose hands are not empty, but who hath store laid up besides; thou bearest yonder burden with thee; and thou art soon to look upon the woes within thy house.

Cr. And what worse ill is yet to follow upon ills?

Me. Thy queen hath died, true mother of yon corpse—ah, hapless lady!—by blows newly dealt.

ant. 1.Cr. Oh Hades, all-receiving, whom no sacrifice can appease! Hast thou, then, no mercy for me? O thou herald of evil, bitter tidings, what word dost thou utter? Alas, I was already as dead, and thou hast smitten me anew! What sayest thou, my son? What is this new message that thou bringest—woe, woe is me!—of a wife's doom,—of slaughter heaped on slaughter?

Ch. Thou canst behold: 'tis no longer hidden within.

[*The doors of the palace are opened, and the corpse of*Eurydice*is disclosed.*

ant. 2.Cr. Ah me,—yonder I behold a new, a second woe! What destiny, ah what, can yet await me? I have but now raised my son in my arms,—and there, again, I see a corpse before me! Alas, alas, unhappy mother! Alas, my child!

Me. There, at the altar, self-stabbed with a keen knife, she suffered her darkening eyes to close, when she had wailed for the noble fate of Megareus who died before, and then for his fate who lies there,—and when, with her last breath, she had invoked evil fortunes upon thee, the slayer of thy sons.

str. 3.Cr. Woe, woe! I thrill with dread. Is there none to strike me to the heart with two-edged sword?—O miserable that I am, and steeped in miserable anguish!

Me. Yea, both this son's doom, and that other's, were laid to thy charge by her whose corpse thou seest.

Cr. And what was the manner of the violent deed by which she passed away?

Me. Her own hand struck her to the heart, when she had learned her son's sorely lamented fate.

str. 4.Cr. Ah me, this guilt can never be fixed on any other of mortal kind, for my acquittal! I, even I, was thy slayer, wretched that I am—I own the truth. Lead me away, O my servants, lead me hence with all speed, whose life is but as death!

Ch. Thy counsels are good, if there can be good with ills; briefest is best, when trouble is in our path.

ant. 3.Cr. Oh, let it come, let it appear, that fairest of fates for me, that brings my last day,—aye, best fate of all! Oh, let it come, that I may never look upon to-morrow's light.

Ch. These things are in the future; present tasks claim our care: the ordering of the future rests where it should rest.

Cr. All my desires, at least, were summed in that prayer.

Ch. Pray thou no more; for mortals have no escape from destined woe.

ant. 4.Cr. Lead me away, I pray you; a rash, foolish man; who have slain thee, ah my son, unwittingly, and thee, too, my wife—unhappy that I am! I know not which way I should bend my gaze, or where I should seek support; for all is amiss with that which is in my hands,—and yonder, again, a crushing fate hath leapt upon my head.

[*As* Creon *is being conducted into the house, the Coryphaeus speaks the closing verses.*

Ch. Wisdom is the supreme part of happiness; and reverence towards the gods must be inviolate. Great words of prideful men are ever punished with great blows, and, in old age, teach the chastened to be wise.

AJAX

PERSONS OF THE DRAMA.

Athena.
Ajax.
Odysseus.
Tecmessa.
Teucer.
Menelaus.
Agamemnon.
Chorus of Salaminian Sailors.

MUTE PERSONS.

The child Eurysaces and his attendant.—Two heralds, accompanying Menelaus (v. 1046: see v. 1115).—Two bodyguards, in attendance on Agamemnon.—Attendants of Teucer (v. 1003: cp. vv. 1402 ff.).

Scene: (1) At first, before the tent of Ajax, at the eastern end of the Greek camp, near Cape Rhoeteum on the northern coast of the Troad. (2) After verse 814, a lonely place on the shore of the Hellespont, with underwood or bushes.

After the death of Achilles in the war at Troy, Ajax and Odysseus were rivals for the honour of inheriting his armour. The Greek chiefs, with the two Atreidae at their head, were the judges; and they awarded the prize to Odysseus. Distempered in mind by his rejection, Ajax went out at night with the purpose of slaying Agamemnon and Menelaus. He was at the very doors of their quarters, when Athena, whom he had angered in past days, smote him with raging madness. He fell on the flocks and herds of the Greek army, fancying that they were his human foes; cut down the shepherds and herdsmen, slaughtered numbers of the animals, and led others captive to his tent.

When the drama begins, it is early on the morning after this midnight raid. Rumour already points to the son of Telamon as the author of the outrage. Odysseus, acting on the hint of an informant who had caught a glimpse of the maniac, has followed up the tracks which he found in the plain; and these have led him to the tent of Ajax. He is now closely scanning the footprints near it, in order to judge whether Ajax is still within the tent, or has again gone forth. While thus engaged, he hears the voice of his guardian goddess.

ATHENA.

Ever have I seen thee, son of Lartius, seeking to snatch some occasion against thy foes; and now at the tent of Ajax by the ships, where he hath his station at the camp's utmost verge, I see thee long while pausing on his trail and scanning his fresh tracks, to find whether he is within or abroad. Well doth it lead thee to thy goal, thy course keen-scenting as a Laconian hound's. For the man is even now gone within, sweat streaming10 from his face and from hands that have slain with the sword. And there is no further need for thee to peer within these doors; but say what is thine aim in this eager quest, that thou mayest learn from her who can give thee light.

ODYSSEUS.

Voice of Athena, dearest to me of the Immortals, how clearly, though thou be unseen, do I hear thy call and seize it in my soul, as when a Tyrrhenian clarion speaks from mouth of bronze! And now thou hast discerned aright that I am hunting to and fro on the trail of a foeman, even Ajax of the mighty shield. 'Tis he, and no other, that I have been tracking so long.20

This night he hath done to us a thing which passes thought,—if he is indeed the doer; for we know nothing certain, but drift in doubt; and I took upon me the burden of this search. We have lately found the cattle, our spoil, dead—yea, slaughtered by human hand—and dead, beside them, the guardians of the flock.

Now, all men lay this crime to him. And a scout30 who had descried him bounding alone over the plain with reeking sword brought me tidings, and declared the matter. Then straightway I rushed upon his track; and sometimes I recognise the footprints as his, but sometimes I am bewildered, and cannot read whose they are. Thy succour is timely; thine is the hand that ever guides my course,—as in the past, so for the days to come.

Ath. I know it, Odysseus, and came early on the path, a watcher friendly to thy chase.

Od. Dear mistress, do I toil to purpose?

Ath. Know that yon man is the doer of these deeds.

Od.40 And why was his insensate hand put forth so fiercely?

Ath. In bitter wrath touching the arms of Achilles.

Od. Why, then, this furious onslaught upon the flocks?

Ath. 'Twas in your blood, as he deemed, that he was dyeing his hand.

Od. What? Was this design aimed against the Greeks?

Ath. He would have accomplished it, too, had I been careless.

Od. And how had he laid these bold plans? What could inspire such hardihood?

Ath. In the night he went forth against you, by stealth, and alone.

Od. And did he come near us? Did he reach his goal?

Ath. He was already at the doors of the two chiefs.

Od. What cause, then, stayed his eager hand from50 murder?

Ath. I, even I, withheld him, for I cast upon his eyes the tyrannous fancies of his baneful joy; and I turned his fury aside on the flocks of sheep, and the confused droves guarded of herdsmen, the spoil which ye had not yet divided. Then he fell on, and dealt death among the horny throng, as he hewed them to the earth around him; and now he deemed that the two Atreidae were the prisoners whom he slew with his hand, now 'twas this chief, now 'twas that, at each new onset. And while the man raved in the throes of frenzy, I still urged him, hurled him into the toils of doom.60 Anon, when he rested from this work, he bound together the living oxen, with all the sheep, and brought them home, as though his captives were men, not goodly kine. And now he torments them, bound together, in the house.

But to thee also will I show this madness openly, that when thou hast seen it thou mayest proclaim it to all the Greeks. And be thou steadfast and of a good courage, nor look for evil from the man; for I will turn away the vision of his eyes, and keep them from beholding70 thy face.

Ho, thou who art binding with cords the back-bent arms of thy captives, I call thee, come hither! Ajax, what ho! come forth from the house!

Od. What dost thou, Athena? Never call him forth.

Ath. Hold thy peace! Do not earn the name of coward!

Od.80 Forbear, I pray thee; be content that he stay within.

Ath. What is the danger? Was he not a man before?

Od. Yea, a foeman to thy servant, and still is.

Ath. And to mock at foes—is not that the sweetest mockery?

Od. Enough for me that he abide within his doors.

Ath. Thou fearest to see a madman in full view?

Od. No fear had made me shun him, if he were sane.

Ath. Nay, even now, he shall not see thee, though thou art near.

Od. How so, if he still sees with the same eyes?

Ath. I will darken them, though they are open.

Od. Well, all is possible when a god contrives.

Ath. Stand silent, then, and stay where thou art.

Od. I must stay.—Would that I were far from here!

Ath.90 What ho, Ajax, once again I call thee! is this thy scanty regard for thine ally?

Enter Ajax, *holding a blood-stained scourge in his hand.*

Aj. Hail, Athena! Hail, Zeus-born maid! How well hast thou stood by me! Yea, I will crown thy shrine with trophies of pure gold for this prize!

Ath. 'Tis fairly spoken. But tell me this—hast thou dyed thy sword well in the Greek camp?

Aj. That vaunt is mine; I disclaim it not.

Ath. And perchance turned thine armed hand on the Atreidae?

Aj. So that nevermore will they dishonour Ajax.

Ath. The men are dead, as I take thy meaning:

Aj. Dead: now let them rob me of my arms!

Ath. Good: and then the son of Laertius—in what plight hast thou left him? Hath he escaped thee?

Aj. What, thou askest me of that accursed fox?

Ath. Yea, in sooth—of Odysseus, thine adversary.

Aj. No guest so welcome, Lady: he is sitting in the house—in bonds: I do not mean him to die just yet.

Ath. What wouldst thou do first? What larger advantage wouldst thou win?

Aj. First, he shall be bound to a pillar beneath my roof—

Ath. The hapless man—what despite wilt thou do unto him?

Aj. — and have his back crimsoned with the scourge, ere he die.

Ath. Nay, do not torture the wretch so cruelly.

Aj. In all else, Athena, I say, have thy will; but *his* doom shall be none but this.

Ath. Nay, then, since it delights thee to do thus, hold not thy hand, abate no jot of thine intent.

Aj. I go to my work:—but thou, I charge thee, stand ever at my side as thou hast stood to-day!

[*Exit* Ajax.

Ath. Seest thou, Odysseus, how great is the strength of the gods? Whom couldest thou have found more prudent than this man, or more valiant for the service of the time?

Od. I know none; and I pity him in his misery, for all that he is my foe, because he is bound fast to a dread doom: I think of mine own lot no less than his. For I see that we are but phantoms, all we who live, or fleeting shadows.

Ath. Therefore, beholding such things, look that thine own lips never speak a haughty word against the gods, and assume no swelling port, if thou prevailest above another in prowess or by store of ample wealth. For a day can humble all human things, and a day can lift them up; but the wise of heart are loved of the gods, and the evil are abhorred.

Enter the Chorus *of Salaminian Sailors, followers of Ajax.*

Ch. Son of Telamon, thou whose wave-girt Salamis is firmly throned upon the sea, when thy fortunes are fair, I rejoice: but when the stroke of Zeus comes on thee, or the angry rumour of the Danai with noise of evil tongues, then I quake exceedingly and am sore afraid, like a winged dove with troubled eye.

And so, telling of the night now spent, loud murmurs beset us for our shame; telling how thou didst visit the meadow wild with steeds, and didst destroy the cattle of the Greeks, their spoil,—prizes of the spear which had not yet been shared,—slaying them with flashing sword.

Such are the whispered slanders that Odysseus breathes into all ears; and he wins large belief. For now the tale that he tells of thee is specious; and each hearer rejoices more than he who told, despitefully exulting in thy woes.

Yea, point thine arrow at a noble spirit, and thou shalt not miss; but should a man speak such things against me, he would win no faith. 'Tis on the powerful that envy creeps. Yet the small without the great can ill be trusted to guard the walls; lowly leagued with great will prosper best, great served by less.

But foolish men cannot be led to learn these truths. Even such are the men who rail against thee, and we are helpless to repel these charges, without thee, O king. Verily, when they have escaped thine eye, they chatter like flocking birds: but, terrified by the mighty vulture, suddenly, perchance—if thou shouldst appear—they will cower still and dumb.

str. Was it the Tauric Artemis, child of Zeus, that drave thee—O dread rumour, parent of my shame!—against the herds of all our host,—in revenge, I ween, for a victory that had paid no tribute, whether it was that she had been disappointed of glorious spoil, or because a stag had been slain without a thank-offering? Or can it have been the mail-clad Lord of War that was wroth for dishonour to his aiding spear, and took vengeance by nightly wiles?

ant. Never of thine own heart, son of Telamon, wouldst thou have gone so far astray as to fall upon the flocks. Yea, when the gods send madness, it must come; but may Zeus and Phoebus avert the evil rumour of the Greeks!

And if the great chiefs charge thee falsely in the furtive rumours which they spread, or sons of the wicked line of Sisyphus, forbear, O my king, forbear to win me an evil name, by still keeping thy face thus hidden in the tent by the sea.

ep. Nay, up from thy seat, wheresoever thou art brooding in this pause of many days from battle, making the flame of mischief blaze up to heaven! But the insolence of thy foes goes abroad without fear in the breezy glens, while all men mock with taunts most grievous; and my sorrow passes not away.

Enter Tecmessa.

Te. Mariners of Ajax, of the race that springs from the Erechtheidae, sons of the soil,—mourning is our portion who care for the house of Telamon afar. Ajax, our dread lord of rugged might, now lies stricken with a storm that darkens the soul.

Ch. And what is the heavy change from the fortune of yesterday which this night hath brought forth? Daughter of the Phrygian Teleutas, speak: for to thee, his spear-won bride, bold Ajax hath borne a constant love; therefore mightest thou hint the answer with knowledge.

Te. Oh, how shall I tell a tale too dire for words? Terrible as death is the hap which thou must hear. Seized with madness in the night, our glorious Ajax hath been utterly undone. For token, thou mayest see within his dwelling the butchered victims weltering in their blood, sacrifices of no hand but his.

str. Ch. What tidings of the fiery warrior hast thou told, not to be borne, nor yet escaped,—tidings which the mighty Danai noise abroad, which their strong rumour spreads! Woe is me, I dread the doom to come: shamed before all eyes, the man will die, if his frenzied hand hath slain with dark sword the herds and the horse-guiding herdsmen.

Te. Alas! 'twas thence, then,—from those pastures,—that he came to me with his captive flock! Of part, he cut the throats on the floor within; some, hewing their sides, he rent asunder. Then he caught up two white-footed rams; he sheared off the head of one, and the tongue-tip, and flung them away; the other he bound upright to a pillar, and seized a heavy thong of horse-gear, and flogged with shrill, doubled lash, while he uttered revilings which a god, and no mortal, had taught.

ant. Ch. The time hath come for each of us to veil his head and betake him to stealthy speed of foot, or to sit on the bench at the quick oar, and give her way to the sea-faring ship. Such angry threats are hurled against us by the brother-kings, the sons of Atreus: I fear to share a bitter death by stoning, smitten at this man's side, who is swayed by a fate to which none may draw nigh.

Te. It sways him no longer: the lightnings flash no more; like a southern gale, fierce in its first onset, his rage abates; and now, in his right mind, he hath new pain. To look on self-wrought woes, when no other hath had a hand therein—this lays sharp pangs to the soul.

Ch. Nay, if his frenzy hath ceased, I have good hope that all may yet be well: the trouble is of less account when once 'tis past.

Te. And which, were the choice given thee, wouldst thou choose—to pain thy friends, and have delights thyself, or to share the grief of friends who grieve?

Ch. The twofold sorrow, lady, is the greater ill.

Te. Then are we losers now, although the plague is past.

Ch. What is thy meaning? I know not how thou meanest.

Te. Yon man, while frenzied, found his own joy in the dire fantasies that held him, though his presence was grievous to us who were sane; but now, since he hath had pause and respite from the plague, *he* is utterly afflicted with sore grief, and we likewise, no less than before. Have we not here two sorrows, instead of one?

Ch. Yea verily: and I fear lest the stroke of a god hath fallen. How else, if his spirit is no lighter, now that the malady is overpast, than when it vexed him?

Te. Thus stands the matter, be well assured.

Ch. And in what wise did the plague first swoop upon him? Declare to us, who share thy pain, how it befell.

Te. Thou shalt hear all that chanced, as one who hath part therein. At dead of night, when the evening lamps no longer burned, he seized a two-edged sword, and was fain to go forth on an aimless path. Then I chid him, and said; 'What dost thou, Ajax? why wouldst thou make this sally unsummoned,—not called by messenger, not warned by trumpet? Nay, at present the whole army sleeps.'

But he answered me in curt phrase and trite: 'Woman, silence graces women.' And I, thus taught, desisted; but he rushed forth alone. What happened abroad, I cannot tell: but he came in with his captives bound together,—bulls, shepherd dogs, and fleecy prisoners. Some he beheaded; of some, he cut the back-bent throat, or cleft the chine; others, in their bonds, he tormented as though they were men, with onslaughts on the cattle.

At last, he darted forward through the door, and began ranting to some creature of his brain,—now against the Atreidae, now about Odysseus,—with many a mocking vaunt of all the despite that he had wreaked on them in his raid. Anon, he rushed back once more into the house; and then, by slow, painful steps, regained his reason.

And as his gaze ranged over the room full of his wild work, he struck his head, and uttered a great cry: he fell down, a wreck amid the wrecks of the slaughtered sheep, and there he sat, with clenched nails tightly clutching his hair. At first, and for a long while, he sat dumb: then he threatened me with those dreadful threats, if I declared not all the chance that had befallen; and asked in what strange plight he stood. And I, friends, in my fear, told all that had been done, so far as I surely knew it. But he straightway broke into bitter lamentations, such as never had I heard from him before. For he had ever taught that such wailing was for craven and low-hearted men; no cry of shrill complaint would pass his lips; only a deep sound, as of a moaning bull.

But now, prostrate in his utter woe, tasting not of food or drink, the man sits quiet where he has fallen, amidst the sword-slain cattle. And plainly he yearns to do some dread deed: there is some such meaning in his words and his laments. Ah, my friends—indeed, this was my errand—come in and help, if in any wise ye can. Men in his case can be won by the words of friends.

Ch. Tecmessa, daughter of Teleutas, dread are thy tidings, that our lord hath been frenzied by his sorrows.

Aj. (*within*). Woe, woe is me!

Te. Soon there will be worse, belike.—Heard ye not Ajax,—heard ye not that resounding cry?

Aj. Woe, woe is me!

Ch. The man seems to be distempered, or else to be grieving for the distempers which lately vexed him, when he sees their work.

Aj. O my son, my son!

Te. Ah me! Eurysaces, 'tis for thee he calls! What can be his purpose? Where art thou? Unhappy that I am!

Aj. Ho, Teucer! Where is Teucer? Will his foray last for ever? And I perish!

Ch. He seems to be sane. Come, open there! open—perchance e'en at the sight of me he may come to a more sober mood.

Te. Behold, I open: thou canst look on yon man's deeds, and his own plight.

Ajax is discovered sitting amidst the slaughtered cattle.

str. 1.Aj. Alas, good sailors, alone of my friends, alone still constant to your loyalty, behold what a wave hath but now surged around me and hemmed me in, under stress of a deadly storm!

Ch. Ah, lady, how sadly true seems thy report! The fact proves that no sane mind is here.

ant. 1.Aj. Alas, ye mates staunch in sea-craft, ye who manned the ship and made the oar-blade flash upon the brine,—in you, in you alone I see a defence against misery: come, slay me also!

Ch. Hush thy wild lips: cure not ill by ill, nor increase the anguish of the doom.

str. 2.Aj. Seest thou the bold, the strong of heart, the dauntless in battles with the foe,—seest thou how I have shown my prowess on creatures that feared no harm? Alas, the mockery! How then have I been shamed!

Te. Ajax, my lord, I implore thee, speak not thus!

Aj. Hence! out with thee! avaunt—begone!—Woe is me! woe is me!

Ch. For the gods' love, yield to counsel, and learn wisdom!

Aj. Wretch that I am, who suffered the accursed men to slip through my hands, but fell on horned kine and goodly flocks, and made their dark blood flow!

Ch. Why grieve when the deed is past recall? These things can never be but as they are.

ant. 2.Aj. Ah, thou who watchest all things, thou ready tool of every crime, ah, son of Lartius, thou foulest knave in all the host, I warrant thou laughest loud and long for joy!

Ch. As the god gives, so every man laughs or mourns.

Aj. Yet would that I could see him, shattered though I am! Ah me, ah me!

Ch. Speak no proud word: seest thou not to what a plight thou hast come?

Aj. O Zeus, father of my sires, would that I might slay that deep dissembler, that hateful knave, and the two brother-chiefs, and lastly die myself also!

Te. When thou makest that prayer, pray therewith for me also that I die: wherefore should I live when thou art dead?

str. 3.Aj. Alas, thou darkness, my sole light! O thou nether gloom, fairer for me than any sunshine! take me to dwell with you,—yea, take me; for I am no longer worthy to look for help to the race of the gods, or for any good from men, the children of a day.

No, the daughter of Zeus, the strong goddess, torments me to the death. Whither then shall a man flee? Whither shall I go to find rest? If my past fame is destroyed, my friends, along with such victims as these near me—if I have set myself to win a madman's triumphs, and all the host, with sword uplifted in both hands, would strike me dead!

Te. Ah me unhappy, that a good man and true should utter such words,—words that, till now, he ne'er would have deigned to speak!

ant. 3.Aj. Alas, ye paths of the sounding wave, ye sea-caves and wooded pastures by the shore, long time, long time and very weary have ye known me tarrying at Troy;

but no more shall ye know me,—no more with the breath of life: of so much let sane men be sure.

Ah, streams of Scamander near us, kindly to the Greeks, never shall ye look on Ajax more; whose peer in the host—for I will utter a proud word—never hath Troy seen come from the land of Hellas: but now, behold, he hath been humbled to the dust!

Ch. In sooth I know not how to restrain thee, or how suffer thee to speak, whom woes so grievous have befallen.

Aj. Ay me! Who could e'er have thought that my name would chime so meetly with my doom? For well may I now mourn,—yea, twice and three times mourn,—in those sad syllables that shape my name; such heavy griefs are mine, whose sire by his prowess won the fairest prize of all the host, and brought all glory home from this land of Ida; but I his son, who came after him in might not less to this same ground of Troy, and proved the service of mine hand in no meaner deeds, thus perish, dishonoured of the Greeks. Yet, methinks, of thus much am I sure; if Achilles lived, and had been called to decree the first place in valour to any claimant of his arms, no one would have grasped them before me. But now the Atreidae have conveyed them to a villain, and thrust away the high deeds of Ajax.

And if these eyes, if this warped mind had not swerved from the purpose that was mine, never would they have procured such a judgment against another man. As it was, the daughter of Zeus, the fierce-eyed, unconquerable goddess, foiled me at the instant when I was making ready my hand against them,—struck me with a plague of frenzy,—made me imbrue my hands in the blood of these poor cattle. And yon men exult to have escaped me,—by no good-will of mine; but if a god send harm, verily e'en the base man can elude the worthier.

And now what shall I do; who plainly am hateful to the gods, abhorred by the Greek host, hated by all Troy and all these plains? Shall I forsake the station of the ships, and leave the Atreidae forlorn, and go homeward across the Aegean? And what face shall I show to my father when I come,—to Telamon? How will he find heart to look on me, when I stand before him ungraced—without that meed of valour whereby *he* won a great crown of fame? 'Tis not to be endured.

But then shall I go to the stronghold of the Trojans,—attack alone, where all are foes,—and, in doing some good service, lastly die? Nay, thus I might haply gladden the Atreidae. It must not be. Some emprise must be sought whereby I may prove to mine aged sire that in heart, at least, his son is not a dastard.

'Tis base for a man to crave the full term of life, who finds no varying in his woes. What joy is there in day following day,—now pushing us forward, now drawing us back, on the verge—of death? I rate that man as nothing worth, who feels the glow of idle hopes. Nay, one of generous strain should nobly live, or forthwith nobly die: thou hast heard all.

Ch. No man shall say that thou hast spoken a bastard word, Ajax, or one not bred of thy true soul. Yet forbear: dismiss these thoughts, and suffer friends to overrule thy purpose.

Te. Ajax, my lord, the doom given by fate is the hardest of evils among men. I was the daughter of a free-born sire, wealthy and mighty, if any Phrygian was; and now I am a slave: for so the gods ordained, I ween, and chiefly thy strong hand. Therefore, since wedlock hath made me thine, I wish thee well; and I do entreat thee, by the Zeus of our hearth, by the marriage that hath made us one, doom me not to the cruel rumour of thy foes,—abandon me not to the hand of a stranger! On what day soever thou die and leave me lonely by thy death, on that same day, be sure, I also shall be seized forcibly by the Greeks, and, with thy son, shall have the portion of a slave. Then shall some one of my masters name me in bitter phrase, with keen taunts: 'See the concubine of Ajax, his, who was the mightiest of the host; see what menial tasks are hers, who had such bliss!' Thus shall men speak; and destiny will afflict me; but these words will be shameful for thee and for thy race.

Nay, have thought for thy father, whom thou forsakest in a drear old age; for thy mother,—and hers are many years,—who oft prays to the gods that thou come home alive; and pity, O king, thy son, if, bereft of fostering care, he must spend his days forlorn of thee, the ward of unloving guardians; think how great is this sorrow, which at thy death thou wilt bequeath to him and me.

I have nothing left whereunto I can look, save thee. Thou didst ravage my country with the spear, and another doom hath laid low my mother and my sire, that they should dwell with Hades in their death. What home, then, could I find, if I lost thee? What wealth? On thee hangs all my welfare. Nay, have thought for me also: a true man should cherish remembrance, if anywhere he reap a joy. 'Tis kindness that still begets kindness. But whosoever suffers the memory of benefits to slip from him, that man can no more rank as noble.

Ch. Ajax, I would that pity touched thy soul as it doth mine: so wouldst thou approve her words.

Aj. Verily she shall have approval on my part, if only she take heart to do my bidding well.

Te. Nay, dear Ajax, I will obey in all things.

Aj. Then bring me my son, that I may see him.

Te. Oh, but in those fears I released him from my keeping.

Aj. During these troubles of mine? Or what meanest thou?

Te. Yea, lest haply the poor child should meet thee, and die.

Aj. Aye truly, that would have been worthy of my fortune.

Te. Well, at least I was watchful to avert *that* woe.

Aj. I praise thy deed, and the foresight which thou hast shown.

Te. How, then, can I serve thee, as the case stands now?

Aj. Let me speak to him, and see him face to face.

Te. Oh yes—he is close by, in charge of attendants.

Aj. Then wherefore is his coming delayed?

Te. My child, thy father calls thee.—Bring him hither, servant, whosoever of you is guiding his steps.

Aj. Comes the man at thy call? Or hath he failed to hear thy words?

Te. Even now one of the servants there draws near with him.

Enter Attendant *with* Eurysaces.

Aj. Lift him, lift him to mine arms. He will feel no dread, I ween, in looking on this newly shed blood, if he is indeed my true-born son. But he must at once be broken into his father's rugged ways, and moulded to the likeness of his nature. Ah, boy, mayest thou prove happier than thy sire, but in all else like him; and thou wilt prove not base. Yet even now I may well envy thee for this, that thou hast no sense of these ills. Yea, life is sweetest before the feelings are awake, [for lack of feeling is

103

a painless ill,]—until one learns to know joy or pain. But when thou shalt come unto that knowledge, then must thou see to prove among thy father's foes of what mettle and what sire thou art.

Meanwhile feed on light breezes, and nurse thy tender life, for this thy mother's joy. No fear, I wot, lest any of the Greeks assail thee with cruel outrage, even when thou hast me no more. So trusty is the warder whom I will leave to guard thee, even Teucer; who will not falter in his care for thee, albeit now he is following a far path, busied with chase of foes.

O my warriors, seafaring comrades! On you, as on him, I lay this task of love; and give ye my behest to Teucer, that he take this child to mine own home, and set him before the face of Telamon, and of my mother, Eriboea, that so he may prove the comfort of their age evermore [until they come unto the deep places of the nether god]. And charge him that no stewards of games, nor he who worked my ruin, make mine arms a prize for the Greeks. No,—*this* take thou, my son,—the broad shield from which thou hast thy name,—hold and wield it by the well-wrought thong, that sevenfold, spear-proof targe! But the rest of my armour shall be buried in my grave.

(*To* Tecmessa.) Come, tarry not; take the child straightway, make fast the doors, and utter no laments before the house: in sooth a woman is a plaintive thing. Quick, close the house! It is not for a skilful leech to whine charms over a sore that craves the knife.

Ch. I am afraid when I mark this eager haste: I like not the keen edge of thy speech.

Te. Ajax, my lord, on what deed can thy mind be set?

Aj. Ask not, inquire not; 'tis good to be discreet.

Te. Ah, my heavy heart! Now, by thy child,—by the gods,—I implore thee, be not guilty of forsaking us!

Aj. Nay, thou vexest me over much: knowest thou not that I no longer owe aught of service to the gods?

Te. Hush, hush! Aj. Speak to those who hear.

Te. And wilt *thou* not hearken? Aj. Already thy words have been too many.

Te. I am afraid, O prince! Aj. (*To the Attendants.*) Close the doors, I say, this instant!

Te. For the gods' love, be softened! Aj. 'Tis a foolish hope, methinks, if thou wouldst begin now to school my temper.

[Ajax *is shut into the tent.—Exit* Tecmessa *with* Eurysaces.

str. 1.Ch. O famous Salamis, thou, I ween, hast thy happy seat among the waves that lash thy shore, the joy of all men's eyes for ever; but I, hapless, have long been tarrying here, still making my couch, through countless months, in the camp on the fields of Ida,—worn by time, and darkly looking for the day when I shall pass to Hades, the abhorred, the unseen.

ant. 1.And now I must wrestle with a new grief, woe is me!—the incurable malady of Ajax, visited by a heavensent frenzy; whom in a bygone day thou sentest forth from thee, mighty in bold war; but now, a changed man who nurses lonely thoughts, he hath been found a heavy sorrow to his friends. And the former deeds of his hands, deeds of prowess supreme, have fallen dead, nor won aught of love from the loveless, the miserable Atreidae.

str. 2.Surely his mother, full of years and white with eld, will uplift a voice of wailing when she hears that he hath been stricken with the spirit's ruin: not in the nightingale's plaintive note will she utter her anguish: in shrill-toned strains the dirge will rise, with sound of hands that smite the breast, and with rending of hoary hair.

ant. 2.Yes, better hid with Hades is he whom vain fancies vex; he who by the lineage whence he springs is noblest of the war-tried Achaeans, yet now is true no more to the promptings of his inbred nature, but dwells with alien thoughts.

Ah, hapless sire, how heavy a curse upon thy son doth it rest for thee to hear, a curse which never yet hath clung to any life of the Aeacidae save his!

*Enter*Ajax,*with a sword in his hand.*

Aj. All things the long and countless years first draw from darkness, then bury from light; and there is nothing for which man may not look; the dread oath is vanquished, and the stubborn will. For even I, erst so wondrous firm,—yea, as iron hardened in the dipping,—felt the keen edge of my temper softened by yon woman's words; and I feel the pity of leaving her a widow with my foes, and the boy an orphan.

But I will go to the bathing-place and the meadows by the shore, that in purging of my stains I may flee the heavy anger of the goddess. Then I will seek out some untrodden spot, and bury this sword, hatefullest of weapons, in a hole dug where none shall see; no, let Night and Hades keep it underground! For since my hand took this gift from Hector, my worst foe, to this hour I have had no good from the Greeks. Yes, men's proverb is true: *The gifts of enemies are no gifts, and bring no good.*

Therefore henceforth I shall know how to yield to the gods, and learn to revere the Atreidae. They are rulers, so we must submit. How else? Dread things and things most potent bow to office; thus it is that snow-strewn winter gives place to fruitful summer; and thus night's weary round makes room for day with her white steeds to kindle light; and the breath of dreadful winds can allow the groaning sea to slumber; and, like the rest, almighty Sleep looses whom he has bound, nor holds with a perpetual grasp.

And we—must we not learn discretion? I, at least, will learn it; for I am newly aware that our enemy is to be hated but as one who will hereafter be a friend; and towards a friend I would wish but thus far to show aid and service, as knowing that he will not always abide. For to most men the haven of friendship is false.

But concerning these things it will be well.—Woman, go thou within, and pray to the gods that in all fulness the desires of my heart may be fulfilled. And ye, my friends,—honour ye these my wishes even as she doth; and bid Teucer, when he comes, have care for me, and good-will towards you withal. For I will go whither I must pass; but do ye what I bid; and ere long, perchance, though now I suffer, ye will hear that I have found peace. [*Exit*Ajax.

*str.*Ch. I thrill with rapture, I soar on the wings of sudden joy! O Pan, O Pan, appear to us, O Pan, roving o'er the sea, from the craggy ridge of snow-beaten Cyllenè, king who makest dances for the gods, that with me thou mayest move blithely in the measures that none hath taught thee, the measures of Nysa and of Cnosus! For now am I fain to dance. And may Apollo, lord of Delos, come over the Icarian waters to be with me, in presence manifest and spirit ever kind!

*ant.*The destroying god hath lifted the cloud of dread trouble from our eyes. Joy, joy! Now, once again, now, O Zeus, can the pure brightness of good days come to the swift sea-cleaving ships; since Ajax again forgets his trouble, and hath turned to perform the law of the gods with all due rites, in perfectness of loyal worship.

The strong years make all things fade; nor would I say that aught was too strange for belief, when thus, beyond our hopes, Ajax hath been led to repent of his wrath against the Atreidae, and his dread feuds.

Enter Messenger *from the Greek camp.*

Me. Friends, I would first tell you this—Teucer is but now returned from the Mysian heights; he hath come to the generals' quarters in mid camp, and is being reviled by all the Greeks at once. They knew him from afar as he drew near,—gathered around him,—and then assailed him with taunts from this side and from that, every man of them,—calling him 'that kinsman of the maniac, of the plotter against the host,'—saying that he should not save himself from being mangled to death by stoning. And so they had come to this, that swords plucked from sheaths were drawn in men's hands; then the strife, when it had run well-nigh to the furthest, was allayed by the soothing words of elders. But where shall I find Ajax, to tell him this? He whom most it touches must hear all the tale.

Ch. He is not within; he hath gone forth but now; for he hath yoked a new purpose to his new mood.

Me. Alas! Alas! Too late, then, was he who sent me on this errand,—or I have proved a laggard.

Ch. And what urgent business hath been scanted here?

Me. Teucer enjoined that the man should not go forth from the house, until he himself should come.

Ch. Well, he is gone, I tell thee,—intent on the purpose that is best for him,—to make his peace with the gods.

Me. These are the words of wild folly, if there is wisdom in the prophecy of Calchas.

Ch. What doth he prophesy? And what knowledge of this matter dost thou bring?

Me. Thus much I know,—for I was present. Leaving the circle of chiefs who sat in council, Calchas drew apart from the Atreidae: then he put his right hand with all kindness in the hand of Teucer, and straitly charged him that, by all means in his power, he should keep Ajax within the house for this day that now is shining on us, and suffer him not to go abroad,—if he wished ever to behold him alive. This day alone will the wrath of divine Athena vex him;—so ran the warning.

'Yea,' said the seer, 'lives that have waxed too proud, and avail for good no more, are struck down by heavy misfortunes from the gods, as often as one born to man's estate forgets it in thoughts too high for man. But Ajax, even at his first going forth from home, was found foolish, when his sire spake well. His father said unto him: "My son, seek victory in arms, but seek it ever with the help of heaven." Then haughtily and foolishly he answered: "Father, with the help of gods e'en a man of nought might win the mastery; but I, even without their aid, trust to bring that glory within my grasp." So proud was his vaunt. Then once again, in answer to divine Athena,—when she was urging him onward and bidding him turn a deadly hand upon his foes,—in that hour he uttered a speech too dread for mortal lips: "Queen, stand thou beside the other Greeks; where Ajax stands, battle will never break our line." By such words it was that he brought upon him the appalling anger of the goddess, since his thoughts were too great for man. But if he lives this day, perchance with the god's help we may find means to save him.'

Thus far the seer: and Teucer had no sooner risen from where they sat than he sent me with these mandates for thy guidance. But if we have been foiled, that man lives not, or Calchas is no prophet.

Ch. Hapless Tecmessa, born to misery, come forth and see what tidings yon man tells; this peril touches us too closely for our peace.

*Enter*Tecmessa.

Te. Why do ye break my rest again, ah me, when I had but just found peace from relentless woes?

Ch. Hearken to yon man, and the tidings of Ajax that he hath brought us, to my grief.

Te. Alas, what sayest thou, man? Are we undone?

Me. I know not of thy fortune, but only that, if Ajax is abroad, my mind is ill at ease for him.

Te. He is abroad indeed, so that I am in anguish to know thy meaning.

Me. Teucer straitly commands that ye keep Ajax under shelter of the roof, and suffer him not to go forth alone.

Te. And where is Teucer, and wherefore speaks he thus?

Me. He hath but now returned; and forbodes that this going forth is fraught with death to Ajax.

Te. Unhappy me! from whom can he have learned this?

Me. From Thestor's son, the seer, this day,—when the issue is one of life or death for Ajax.

Te. Ah me, my friends, protect me from the doom threatened by fate! Speed, some of you, to hasten Teucer's coming; let others go to the westward bays, and others to the eastward, and seek the man's ill-omened steps. I see now that I have been deceived by my lord, and cast out of the favour that once I found with him. Ah me, my child, what shall I do? We must not sit idle:—nay, I too will go as far as I have strength. Away—let us be quick—'tis no time to rest, if we would save a man who is in haste to die.

Ch. I am ready, and will show it in more than word; speed of act and foot shall go therewith.

*The scene changes to a lonely place on the sea-shore. Enter*Ajax.

Aj. The slayer stands so that he shall do his work most surely,—if leisure serves for so much thought,—the gift of Hector, that foeman-friend who was most hateful to my soul and to my sight; 'tis fixed in hostile soil, the land of Troy, with a new edge from the iron-biting whet; and I have planted it with heedful care, so that it should prove most kindly to me in a speedy death.

Thus on my part all is ready; and next be thou, O Zeus—as is meet—the first to aid me: 'tis no large boon that I will crave. Send, I pray thee, some messenger with the ill news to Teucer, that he may be the first to raise me where I have fallen on this reeking sword, lest I be first espied by some enemy, and cast forth a prey to dogs and birds. For thus much, O Zeus, I entreat thee; and I call also on Hermes, guide to the nether world, that he lay me softly asleep, without a struggle, at one quick bound, when I have driven this sword into my side.

And I call for help to the maidens who live for ever, and ever look on all the woes of men, the dread, far-striding Furies; let them mark how my miserable life is blasted by the Atreidae. And may they overtake those evil men with doom most evil and with utter blight [even as they behold me fall self-slain, so, slain by kinsfolk, may those men perish at the hand of their bestloved offspring]. Come, ye swift and vengeful Furies, glut your wrath on all the host, and spare not!

And thou whose chariot-wheels climb the heights of heaven, thou Sun-god, when thou lookest on the land of my sires, draw in thy rein o'erspread with gold, and tell my disasters and my death to mine aged father and to the hapless woman who reared me. Poor mother! I think, when she hears those tidings, her loud wail will ring through all the city. But it avails not to make idle moan: now for the deed, as quickly as I may.

O Death, Death, come now and look upon me! Nay, to thee will I speak in that other world also, when I am with thee. But thee, thou present beam of the bright day, and the Sun in his chariot, I accost for the last, last time,—as never more hereafter. O sunlight! O sacred soil of mine own Salamis, firm seat of my father's hearth! O famous Athens, and thy race kindred to mine! And ye, springs and rivers of this land—and ye plains of Troy, I greet you also—farewell, ye who have cherished my life! This is the last word that Ajax speaks to you: henceforth he will speak in Hades with the dead. [Ajax *falls upon his sword.*

The Chorus *re-enters, in two bands.*

First Semi-Chorus. Toil follows toil, and brings but toil! Where, where have my steps not been? And still no place is conscious of a secret that I share.—Hark—a sudden noise!

Second Semi-Chor. 'Tis we, the shipmates of your voyage.

Semi-Ch. 1. How goes it?

Semi-Ch. 2. All the westward side of the ships hath been paced.

Semi-Ch. 1. Well, hast thou found aught?

Semi-Ch. 2. Only much toil, and nothing more to see.

Semi-Ch. 1. And clearly the man hath not been seen either along the path that fronts the morning ray.

str. Ch. O for tidings from some toiling fisher, busy about his sleepless quest,— or from some nymph of the Olympian heights, or of the streams that flow toward Bosporus,—if anywhere such hath seen the man of fierce spirit roaming! 'Tis hard that I, the wanderer who have toiled so long, cannot come near him with prospered course, but fail to descry where the sick man is.

Te. Ah me, ah me!

Ch. Whose cry broke from the covert of the wood near us?

Te. Ah, miserable!

Ch. I see the spear-won bride, hapless Tecmessa: her soul is steeped in the anguish of that wail.

Te. I am lost, undone, left desolate, my friends!

Ch. What ails thee?

Te. Here lies our Ajax, newly slain,—a sword buried and sheathed in his corpse.

Ch. Alas for my hopes of return! Ah, prince, thou hast slain me, the comrade of thy voyage! Hapless man,—broken-hearted woman!

Te. Even thus is it with him: 'tis ours to wail.

Ch. By whose hand, then, can the wretched man have done the deed?

Te. By his own; 'tis well seen: this sword, which he planted in the ground, and on which he fell, convicts him.

Ch. Alas for my blind folly, all alone, then, thou hast fallen in blood, unwatched of friends! And I took no heed, so dull was I, so witless! Where, where lies Ajax, that wayward one, of ill-boding name?

Te. No eye shall look on him: nay, in this enfolding robe I will shroud him wholly; for no man who loved him could bear to see him, as up to nostril and forth from red gash he spirts the darkened blood from the self-dealt wound. Ah me, what shall I do? What friend shall lift thee in his arms? Where is Teucer? How timely would be his arrival, might he but come, to compose the corpse of this his brother! Ah, hapless Ajax, from what height fallen how low! How worthy, even in the sight of foes, to be mourned!

ant.Ch. Thou wast fated, hapless one, thou wast fated, then, with that unbending soul, at last to work out an evil doom of woes untold! Such was the omen of those complainings which by night and by day I heard thee utter in thy fierce mood, bitter against the Atreidae with a deadly passion. Aye, that time was a potent source of sorrows, when the golden arms were made the prize in a contest of prowess!

Te. Woe, woe is me!

Ch. The anguish pierces, I know, to thy true heart.

Te. Woe, woe is me!

Ch. I marvel not, lady, that thou shouldst wail, and wail again, who hast lately been bereft of one so loved.

Te. 'Tis for thee to conjecture of these things,—for me, to feel them but too sorely.

Ch. Yea, even so.

Te. Alas, my child, to what a yoke of bondage are we coming, seeing what task-masters are set over thee and me!

Ch. Oh, the two Atreidae would be ruthless—those deeds of theirs would be unspeakable, which thou namest in hinting at such a woe! But may the gods avert it!

Te. Never had these things stood thus, save by the will of the gods.

Ch. Yea, they have laid on us a burden too heavy to be borne.

Te. Yet such the woe that the daughter of Zeus, the dread goddess, engenders for Odysseus' sake.

Ch. Doubtless, the patient hero exults in his dark soul, and mocks with keen mockery at these sorrows born of frenzy. Alas! And with him, when they hear the tidings, laugh the royal brothers, the Atreidae.

Te. Then let them mock, and exult in this man's woes. Perchance, though they missed him not while he lived, they will bewail him dead, in the straits of warfare. Ill-judging men know not the good that was in their hands, till they have lost it. To my pain hath he died more than for their joy, and to his own content. All that he yearned to win hath he made his own,—the death for which he longed. Over this man, then, wherefore should they triumph? His death concerns the gods, not them—no, verily. Then let Odysseus revel in empty taunts. Ajax is for them no more: to me he hath left anguish and mourning—and is gone.

Teucer,*approaching.*

Woe, woe is me!

Ch. Hush—methinks I hear the voice of Teucer, raised in a strain that hath regard to this dire woe.

Enter Teucer.

Teu. Beloved Ajax, brother whose face was so dear to me—hast thou indeed fared as rumour holds?

Ch. He hath perished, Teucer: of that be sure.

Teu. Woe is me, then, for my heavy fate!

Ch. Know that thus it stands— Teu. Hapless, hapless that I am!

Ch. And thou hast cause to mourn. Teu. O fierce and sudden blow!

Ch. Thou sayest but too truly, Teucer. Teu. Ay me!—But tell me of yon man's child—where shall I find him in the land of Troy?

Ch. Alone, by the tent.

Teu. (*To* Tecmessa.) Then bring him hither with all speed, lest some foeman snatch him up, as a whelp from a lioness forlorn! Away—haste—bear help! 'Tis all men's wont to triumph o'er the dead, when they lie low. [*Exit* Tecmessa.

Ch. Yea, while he yet lived, Teucer, yon man charged thee to have care for the child, even as thou hast care indeed.

Teu. O sight most grievous to me of all that ever mine eyes have beheld! O bitter to my heart above all paths that I have trod, the path that now hath led me hither, when I learned thy fate, ah best-loved Ajax, as I was pursuing and tracking out thy footsteps! For a swift rumour about thee, as from some god, passed through the Greek host, telling that thou wast dead and gone. I heard it, ah me, while yet far off, and groaned low; but now the sight breaks my heart!

Come—lift the covering, and let me see the worst.

[*The corpse of* Ajax *is uncovered.*

O thou form dread to look on, wherein dwelt such cruel courage, what sorrows hast thou sown for me in thy death!

Whither can I betake me, to what people, after bringing thee no succour in thy troubles? Telamon, methinks, thy sire and mine, is like to greet me with sunny face and gracious mien, when I come without thee. Aye, surely—he who, even when good fortune befalls him, is not wont to smile more brightly than before.

What will such an one keep back? What taunt will he not utter against the bastard begotten from the warprize of his spear,—against him who betrayed thee, beloved Ajax, like a coward and a craven—or by guile, that, when thou wast dead, he might enjoy thy lordship and thy house? So will he speak,—a passionate man, peevish in old age, whose wrath makes strife even without a cause. And in the end I shall be thrust from the realm, and cast off,—branded by his taunts as no more a freeman but a slave.

Such is my prospect at home; while at Troy I have many foes, and few things to help me. All this have I reaped by thy death! Ah me, what shall I do? how draw thee, hapless one, from the cruel point of this gleaming sword, the slayer, it seems, to whom thou hast yielded up thy breath? Now seest thou how Hector, though dead, was to destroy thee at the last?

Consider, I pray you, the fortune of these two men. With the very girdle that had been given to him by Ajax, Hector was gripped to the chariot-rail, and mangled till he gave up the ghost. 'Twas from Hector that Ajax had this gift, and by this hath he perished in his deadly fall. Was it not the Fury who forged this blade, was not that

110

girdle wrought by Hades, grim artificer? I, at least, would deem that these things, and all things ever, are planned by gods for men; but if there be any in whose mind this wins no favour, let him hold to his own thoughts, as I hold to mine.

Ch. Speak not at length, but think how thou shalt lay the man in the tomb, and what thou wilt say anon: for I see a foe, and perchance he will come with mocking of our sorrows, as evil-doers use.

Teu. And what man of the host dost thou behold?

Ch. Menelaüs, for whom we made this voyage.

Teu. I see him; he is not hard to know, when near.

*Enter*Menelaus.

Me. Sirrah, I tell thee to bear no hand in raising yon corpse, but to leave it where it lies.

Teu. Wherefore hast thou spent thy breath in such proud words?

Me. 'Tis my pleasure, and his who rules the host.

Teu. And might we hear what reason thou pretendest?

Me. This—that, when we had hoped we were bringing him from home to be an ally and a friend for the Greeks, we found him, on trial, a worse than Phrygian foe; who plotted death for all the host, and sallied by night against us, to slay with the spear; and, if some god had not quenched this attempt, ours would have been the lot which he hath found, to lie slain by an ignoble doom, while he would have been living. But now a god hath turned his outrage aside, to fall on sheep and cattle.

Wherefore there is no man so powerful that he shall entomb the corpse of Ajax; no, he shall be cast forth somewhere on the yellow sand, and become food for the birds by the sea. Then raise no storm of angry threats. If we were not able to control him while he lived, at least we shall rule him in death, whether thou wilt or not, and control him with our hands; since, while he lived, there never was a time when he would hearken to my words.

Yet 'tis the sign of an unworthy nature when a subject deigns not to obey those who are set over him. Never can the laws have prosperous course in a city where dread hath no place; nor can a camp be ruled discreetly any more, if it lack the guarding force of fear and reverence. Nay, though a man's frame have waxed mighty, he should look to fall, perchance, by a light blow. Whoso hath fear, and shame therewith, be sure that he is safe; but where there is licence to insult and act at will, doubt not that such a State, though favouring gales have sped her, some day, at last, sinks into the depths.

No, let me see fear, too, where fear is meet, established; let us not dream that we can do after our desires, without paying the price in our pains. These things come by turns. This man was once hot and insolent; now 'tis my hour to be haughty. And I warn thee not to bury him, lest through that deed thou thyself shouldst come to need a grave.

Ch. Menelaüs, after laying down wise precepts, do not thyself be guilty of outrage on the dead.

Teu. Never, friends, shall I wonder more if a lowborn man offends after his kind, when they who are accounted of noble blood allow such scandalous words to pass their lips.

Come, tell me from the first once more—Sayest thou that *thou* broughtest the man hither to the Greeks, as an ally found by *thee*? Sailed he not forth of his own act,—as his own master? What claim hast thou to be his chief? On what ground hast thou a right to kingship of the lieges whom he brought from home? As Sparta's king thou camest, not as master over us. Nowhere was it laid down among thy lawful powers that thou shouldst dictate to him, any more than he to thee. Under the command of others didst thou sail hither, not as chief of all, so that thou shouldst ever be captain over Ajax.

No, lord it over them whose lord thou art,—lash *them* with thy proud words: but this man will I lay duly in the grave, though thou forbid it,—aye, or thy brotherchief,—nor shall I tremble at thy word. 'Twas not for thy wife's sake that Ajax came unto the war, like yon toil-worn drudges,—no, but for the oath's sake that bound him,—no whit for thine; he was not wont to reck of nobodies. So, when thou comest again, bring more heralds, and the Captain of the host; at *thy* noise I would not turn my head, while thou art the man that thou art now.

Ch. Such speech again, in the midst of ills, I love not; for harsh words, how just soever, sting.

Me. The bowman, methinks, hath no little pride.

Teu. Even so; 'tis no sordid craft that I profess.

Me. How thou wouldst boast, wert thou given a shield!

Teu. Without a shield, I were a match for thee full-armed.

Me. How dreadful the courage that inspires thy tongue!

Teu. When right is with him, a man's spirit may be high.

Me. Is it right that this my murderer should have honour?

Teu. Murderer? A marvel truly, if, though slain, thou livest.

Me. A god rescued me: in yon man's purpose, I am dead.

Teu. The gods have saved thee: then dishonour not the gods.

Me. What, would *I* disparage the laws of Heaven?

Teu. If thou art here to forbid the burying of the dead.

Me. Yea, of my country's foes: for it is not meet.

Teu. Did Ajax e'er confront thee as public foe?

Me. There was hate betwixt us; thou, too, knewest this.

Teu. Yea, 'twas found that thou hadst suborned votes, to rob him.

Me. At the hands of the judges, not at mine, he had that fall.

Teu. Thou couldst put a fair face on many a furtive villainy.

Me. That saying tends to pain—I know, for whom.

Teu. Not greater pain, methinks, than we shall inflict.

Me. Hear my last word—that man must not be buried.

Teu. And hear my answer—he shall be buried forthwith.

Me. Once did I see a man bold of tongue, who had urged sailors to a voyage in time of storm, in whom thou wouldst have found no voice when the stress of the tempest was upon him, but, hidden beneath his cloak, he would suffer the crew to trample on him at will. And so with thee and thy fierce speech—perchance a great tempest, though its breath come from a little cloud, shall quench thy blustering.

Teu. Yea, and I have seen a man full of folly, who triumphed in his neighbour's woes; and it came to pass that a man like unto me, and of like mood, beheld him, and spake such words as these: 'Man, do not evil to the dead; for, if thou dost, be sure that thou wilt come to harm.' So warned he the misguided one before him; and know that I see that man, and methinks he is none else but thou: have I spoken in riddles?

Me. I will go:—it were a disgrace to have it known that I was chiding when I have the power to compel.

Teu. Begone then! For me 'tis the worse disgrace that I should listen to a fool's idle prate.

[*Exit*Menelaus.

Ch. A dread strife will be brought to the trial. But thou, Teucer, with what speed thou mayest, haste to seek a hollow grave for yon man, where he shall rest in his dark, dank tomb, that men shall ever hold in fame.

*Enter*Tecmessa*and* Child.

Teu. Lo, just in time our lord's child and his wife draw nigh, to tend the burial of the hapless corpse.

My child, come hither: take thy place near him, and lay thy hand, as a suppliant, upon thy sire. And kneel as one who implores help, with locks of hair in thy hand,—mine, hers, and thirdly thine,—the suppliant's store. But if any man of the host should tear thee by violence from this dead, then, for evil doom on evil deed, may he perish out of the land and find no grave, and with him be his race cut off, root and branch, even as I sever this lock. Take it, boy, and keep; and let no one move thee, but kneel there, and cling unto the dead.

And ye, be not as women at his side, but bear you like men for his defence, till I return, when I have prepared a grave for this man, though all the world forbid.

[*Exit*Teucer.

str. 1.Ch. When, ah when, will the number of the restless years be full, at what term will they cease, that bring on me the unending woe of a warrior's toils throughout the wide land of Troy, for the sorrow and the shame of Greece?

ant. 1.Would that the man had passed into the depths of the sky, or to all-receiving Hades, who taught Greeks how to league themselves for war in hateful arms! Ah, those toils of his, from which so many toils have sprung! Yea, he it was who wrought the ruin of men.

str. 2.No delight of garlands or bounteous wine-cups did that man give me for my portion, no sweet music of flutes, the wretch, or soothing rest in the night; and from love, alas, from love he hath divorced my days.

And here I have my couch, uncared for, while heavy dews ever wet my hair, lest I should forget that I am in the cheerless land of Troy.

ant. 2.Erewhile, bold Ajax was alway my defence against nightly terror and the darts of the foe; but now he hath become the sacrifice of a malignant fate. What joy, then, what joy shall crown me more?

O to be wafted where the wooded sea-cape stands upon the laving sea, O to pass beneath Sunium's level summit, that so we might greet sacred Athens!

*Enter*Teucer,*followed by*Agamemnon.

Teu. Lo, I am come in haste, for I saw the Captain of the host, Agamemnon, moving hither apace; and I wot he will not bridle perverse lips.

Agamemnon. So 'tis thou, they tell me, who hast dared to open thy mouth with such blustering against us—and hast yet to smart for it? Yea, I mean thee,—thee, the captive woman's son. Belike, hadst thou been bred of well-born mother, lofty had been thy vaunt and proud thy strut, when, nought as thou art, thou hast stood up for him who is as nought, and hast vowed that we came out with no title on sea or land to rule the Greeks or thee; no, as chief in his own right, thou sayest, sailed Ajax forth.

Are not these presumptuous taunts for us to hear from slaves? What was the man whom thou vauntest with such loud arrogance? Whither went he, or where stood he, where I was not? Have the Greeks, then, no other men but him? Methinks we shall rue that day when we called the Greeks to contest the arms of Achilles, if, whatever the issue, we are to be denounced as false by Teucer, and if ye never will consent, though defeated, to accept that doom for which most judges gave their voice, but must ever assail us somewhere with revilings, or stab us in the dark,—ye, the losers in the race.

Now, where such ways prevail, no law could ever be firmly stablished, if we are to thrust the rightful winners aside, and bring the rearmost to the front. Nay, this must be checked. 'Tis not the burly, broad-shouldered men that are surest at need; no, 'tis the wise who prevail in every field. A large-ribbed ox is yet kept straight on the road by a small whip. And this remedy, methinks, will visit thee ere long, if thou fail to gain some measure of wisdom; thou who, when the man lives no more, but is now a shade, art so boldly insolent, and givest such licence to thy tongue. Sober thyself, I say;—recall thy birth;—bring hither some one else,—a freeborn man,—who shall plead thy cause for thee before us. When thou speakest, I can take the sense no more; I understand not thy barbarian speech.

Ch. Would that ye both could learn the wisdom of a temperate mind! No better counsel could I give you twain.

Teu. Ah, gratitude to the dead—in what quick sort it falls away from men and is found a traitor, if this man hath no longer the slightest tribute of remembrance for thee, Ajax,—he for whom thou didst toil so often, putting thine own life to the peril of the spear! No—'tis all forgotten,—all flung aside!

Man who but now hast spoken many words and vain, hast thou no more memory of the time when ye were shut within your lines,—when ye were as lost in the turning back of your battle,—and he came alone and saved you,—when the flames were already wrapping the decks at your ships' stern, and Hector was bounding high over the trench towards the vessels? Who averted that? Were these deeds not his, who, thou sayest, nowhere set foot where thou wast not?

Would ye allow that he did his duty there? Or when, another time, all alone, he confronted Hector in single fight,—not at any man's bidding, but by right of ballot, for the lot which he cast in was not one to skulk behind, no lump of moist earth, but such as would be the first to leap lightly from the crested helm! His were these deeds, and at his side was I,—the slave, the son of the barbarian mother.

Wretch, how canst thou be so blind as to rail thus? Knowst thou not that thy sire's sire was Pelops of old,—a barbarian, a Phrygian? That Atreus, who begat thee, set before his brother a most impious feast,—the flesh of that brother's children? And thou thyself wert born of a Cretan mother, with whom her sire found a paramour, and doomed her to be food for the dumb fishes? Being such, makest thou his origin a reproach to such as I am? The father from whom I sprang is Telamon, who, as prize for valour peerless in the host, won my mother for his bride, by birth a princess, daughter of Laomedon; and as the flower of the spoil was she given to Telamon by Alcmena's son.

Thus nobly born from two noble parents, could I disgrace my kinsman, whom, now that such sore ills have laid him low, thou wouldst thrust forth without burial,—yea, and art not ashamed to say it? Now be thou sure of this,—wheresoever ye cast this man, with him ye will cast forth our three corpses also. It beseems me to die in his cause, before all men's eyes, rather than for thy wife,—or thy brother's, should I say? Be prudent, therefore, not for my sake, but for thine own also; for, if thou harm me, thou wilt wish anon that thou hadst been a very coward, ere thy rashness had been wreaked on me.

Enter Odysseus.

Ch. King Odysseus, know that thou hast come in season, if thou art here, not to embroil, but to mediate.

Od. What ails you, friends? Far off I heard loud speech of the Atreidae over this brave man's corpse.

Ag. Nay, King Odysseus, have we not been hearing but now most shameful taunts from yonder man?

Od. How was that? I can pardon a man who is reviled if he engage in wordy war.

Ag. I *had* reviled him; for his deeds toward me were vile.

Od. And what did he unto thee, that thou hast a wrong?

Ag. He says that he will not leave yon corpse ungraced by sepulture, but will bury it in my despite.

Od. Now may a friend speak out the truth, and still, as ever, ply his oar in time with thine?

Ag. Speak: else were I less than sane; for I count thee my greatest friend of all the Greeks.

Od. Listen, then. For the love of the gods, take not the heart to cast forth this man unburied so ruthlessly; and in no wise let violence prevail with thee to hate so utterly that thou shouldest trample justice under foot.

To me also this man was once the worst foe in the army,—from the day that I became master of the arms of Achilles; yet, for all that he was such toward me, never would I requite him with indignity, or refuse to avow that, in all our Greek host which came to Troy, I have seen none who was his peer, save Achilles. It were not just, then, that he should suffer dishonour at thy hand; 'tis not he, 'tis the law of Heaven that thou wouldst hurt. When a brave man is dead, 'tis not right to do him scathe—no, not even if thou hate him.

Ag. *Thou*, Odysseus, thus his champion against me?

Od. I am; yet hated him, when I could honourably hate.

Ag. And shouldst thou not also set thy heel on him in death?

Od. Delight not, son of Atreus, in gains which sully honour.

Ag. 'Tis not easy for a king to observe piety.

Od. But he can show respect to his friends, when they counsel well.

Ag. A loyal man should hearken to the rulers.

Od. Enough:—the victory is thine, when thou yieldest to thy friends.

Ag. Remember to what a man thou showest the grace.

Od. Yon man was erst my foe, yet noble.

Ag. What canst thou mean? Such reverence for a dead foe?

Od. His worth weighs with me far more than his enmity.

Ag. Nay, such as thou are the unstable among men.

Od. Full many are friends at one time, and foes anon.

Ag. Dost thou approve, then, of our making such friends?

Od. 'Tis not my wont to approve a stubborn soul.

Ag. Thou wilt make us appear cowards this day.

Od. Not so, but just men in the sight of all the Greeks.

Ag. So thou wouldst have me allow the burying of the dead?

Od. Yea: for I too shall come to that need.

Ag. Truly in all things alike each man works for himself!

Od. And for whom should I work rather than for myself?

Ag. It must be called thy doing, then, not mine.

Od. Call it whose thou wilt, in any case thou wilt be kind.

Ag. Nay, be well assured that I would grant *thee* a larger boon than this; yon man, however, as on earth, so in the shades, shall have my hatred. But thou canst do what thou wilt. [*Exit* Agamemnon.

Ch. Whoso saith, Odysseus, that thou hast not inborn wisdom, being such as thou art, that man is foolish.

Od. Yea, and I tell Teucer now that henceforth I am ready to be his friend—as staunch as I was once a foe. And I would join in the burying of your dead, and partake your cares, and omit no service which mortals should render to the noblest among men.

Teu. Noble Odysseus, I have only praise to give thee for thy words; and greatly hast thou belied my fears. Thou wast his deadliest foe of all the Greeks, yet thou alone hast stood by him with active aid; thou hast found no heart, in this presence, to heap the insults of the living on the dead,—like yon crazed chief that came, he and his brother, and would have cast forth the outraged corpse without burial. Therefore may the Father supreme in the heaven above us, and the remembering Fury, and Justice that brings the end, destroy those evil men with evil doom, even as they sought to cast forth this man with unmerited despite.

But, son of aged Laertes, I scruple to admit thy helping hand in these funeral rites, lest so I do displeasure to the dead; in all else be thou indeed our fellow-worker; and if thou wouldst bring any man of the host, we shall make thee welcome. For the rest, I will make all things ready; and know that to us thou hast been a generous friend.

Od. It was my wish; but if it is not pleasing to thee that I should assist here, I accept thy decision, and depart. [*Exit* Odysseus.

Teu. Enough: already the delay hath been long drawn out. Come, haste some of you to dig the hollow grave,—place, some, the high-set caldron girt with fire, in readiness for holy ablution; and let another band bring the body-armour from the tent.

And thou, too, child, with such strength as thou hast, lay a loving hand upon thy sire, and help me to uplift this prostrate form; for still the warm channels are spouting upward their dark tide.

Come, each one here who owns the name of friend,—haste, away, in service to this man of perfect prowess; and never yet was service rendered to a nobler among men.

Ch. Many things shall mortals learn by seeing; but, before he sees, no man may read the future, or his fate.

ELECTRA

PERSONS OF THE DRAMA.

Orestes,*son of Agamemnon and Clytaemnestra.*
Electra,} *sisters of Orestes.*
Chrysothemis,
An Old Man,*formerly the*Paedagogus*or Attendant of Orestes.*
Clytaemnestra.
Aegisthus.
Chorus of Women of Mycenae.

MUTE PERSONS.

Pylades,*son of Strophius king of Crisa, the friend of Orestes.*—A handmaid of Clytaemnestra (v. 634).—Two attendants of Orestes (v. 1123).

Scene: At Mycenae, before the Palace of the Pelopidae.

Agamemnon, on his return from Troy, was murdered in the palace at Mycenae by his wife Clytaemnestra and her paramour Aegisthus. Orestes, the victim's son and heir, then a child, was saved by his sister Electra. She gave him to a faithful retainer, who carried him to Phocis. There he grew up in the house of Strophius, King of Crisa near Delphi, the father of his friend Pylades.

Many years have passed since then. Electra has perforce continued to live under the same roof with the murderers. While her sisters, Chrysothemis and Iphianassa, have been taught by prudence to hide their feelings, she has made no concealment of her loyalty to her father's memory, or of her inconsolable grief. Every kind of hardship and of insult is her portion at the hands of her mother and the dastardly Aegisthus; no slave could fare worse than she does in the house that was her father's. Clytaemnestra's hatred has been embittered, from time to time, by some false rumour as to the return of Orestes,—the one terror that still haunts the guilty pair. Meanwhile Electra herself, worn out with misery and with waiting, has begun to falter in the one hope which has hitherto borne her up,—that the brother from whom she parted so long ago would be sent back by the gods as an avenger.

It is morning, the new-risen sun is bright and the birds are singing, as the old man, accompanied by two youths, arrives on the high ground in front of the palace at Mycenae.

PAEDAGOGUS.

Son of him who led our hosts at Troy of old, son of Agamemnon!—now thou mayest behold with thine eyes all that thy soul hath desired so long. There is the ancient Argos of thy yearning,—that hallowed scene whence the gad-fly drove the daughter of Inachus; and there, Orestes, is the Lycean Agora, named from the wolf-slaying god; there, on the left, Hera's famous temple; and in this place to which we have come, deem that thou seest Mycenae rich in gold, with the house of the Pelopidae there, so often stained with bloodshed;10 whence I carried thee of yore, from the slaying of thy father, as thy kinswoman, thy sister, charged me; and saved thee, and reared thee up to manhood, to be the avenger of thy murdered sire.

Now, therefore, Orestes, and thou, best of friends, Pylades, our plans must be laid quickly; for lo, already the sun's bright ray is waking the songs of the birds into clearness, and the dark night of stars is spent. Before, then, anyone comes forth from the house, take counsel;20 seeing that the time allows not of delay, but is full ripe for deeds.

ORESTES.

True friend and follower, how well dost thou prove thy loyalty to our house! As a steed of generous race, though old, loses not courage in danger, but pricks his ear, even so thou urgest us forward, and art foremost in our support. I will tell thee, then, what I have determined;30 listen closely to my words, and correct me, if I miss the mark in aught.

When I went to the Pythian oracle, to learn how I might avenge my father on his murderers, Phoebus gave me the response which thou art now to hear:—that alone, and by stealth, without aid of arms or numbers, I should snatch the righteous vengeance of my hand. Since, then, the god spake to us on this wise, thou must go into yonder house, when opportunity gives thee40 entrance, and learn all that is passing there, so that thou mayest report to us from sure knowledge. Thine age, and the lapse of time, will prevent them from recognising thee; they will never suspect who thou art, with that silvered hair. Let thy tale be that thou art a Phocian stranger, sent by Phanoteus; for he is the greatest of their allies. Tell them, and confirm it with thine oath, that Orestes hath perished by a fatal chance,—hurled, at the Pythian games, from his rapid chariot;50 be that the substance of thy story.

We, meanwhile, will first crown my father's tomb, as the god enjoined, with drink-offerings and the luxuriant tribute of severed hair; then come back, bearing in our hands an urn of shapely bronze,—now hidden in the brushwood, as I think thou knowest,—so to gladden them with the false tidings that this my body is no more, but has been consumed with fire and turned to ashes. Why should the omen trouble me, when by a feigned death I find life indeed, and win renown? I60 trow, no word is ill-omened, if fraught with gain. Often ere now have I seen wise men die in vain report; then, when they return home, they are held in more abiding honour: as I trust that from this rumour I also shall emerge in radiant life, and yet shine like a star upon my foes.

O my fatherland, and ye gods of the land, receive me with good fortune in this journey,—and ye also, halls of my fathers, for I come with a divine mandate to cleanse70 you righteously; send me not dishonoured from the land, but grant that I may rule over my possessions, and restore my house!

Enough;—be it now thy care, old man, to go and heed thy task; and we twain will go forth; for so occasion bids, chief ruler of every enterprise for men.

Electra (*within*).

Ah me, ah me!

Pae. Hark, my son,—from the doors, methought, came the sound of some handmaid moaning within.

Or. Can it be the hapless Electra? Shall we stay80 here, and listen to her laments?

Pae. No, no: before all else, let us seek to obey the command of Loxias, and thence make a fair beginning, by pouring libations to thy sire; that brings victory within our grasp, and gives us the mastery in all that we do.

[*Exeunt*Paedagogus (*on the spectator's left*), Orestes and Pylades (*on the right*).—
*Enter*Electra,*from the house.*

*syst.*El. O thou pure sunlight, and thou air, earth's canopy, how often have ye heard the strains of my90 lament, the wild blows dealt against this bleeding breast, when dark night fails! And my wretched couch in yonder house of woe knows well, ere now, how I keep the watches of the night,—how often I bewail my hapless sire; to whom deadly Ares gave not of his gifts in a strange land, but my mother, and her mate Aegisthus, cleft his head with murderous axe, as woodmen fell an oak. And for this no plaint bursts from any lip save mine, when thou, my father, hath died a death so cruel and so piteous!

*antisyst.*But never will I cease from dirge and sore lament, while I look on the trembling rays of the bright stars, or on this light of day; but like the nightingale, slayer of her offspring, I will wail without ceasing, and cry aloud to all, here, at the doors of my father.

O home of Hades and Persephone! O Hermes of the shades! O potent Curse, and ye, dread daughters of the gods, Erinyes,—ye who behold when a life is reft by violence, when a bed is dishonoured by stealth,—come, help me, avenge the murder of my sire,—and send to me my brother; for I have no more the strength to bear up alone against the load of grief that weighs me down.

CHORUS.

str. 1.Ah, Electra, child of a wretched mother, why art thou ever pining thus in ceaseless lament for Agamemnon, who long ago was wickedly ensnared by thy false mother's wiles, and betrayed to death by a dastardly hand? Perish the author of that deed, if I may utter such a prayer!

El. Ah, noble-hearted maidens, ye have come to soothe my woes. I know and feel it, it escapes me not; but I cannot leave this task undone, or cease from mourning for my hapless sire. Ah, friends whose love responds to mine in every mood, leave me to rave thus,—oh leave me, I entreat you!

ant. 1.Ch. But never by laments or prayers shalt thou recall thy sire from that lake of Hades to which all must pass. Nay, thine is a fatal course of grief, passing ever from due bounds into a cureless sorrow; wherein there is no deliverance from evils. Say, wherefore art thou enamoured of misery?

El. Foolish is the child who forgets a parent's piteous death. No, dearer to my soul is the mourner that laments for Itys, Itys, evermore, that bird distraught with grief, the messenger of Zeus. Ah, queen of sorrow, Niobe, thee I deem divine,— thee, who evermore weepest in thy rocky tomb!

str. 2.Ch. Not to thee alone of mortals, my daughter, hath come any sorrow which thou bearest less calmly than those within, thy kinswomen and sisters, Chrysothemis and Iphianassa, who still live,—as he, too, lives, sorrowing in a secluded youth, yet happy in that this famous realm of Mycenae shall one day welcome him to his heritage, when the kindly guidance of Zeus shall have brought him to this land,— Orestes.

El. Yes, I wait for him with unwearied longing, as I move on my sad path from day to day, unwed and childless, bathed in tears, bearing that endless doom of woe; but he forgets all that he has suffered and heard. What message comes to me, that is not belied? He is ever yearning to be with us, but, though he yearns, he never resolves.

ant. 2.Ch. Courage, my daughter, courage; great still in heaven is Zeus, who sees and governs all: leave thy bitter quarrel to him; forget not thy foes, but refrain from excess of wrath against them; for Time is a god who makes rough ways smooth. Not heedless is the son of Agamemnon, who dwells by Crisa's pastoral shore; not heedless is the god who reigns by Acheron.

El. Nay, the best part of life hath passed away from me in hopelessness, and I have no strength left; I, who am pining away without children,—whom no loving champion shields,—but, like some despised alien, I serve in the halls of my father, clad in this mean garb, and standing at a meagre board.

str. 3.Ch. Piteous was the voice heard at his return, and piteous, as thy sire lay on the festal couch, when the straight, swift blow was dealt him with the blade of bronze. Guile was the plotter, Lust the slayer, dread parents of a dreadful shape; whether it was mortal that wrought therein, or god.

El. O that bitter day, bitter beyond all that have come to me; O that night, O the horrors of that unutterable feast, the ruthless death-strokes that my father saw from the hands of twain, who took my life captive by treachery, who doomed me to woe! May the great god of Olympus give them sufferings in requital, and never may their splendour bring them joy, who have done such deeds!

ant. 3.Ch. Be advised to say no more; canst thou not see what conduct it is which already plunges thee so cruelly in self-made miseries? Thou hast greatly aggravated thy troubles, ever breeding wars with thy sullen soul; but such strife should not be pushed to a conflict with the strong.

El. I have been forced to it,—forced by dread causes; I know my own passion, it escapes me not; but, seeing that the causes are so dire, I will never curb these frenzied plaints, while life is in me. Who indeed, ye kindly sisterhood, who that thinks aright, would deem that any word of solace could avail me? Forbear, forbear, my comforters! Such ills must be numbered with those which have no cure; I can never know a respite from my sorrows, or a limit to this wailing.

*ep.*Ch. At least it is in love, like a true-hearted mother, that I dissuade thee from adding misery to miseries.

El. But what measure is there in my wretchedness? Say, how can it be right to neglect the dead? Was that impiety ever born in mortal? Never may I have praise of such; never, when my lot is cast in pleasant places, may I cling to selfish ease, or dishonour my sire by restraining the wings of shrill lamentation!

For if the hapless dead is to lie in dust and nothingness, while the slayers pay not with blood for blood, all regard for man, all fear of heaven, will vanish from the earth.

Ch. I came, my child, in zeal for thy welfare no less than for mine own; but if I speak not well, then be it as thou wilt; for we will follow thee.

El. I am ashamed, my friends, if ye deem me too impatient for my oft complaining; but, since a hard constraint forces me to this, bear with me. How indeed could any woman of noble nature refrain, who saw the calamities of a father's house, as I see them by day and night continually, not fading, but in the summer of their strength? I, who, first, from the mother that bore me have found bitter enmity; next, in mine own home I dwell with my father's murderers; they rule over me, and with them it rests to give or to withhold what I need.

And then think what manner of days I pass, when I see Aegisthus sitting on my father's throne, wearing the robes which he wore, and pouring libations at the hearth where he slew my sire; and when I see the outrage that crowns all, the murderer in our father's bed at our wretched mother's side, if mother she should be called, who is his wife; but so hardened is she that she lives with that accursed one, fearing no Erinys; nay, as if exulting in her deeds, having found the day on which she treacherously slew my father of old, she keeps it with dance and song, and month by month sacrifices sheep to the gods who have wrought her deliverance.

But I, hapless one, beholding it, weep and pine in the house, and bewail the unholy feast named after my sire,—weep to myself alone; since I may not even indulge my grief to the full measure of my yearning. For this woman, in professions so noble, loudly upbraids me with such taunts as these: 'Impious and hateful girl, hast thou alone lost a father, and is there no other mourner in the world? An evil doom be thine, and may the gods infernal give thee no riddance from thy present laments.'

Thus she insults; save when any one brings her word that Orestes is coming: then, infuriated, she comes up to me, and cries;—'Hast not *thou* brought this upon me? Is not this deed thine, who didst steal Orestes from my hands, and privily convey him forth? Yet be sure that thou shalt have thy due reward.' So she shrieks; and, aiding her, the renowned spouse at her side is vehement in the same strain,—that abject dastard, that utter pest, who fights his battles with the help of women. But I, looking ever for Orestes to come and end these woes, languish in my misery. Always intending to strike a blow, he has worn out every hope that I could conceive. In such a case, then, friends, there is no room for moderation or for reverence; in sooth, the stress of ills leaves no choice but to follow evil ways.

Ch. Say, is Aegisthus near while thou speakest thus, or absent from home?

El. Absent, certainly; do not think that I should have come to the doors, if he had been near; but just now he is a-field.

Ch. Might I converse with thee more freely, if this is so?

El. He is not here, so put thy question; what wouldst thou?

Ch. I ask thee, then, what sayest thou of thy brother? Will he come soon, or is he delaying? I fain would know.

El. He promises to come; but he never fulfils the promise.

Ch. Yea, a man will pause on the verge of a great work.

El. And yet I saved *him* without pausing.

Ch. Courage; he is too noble to fail his friends.

El. I believe it; or I should not have lived so long.

Ch. Say no more now; for I see thy sister coming from the house, Chrysothemis, daughter of the same sire and mother, with sepulchral gifts in her hands, such as are given to those in the world below.

*Enter*Chrysothemis.

Chr. Why, sister, hast thou come forth once more to declaim thus at the public doors? Why wilt thou not learn with any lapse of time to desist from vain indulgence of idle wrath? Yet this I know,—that I myself am grieved at our plight; indeed, could I find the strength, I would show what love I bear them. But now, in these troubled waters, 'tis best, methinks, to shorten sail; I care not to seem active, without the power to hurt. And would that thine own conduct were the same! Nevertheless, right is on the side of thy choice, not of that which I advise; but if I am to live in freedom, our rulers must be obeyed in all things.

El. Strange indeed, that thou, the daughter of such a sire as thine, shouldst forget him, and think only of thy mother! All thy admonitions to me have been taught by her; no word is thine own. Then take thy choice,—to be imprudent; or prudent, but forgetful of thy friends: thou, who hast just said that, couldst thou find the strength, thou wouldst show thy hatred of them; yet, when I am doing my utmost to avenge my sire, thou givest no aid, but seekest to turn thy sister from her deed.

Does not this crown our miseries with cowardice? For tell me,—or let me tell thee,—what I should gain by ceasing from these laments? Do I not live?—miserably, I know, yet well enough for me. And I vex *them,* thus rendering honour to the dead, if pleasure can be felt in that world. But thou, who tellest me of thy hatred, hatest in word alone, while in deeds thou art with the slayers of thy sire. I, then, would never yield to them, though I were promised the gifts which now make thee proud; thine be the richly-spread table and the life of luxury. For me, be it food enough that I do not wound mine own conscience; I covet not such privilege as thine,—nor wouldst thou, wert thou wise. But now, when thou mightest be called daughter of the noblest father among men, be called the child of thy mother; so shall thy baseness be most widely seen, in betrayal of thy dead sire and of thy kindred.

Ch. No angry word, I entreat! For both of you there is good in what is urged,— if thou, Electra, wouldst learn to profit by her counsel, and she, again, by thine.

Chr. For my part, friends, I am not wholly unused to her discourse; nor should I have touched upon this theme, had I not heard that she was threatened with a dread doom, which shall restrain her from her long-drawn laments.

El. Come, declare it then, this terror! If thou canst tell me of aught worse than my present lot, I will resist no more.

Chr. Indeed, I will tell thee all that I know. They purpose, if thou wilt not cease from these laments, to send thee where thou shalt never look upon the sunlight, but pass thy days in a dungeon beyond the borders of this land, there to chant thy dreary strain. Bethink thee, then, and do not blame me hereafter, when the blow hath fallen; now is the time to be wise.

El. Have they indeed resolved to treat me thus?

Chr. Assuredly, whenever Aegisthus comes home.

El. If that be all, then may he arrive with speed!

Chr. Misguided one! what dire prayer is this?

El. That he may come, if he hath any such intent.

Chr. That thou mayst suffer—what? Where are thy wits?

El. That I may fly as far as may be from you all.

Chr. But hast thou no care for thy present life?

El. Aye, my life is marvellously fair.

Chr. It might be, couldst thou only learn prudence.

El. Do not teach me to betray my friends.

Chr. I do not,—but to bend before the strong.

El. Thine be such flattery: those are not my ways.

Chr. 'Tis well, however, not to fall by folly.

El. I will fall, if need be, in the cause of my sire.

Chr. But our father, I know, pardons me for this.

El. It is for cowards to find peace in such maxims.

Chr. So thou wilt not hearken, and take my counsel?

El. No, verily; long may be it before I am so foolish.

Chr. Then I will go forth upon mine errand.

El. And whither goest thou? To whom bearest thou these offerings?

Chr. Our mother sends me with funeral libations for our sire.

El. How sayest thou? For her deadliest foe?

Chr. Slain by her own hand—so thou wouldest say.

El. What friend hath persuaded her? Whose wish was this?

Chr. The cause, I think, was some dread vision of the night.

El. Gods of our house! be ye with me—now at last!

Chr. Dost thou find any encouragement in this terror?

El. If thou wouldst tell me the vision, then I could answer.

Chr. Nay, I can tell but little of the story.

El. Tell what thou canst; a little word hath often marred, or made, men's fortunes.

Chr. 'Tis said that she beheld our sire, restored to the sunlight, at her side once more; then he took the sceptre,—once his own, but now borne by Aegisthus,—and planted it at the hearth; and thence a fruitful bough sprang upward, wherewith the whole land of Mycenae was overshadowed. Such was the tale that I heard told by one who was present when she declared her dream to the Sun-god. More than this I know not,—save that she sent me by reason of that fear.—So by the gods of our house I beseech thee, hearken to me, and be not ruined by folly! For if thou repel me now, thou wilt come back to seek me in thy trouble.

El. Nay, dear sister, let none of these things in thy hands touch the tomb; for neither custom nor piety allows thee to dedicate gifts or bring libations to our sire from a hateful wife. No—to the winds with them! or bury them deep in the earth, where none of them shall ever come near his place of rest; but, when she dies, let her find these treasures laid up for her below.

And were she not the most hardened of all women, she would never have sought to pour these offerings of enmity on the grave of him whom she slew. Think now if it is likely that the dead in the tomb should take these honours kindly at her hand, who ruthlessly slew him, like a foeman, and mangled him, and, for ablution, wiped off the blood-stains on his head? Canst thou believe that these things which thou bringest will absolve her of the murder?

It is not possible. No, cast these things aside; give him rather a lock cut from thine own tresses, and on my part, hapless that I am,—scant gifts these, but my best,—this hair, not glossy with unguents, and this girdle, decked with no rich ornament. Then fall down and pray that he himself may come in kindness from the world below, to aid us against our foes; and that the young Orestes may live to set his foot upon his foes in victorious might, that henceforth we may crown our father's tomb with wealthier hands than those which grace it now.

I think, indeed, I think that he also had some part in sending her these appalling dreams; still, sister, do this service, to help thyself, and me, and him, that most beloved of all men, who rests in the realm of Hades, thy sire and mine.

123

Ch. The maiden counsels piously; and thou, friend, wilt do her bidding, if thou art wise.

Chr. I will. When a duty is clear, reason forbids that two voices should contend, and claims the hastening of the deed. Only, when I attempt this task, aid me with your silence, I entreat you, my friends; for, should my mother hear of it, methinks I shall yet have cause to rue my venture.

*str.*Ch. If I am not an erring seer and one who fails in wisdom, Justice, that hath sent the presage, will come, triumphant in her righteous strength,—will come ere long, my child, to avenge. There is courage in my heart, through those new tidings of the dream that breathes comfort. Not forgetful is thy sire, the lord of Hellas; not forgetful is the two-edged axe of bronze that struck the blow of old, and slew him with foul cruelty.

*ant.*The Erinys of untiring feet, who is lurking in her dread ambush, will come, as with the march and with the might of a great host. For wicked ones have been fired with passion that hurried them to a forbidden bed, to accursed bridals, to a marriage stained with guilt of blood. Therefore am I sure that the portent will not fail to bring woe upon the partners in crime. Verily mortals cannot read the future in fearful dreams or oracles, if this vision of the night find not due fulfilment.

O chariot-race of Pelops long ago, source of many a sorrow, what weary troubles hast thou brought upon this land! For since Myrtilus sank to rest beneath the waves, when a fatal and cruel hand hurled him to destruction out of the golden car, this house was never yet free from misery and violence.

*Enter*Clytaemnestra.

Cl. At large once more, it seems, thou rangest,—for Aegisthus is not here, who always kept thee at least from passing the gates, to shame thy friends. But now, since he is absent, thou takest no heed of me; though thou hast said of me oft-times, and to many, that I am a bold and lawless tyrant, who insults thee and thine. I am guilty of no insolence; I do but return the taunts that I often hear from thee.

Thy father—this is thy constant pretext—was slain by me. Yes, by me—I know it well; it admits of no denial; for Justice slew him, and not I alone,—Justice, whom it became thee to support, hadst thou been rightminded; seeing that this father of thine, whom thou art ever lamenting, was the one man of the Greeks who had the heart to sacrifice thy sister to the gods—he, the father, who had not shared the mother's pangs.

Come, tell me now, wherefore, or to please whom, did he sacrifice her? To please the Argives, thou wilt say? Nay, they had no right to slay my daughter. Or if, forsooth, it was to screen his brother Menelaüs that he slew my child, was he not to pay me the penalty for that? Had not Menelaüs two children, who should in fairness have been taken before my daughter, as sprung from the sire and mother who had caused that voyage? Or had Hades some strange desire to feast on my off-spring, rather than on hers? Or had that accursèd father lost all tenderness for the children of my womb, while he was tender to the children of Menelaüs? Was not that the part of a callous and perverse parent? I think so, though I differ from thy judgment; and so would say the dead, if she could speak. For myself, then, I view the past without dismay; but if thou deemest me perverse, see that thine own judgment is just, before thou blame thy neighbour.

124

El. This time thou canst not say that I have done anything to provoke such words from thee. But, if thou wilt give me leave, I fain would declare the truth, in the cause alike of my dead sire and of my sister.

Cl. Indeed, thou hast my leave; and didst thou always address me in such a tone, thou wouldst be heard without pain.

El. Then I will speak. Thou sayest that thou hast slain my father. What word could bring thee deeper shame than that, whether the deed was just or not? But I must tell thee that thy deed was not just; no, thou wert drawn on to it by the wooing of the base man who is now thy spouse.

Ask the huntress Artemis what sin she punished when she stayed the frequent winds at Aulis; or I will tell thee; for we may not learn from her. My father—so I have heard—was once disporting himself in the grove of the goddess, when his footfall startled a dappled and antlered stag; he shot it, and chanced to utter a certain boast concerning its slaughter. Wroth thereat the daughter of Leto detained the Greeks, that, in quittance for the wild creature's life, my father should yield up the life of his own child. Thus it befell that she was sacrificed; since the fleet had no other release, homeward or to Troy; and for that cause, under sore constraint and with sore reluctance, at last he slew her—not for the sake of Menelaüs.

But grant—for I will take thine own plea—grant that the motive of his deed was to benefit his brother;—was that a reason for his dying by thy hand? Under what law? See that, in making such a law for men, thou make not trouble and remorse for thyself; for, if we are to take blood for blood, thou wouldst be the first to die, didst thou meet with thy desert.

But look if thy pretext is not false. For tell me, if thou wilt, wherefore thou art now doing the most shameless deeds of all,—dwelling as wife with that bloodguilty one, who first helped thee to slay my sire, and bearing children to him, while thou hast cast out the earlier-born, the stainless offspring of a stainless marriage. How can I praise these things? Or wilt thou say that this, too, is thy vengeance for thy daughter? Nay, a shameful plea, if so thou plead; 'tis not well to wed an enemy for a daughter's sake.

But indeed I may not even counsel thee,—who shriekest that I revile my mother; and truly I think that to me thou art less a mother than a mistress; so wretched is the life that I live, ever beset with miseries by thee and by thy partner. And that other, who scarce escaped thy hand, the hapless Orestes, is wearing out his ill-starred days in exile. Often hast thou charged me with rearing him to punish thy crime; and I would have done so, if I could, thou mayst be sure:—for that matter, denounce me to all, as disloyal, if thou wilt, or petulant, or impudent; for if I am accomplished in such ways, methinks I am no unworthy child of thee.

Ch. I see that she breathes forth anger; but whether justice be with her, for this she seems to care no longer.

Cl. And what manner of care do I need to use against her, who hath thus insulted a mother, and this at her ripe age? Thinkest thou not that she would go forward to any deed, without shame?

El. Now be assured that I do feel shame for this, though thou believe it not; I know that my behaviour is unseemly, and becomes me ill. But then the enmity on thy part, and thy treatment, compel me in mine own despite to do thus; for base deeds are taught by base.

Cl. Thou brazen one! Truly I and my sayings and my deeds give thee too much matter for words.

El. The words are thine, not mine; for thine is the action; and the acts find the utterance.

Cl. Now by our lady Artemis, thou shalt not fail to pay for this boldness, so soon as Aegisthus returns.

El. Lo, thou art transported by anger, after granting me free speech, and hast no patience to listen.

Cl. Now wilt thou not hush thy clamour, or even suffer me to sacrifice, when I have permitted *thee* to speak unchecked?

El. I hinder not,—begin thy rites, I pray thee; and blame not my voice, for I shall say no more.

Cl. Raise then, my handmaid, the offerings of many fruits, that I may uplift my prayers to this our king, for deliverance from my present fears. Lend now a gracious ear, O Phoebus our defender, to my words, though they be dark; for I speak not among friends, nor is it meet to unfold my whole thought to the light, while *she* stands near me, lest with her malice and her garrulous cry she spread some rash rumour throughout the town: but hear me thus, since on this wise I must speak.

That vision which I saw last night in doubtful dreams—if it hath come for my good, grant, Lycean king, that it be fulfilled; but if for harm, then let it recoil upon my foes. And if any are plotting to hurl me by treachery from the high estate which now is mine, permit them not; rather vouchsafe that, still living thus unscathed, I may bear sway over the house of the Atreidae and this realm, sharing prosperous days with the friends who share them now, and with those of my children from whom no enmity or bitterness pursues me.

O Lycean Apollo, graciously hear these prayers, and grant them to us all, even as we ask! For the rest, though I be silent, I deem that thou, a god, must know it; all things, surely, are seen by the sons of Zeus.

Enter the Paedagogus.

Pae. Ladies, might a stranger crave to know if this be the palace of the king Aegisthus?

Ch. It is, sir; thou thyself hast guessed aright.

Pae. And am I right in surmising that this lady is his consort? She is of queenly aspect.

Ch. Assuredly; thou art in the presence of the queen.

Pae. Hail, royal lady! I bring glad tidings to thee and to Aegisthus, from a friend.

Cl. I welcome the omen; but I would fain know from thee, first, who may have sent thee.

Pae. Phanoteus the Phocian, on a weighty mission.

Cl. What is it, sir? Tell me: coming from a friend, thou wilt bring, I know, a kindly message.

Pae. Orestes is dead; that is the sum.

El. Oh, miserable that I am! I am lost this day!

Cl. What sayest thou, friend, what sayest thou?—listen not to her!

Pae. I said, and say again—Orestes is dead.

El. I am lost, hapless one, I am undone!

Cl. (*to*Electra). See thou to thine own concerns.—But do thou, sir, tell me exactly,—how did he perish?

Pae. I was sent for that purpose, and will tell thee all. Having gone to the renowned festival, the pride of Greece, for the Delphian games, when he heard the loud summons to the foot-race which was first to be decided, he entered the lists, a brilliant form, a wonder in the eyes of all there; and, having finished his course at the point where it began, he went out with the glorious meed of victory. To speak briefly, where there is much to tell, I know not the man whose deeds and triumphs have matched his; but one thing thou must know; in all the contests that the judges announced, he bore away the prize; and men deemed him happy, as oft as the herald proclaimed him an Argive, by name Orestes, son of Agamemnon, who once gathered the famous armament of Greece.

Thus far, 'twas well; but, when a god sends harm, not even the strong man can escape. For, on another day, when chariots were to try their speed at sunrise, he entered, with many charioteers. One was an Achaean, one from Sparta, two masters of yoked cars were Libyans; Orestes, driving Thessalian mares, came fifth among them; the sixth from Aetolia, with chestnut colts; a Magnesian was the seventh; the eighth, with white horses, was of Aenian stock; the ninth, from Athens, built of gods; there was a Boeotian too, making the tenth chariot.

They took their stations where the appointed umpires placed them by lot and ranged the cars; then, at the sound of the brazen trump, they started. All shouted to their horses, and shook the reins in their hands; the whole course was filled with the noise of rattling chariots; the dust flew upward; and all, in a confused throng, plied their goads unsparingly, each of them striving to pass the wheels and the snorting steeds of his rivals; for alike at their backs and at their rolling wheels the breath of the horses foamed and smote.

Orestes, driving close to the pillar at either end of the course, almost grazed it with his wheel each time, and, giving rein to the trace-horse on the right, checked the horse on the inner side. Hitherto, all the chariots had escaped overthrow; but presently the Aenian's hard-mouthed colts ran away, and, swerving, as they passed from the sixth into the seventh round, dashed their foreheads against the team of the Barcaean. Other mishaps followed the first, shock on shock and crash on crash, till the whole race-ground of Crisa was strewn with the wreck of the chariots.

Seeing this, the wary charioteer from Athens drew aside and paused, allowing the billow of chariots, surging in mid course, to go by. Orestes was driving last, keeping his horses behind,—for his trust was in the end; but when he saw that the Athenian was alone left in, he sent a shrill cry ringing through the ears of his swift colts, and gave chase. Team was brought level with team, and so they raced,—first one man, then the other, showing his head in front of the chariots.

Hitherto the ill-fated Orestes had passed safely through every round, steadfast in his steadfast car; at last, slackening his left rein while the horse was turning, unawares he struck the edge of the pillar; he broke the axle-box in twain; he was thrown over the chariotrail; he was caught in the shapely reins; and, as he fell on the ground, his colts were scattered into the middle of the course.

But when the people saw him fallen from the car, a cry of pity went up for the youth, who had done such deeds and was meeting such a doom,—now dashed to earth, now tossed feet uppermost to the sky,—till the charioteers, with difficulty checking the career of his horses, loosed him, so covered with blood that no friend who saw it would have known the hapless corpse. Straightway they burned it on a pyre; and chosen men of Phocis are bringing in a small urn of bronze the sad dust of that mighty form, to find due burial in his fatherland.

Such is my story,—grievous to hear, if words can grieve; but for us, who beheld, the greatest of sorrows that these eyes have seen.

Ch. Alas, alas! Now, methinks, the stock of our ancient masters hath utterly perished, root and branch.

Cl. O Zeus, what shall I call these tidings,—glad tidings? Or dire, but gainful? 'Tis a bitter lot, when mine own calamities make the safety of my life.

Pae. Why art thou so downcast, lady, at this news?

Cl. There is a strange power in motherhood; a mother may be wronged, but she never learns to hate her child.

Pae. Then it seems that we have come in vain.

Cl. Nay, not in vain; how canst thou say 'in vain,' when thou hast brought me sure proofs of his death?—His, who sprang from mine own life, yet forsaking me who had suckled and reared him, became an exile and an alien; and, after he went out of this land, he saw me no more; but, charging me with the murder of his sire, he uttered dread threats against me; so that neither by night nor by day could sweet sleep cover mine eyes, but from moment to moment I lived in fear of death. Now, however—since this day I am rid of terror from him, and from this girl,—that worse plague who shared my home, while still she drained my very life-blood,—now, methinks, for aught that she can threaten, I shall pass my days in peace.

El. Ah, woe is me! Now, indeed, Orestes, thy fortune may be lamented, when it is thus with thee, and thou art mocked by this thy mother! Is it not well?

Cl. Not with thee; but his state is well.

El. Hear, Nemesis of him who hath lately died!

Cl. She hath heard who should be heard, and hath ordained well.

El. Insult us, for this is the time of thy triumph.

Cl. Then will not Orestes and thou silence me?

El. We are silenced; much less should we silence thee.

Cl. Thy coming, sir, would deserve large recompense, if thou hast hushed her clamorous tongue.

Pae. Then I may take my leave, if all is well.

Cl. Not so; thy welcome would then be unworthy of me, and of the ally who sent thee. Nay, come thou in; and leave her without, to make loud lament for herself and for her friends.

[Clytaemnestra *and the* Paedagogus *enter the house.*

El. How think ye? Was there not grief and anguish there, wondrous weeping and wailing of that miserable mother, for the son who perished by such a fate? Nay, she left us with a laugh! Ah, woe is me! Dearest Orestes, how is my life quenched by thy death! Thou hast torn away with thee from my heart the only hopes which still were mine,—that thou wouldst live to return some day, an avenger of thy sire, and of me unhappy. But now—whither shall I turn? I am alone, bereft of thee, as of my father.

Henceforth I must be a slave again among those whom most I hate, my father's murderers. Is it not well with me? But never, at least, henceforward, will I enter the house to dwell with them; nay, at these gates I will lay me down, and here, without a friend, my days shall wither. Therefore, if any in the house be wroth, let them slay me; for 'tis a grace, if I die, but if I live, a pain; I desire life no more.

Ch. Where are the thunderbolts of Zeus, or where is the bright Sun, if they look upon these things, and brand them not, but rest?

El. Woe, woe, ah me, ah me!

Ch. O daughter, why weepest thou?

El. *(with hands outstretched to heaven)*. Alas!

Ch. Utter no rash cry!

El. Thou wilt break my heart!

Ch. How meanest thou?

El. If thou suggest a hope concerning those who have surely passed to the realm below, thou wilt trample yet more upon my misery.

Ch. Nay, I know how, ensnared by a woman for a chain of gold, the prince Amphiaraüs found a grave; and now beneath the earth—

El. ah me, ah me!

Ch. —he reigns in fulness of force.

El. Alas!

Ch. Alas indeed! for the murderess—

El. Was slain.

Ch. Yea.

El. I know it, I know it; for a champion arose to avenge the mourning dead; but to me no champion remains; for he who yet was left hath been snatched away.

Ch. Hapless art thou, and hapless is thy lot!

El. Well know I that, too well,—I, whose life is a torrent of woes dread and dark, a torrent that surges through all the months!

Ch. We have seen the course of thy sorrow.

El. Cease, then, to divert me from it, when no more—

Ch. How sayest thou?

El. —when no more can I have the comfort of hope from a brother, the seed of the same noble sire.

Ch. For all men it is appointed to die.

El. What, to die as that ill-starred one died, amid the tramp of racing steeds, entangled in the reins that dragged him?

Ch. Cruel was his doom, beyond thought!

El. Yea, surely; when in foreign soil, without ministry of my hands—

Ch. Alas!

El. —he is buried, ungraced by me with sepulture or with tears.

Enter Chrysothemis.

Chr. Joy wings my feet, dear sister, not careful of seemliness, if I come with speed; for I bring joyful news, to relieve thy long sufferings and sorrows.

El. And whence couldst *thou* find help for my woes, whereof no cure can be imagined?

Chr. Orestes is with us,—know this from my lips,—in living presence, as surely as thou seest me here.

El. What, art thou mad, poor girl? Art thou laughing at my sorrows, and thine own?

Chr. Nay, by our father's hearth, I speak not in mockery; I tell thee that he is with us indeed.

El. Ah, woe is me! And from whom hast thou heard this tale, which thou believest so lightly?

Chr. I believe it on mine own knowledge, not on hearsay; I have seen clear proofs.

El. What hast thou seen, poor girl, to warrant thy belief? Whither, I wonder hast thou turned thine eyes, that thou art fevered with this baneful fire?

Chr. Then, for the gods' love, listen, that thou mayest know my story, before deciding whether I am sane or foolish.

El. Speak on, then, if thou findest pleasure in speaking.

Chr. Well, thou shalt hear all that I have seen. When I came to our father's ancient tomb, I saw that streams of milk had lately flowed from the top of the mound, and that his sepulchre was encircled with garlands of all flowers that blow. I was astonished at the sight, and peered about, lest haply some one should be close to my side. But when I perceived that all the place was in stillness, I crept nearer to the tomb; and on the mound's edge I saw a lock of hair, freshly severed.

And the moment that I saw it, ah me, a familiar image rushed upon my soul, telling me that there I beheld a token of him whom most I love, Orestes. Then I took it in my hands, and uttered no ill-omened word, but the tears of joy straightway filled mine eyes. And I know well, as I knew then, that this fair tribute has come from none but him. Whose part else was that, save mine and thine? And I did it not, I know,—nor thou; how shouldst thou?—when thou canst not leave this house, even to worship the gods, but at thy peril. Nor, again, does our mother's heart incline to do such deeds, nor could she have so done without our knowledge.

No, these offerings are from Orestes! Come, dear sister, courage! No mortal life is attended by a changeless fortune. Ours was once gloomy; but this day, perchance, will seal the promise of much good.

El. Alas for thy folly! How I have been pitying thee!

Chr. What, are not my tidings welcome?

El. Thou knowest not whither or into what dreams thou wanderest.

Chr. Should I not know what mine own eyes have seen?

El. He is dead, poor girl; and thy hopes in that deliverer are gone: look not to him.

Chr. Woe, woe is me! From whom hast thou heard this?

El. From the man who was present when he perished.

Chr. And where is he? Wonder steals over my mind.

El. He is within, a guest not unpleasing to our mother.

Chr. Ah, woe is me! Whose, then, can have been those ample offerings to our father's tomb?

El. Most likely, I think, some one brought those gifts in memory of the dead Orestes.

Chr. Oh, hapless that I am! And I was bringing such news in joyous haste, ignorant, it seems, how dire was our plight; but now that I have come, I find fresh sorrows added to the old!

El. So stands thy case; yet, if thou wilt hearken to me, thou wilt lighten the load of our present trouble.

Chr. Can I ever raise the dead to life?

El. I meant not that; I am not so foolish.

Chr. What biddest thou, then, for which my strength avails?

El. That thou be brave in doing what I enjoin.

Chr. Nay, if any good can be done, I will not refuse.

El. Remember, nothing succeeds without toil.

Chr. I know it, and will share thy burden with all my power.

El. Hear, then, how I am resolved to act. As for the support of friends, thou thyself must know that we have none; Hades hath taken our friends away, and we two are left alone. I, so long as I heard that my brother still lived and prospered, had hopes that he would yet come to avenge the murder of our sire. But now that he is no more, I look next to thee, not to flinch from aiding me thy sister to slay our father's murderer, Aegisthus:—I must have no secret from thee more.

How long art thou to wait inactive? What hope is left standing, to which thine eyes can turn? Thou hast to complain that thou art robbed of thy father's heritage; thou hast to mourn that thus far thy life is fading without nuptial song or wedded love. Nay, and do not hope that such joys will ever be thine; Aegisthus is not so ill-advised as ever to permit that children should spring from thee or me for his own sure destruction. But if thou wilt follow my counsels, first thou wilt win praise of piety from our dead sire below, and from our brother too; next, thou shalt be called free henceforth, as thou wert born, and shalt find worthy bridals; for noble natures draw the gaze of all.

Then seest thou not what fair fame thou wilt win for thyself and for me, by hearkening to my word? What citizen or stranger, when he sees us, will not greet us with praises such as these?—'Behold these two sisters, my friends, who saved their father's house; who, when their foes were firmly planted of yore, took their lives in their hands and stood forth as avengers of blood! Worthy of love are these twain, worthy of reverence from all; at festivals, and wherever the folk are assembled, let these be honoured of all men for their prowess.' Thus will every one speak of us, so that in life and in death our glory shall not fail.

Come, dear sister, hearken! Work with thy sire, share the burden of thy brother, win rest from woes for me and for thyself,—mindful of this, that an ignoble life brings shame upon the noble.

Ch. In such case as this, forethought is helpful for those who speak and those who hear.

Chr. Yea, and before she spake, my friends, were she blest with a sound mind, she would have remembered caution, as she doth not remember it.

Now whither canst thou have turned thine eyes, that thou art arming thyself with such rashness, and calling me to aid thee? Seest thou not, thou art a woman, not a man, and no match for thine adversaries in strength? And their fortune prospers day by day, while ours is ebbing and coming to nought. Who, then, plotting to vanquish a foe so strong, shall escape without suffering deadly scathe? See that we change not our evil plight to worse, if any one hears these words. It brings us no relief or benefit, if, after winning fair fame, we die an ignominious death; for mere death is not the bitterest, but rather when one who craves to die cannot obtain even that boon.

Nay, I beseech thee, before we are utterly destroyed, and leave our house desolate, restrain thy rage! I will take care that thy words remain secret and harmless;

and learn thou the prudence, at last though late, of yielding, when so helpless, to thy rulers.

Ch. Hearken; there is no better gain for mortals to win than foresight and a prudent mind.

El. Thou hast said nothing unlooked-for; I well knew that thou wouldst reject what I proffered. Well! I must do this deed with mine own hand, and alone; for assuredly I will not leave it void.

Chr. Alas! Would thou hadst been so purposed on the day of our father's death! What mightst thou not have wrought?

El. My nature was the same then, but my mind less ripe.

Chr. Strive to keep such a mind through all thy life.

El. These counsels mean that thou wilt not share my deed.

Chr. No; for the venture is likely to bring disaster.

El. I admire thy prudence; thy cowardice I hate.

Chr. I will listen not less calmly when thou praise me.

El. Never fear to suffer that from me.

Chr. Time enough in the future to decide that.

El. Begone; there is no power to help in thee.

Chr. Not so; but in thee, no mind to learn.

El. Go, declare all this to thy mother!

Chr. But, again, I do not hate thee with such a hate.

El. Yet know at least to what dishonour thou bringest me.

Chr. Dishonour, no! I am only thinking of thy good.

El. Am I bound, then, to follow thy rule of right?

Chr. When thou art wise, then thou shalt be our guide.

El. Sad, that one who speaks so well should speak amiss!

Chr. Thou hast well described the fault to which thou cleavest.

El. How? Dost thou not think that I speak with justice?

Chr. But sometimes justice itself is fraught with harm.

El. I care not to live by such a law.

Chr. Well, if thou must do this, thou wilt praise me yet.

El. And do it I will, no whit dismayed by thee.

Chr. Is this so indeed? Wilt thou not change thy counsels?

El. No, for nothing is more hateful than bad counsel.

Chr. Thou seemest to agree with nothing that I urge.

El. My resolve is not new, but long since fixed.

Chr. Then I will go; thou canst not be brought to approve my words, nor I to commend thy conduct.

El. Nay, go within; never will I follow thee, however much thou mayst desire it; it were great folly even to attempt an idle quest.

Chr. Nay, if thou art wise in thine own eyes, be such wisdom thine; by and by, when thou standest in evil plight, thou wilt praise my words.

str. 1.Ch. When we see the birds of the air, with sure instinct, careful to nourish those who give them life and nurture, why do not we pay these debts in like measure? Nay, by the lightning-flash of Zeus, by Themis throned in heaven, it is not long till sin brings sorrow.

Voice that comest to the dead beneath the earth, send a piteous cry, I pray thee, to the son of Atreus in that world, a joyless message of dishonour;

ant. 1.tell him that the fortunes of his house are now distempered; while, among his children, strife of sister with sister hath broken the harmony of loving days. Electra, forsaken, braves the storm alone; she bewails alway, hapless one, her father's fate, like the nightingale unwearied in lament; she recks not of death, but is ready to leave the sunlight, could she but quell the two Furies of her house. Who shall match such noble child of noble sire?

str. 2.No generous soul deigns, by a base life, to cloud a fair repute, and leave a name inglorious; as thou, too, O my daughter, hast chosen to mourn all thy days with those that mourn, and hast spurned dishonour, that thou mightest win at once a twofold praise, as wise, and as the best of daughters.

ant. 2.May I yet see thy life raised in might and wealth above thy foes, even as now it is humbled beneath their hand! For I have found thee in no prosperous estate; and yet, for observance of nature's highest laws, winning the noblest renown, by thy piety towards Zeus.

Enter Orestes, *with* Pylades *and two attendants.*

Or. Ladies, have we been directed aright, and are we on the right path to our goal?

Ch. And what seekest thou? With what desire hast thou come?

Or. I have been searching for the home of Aegisthus.

Ch. Well, thou hast found it; and thy guide is blameless.

Or. Which of you, then, will tell those within that our company, long desired, hath arrived?

Ch. This maiden,—if the nearest should announce it.

Or. I pray thee, mistress, make it known in the house that certain men of Phocis seek Aegisthus.

El. Ah, woe is me! Surely ye are not bringing the visible proofs of that rumour which we heard?

Or. I know nothing of thy 'rumour'; but the aged Strophius charged me with tidings of Orestes.

El. What are they, sir? Ah, how I thrill with fear!

Or. He is dead; and in a small urn, as thou seest, we bring the scanty relics home.

El. Ah me unhappy! There, at last, before mine eyes, I see that woful burden in your hands!

Or. If thy tears are for aught which Orestes hath suffered, know that yonder vessel holds his dust.

El. Ah, sir, allow me, then, I implore thee, if this urn indeed contains him, to take it in my hands,—that I may weep and wail, not for these ashes alone, but for myself and for all our house therewith!

Or. (*to the attendants*). Bring it and give it her, whoe'er she be; for she who begs this boon must be one who wished him no evil, but a friend, or haply a kinswoman in blood.

[*The urn is placed in* Electra's *hands.*

El. Ah, memorial of him whom I loved best on earth! Ah, Orestes, whose life hath no relic left save this,—how far from the hopes with which I sent thee forth is the manner in which I receive thee back! Now I carry thy poor dust in my hands; but

133

thou wert radiant, my child, when I sped thee forth from home! Would that I had yielded up my breath, ere, with these hands, I stole thee away, and sent thee to a strange land, and rescued thee from death; that so thou mightest have been stricken down on that self-same day, and had thy portion in the tomb of thy sire!

But now, an exile from home and fatherland, thou hast perished miserably, far from thy sister; woe is me, these loving hands have not washed or decked thy corpse, nor taken up, as was meet, their sad burden from the flaming pyre. No! at the hands of strangers, hapless one, thou hast had those rites, and so art come to us, a little dust in a narrow urn.

Ah, woe is me for my nursing long ago, so vain, that I oft bestowed on thee with loving toil! For thou wast never thy mother's darling so much as mine; nor was any in the house thy nurse but I; and by thee I was ever called 'sister.' But now all this hath vanished in a day, with thy death; like a whirlwind, thou hast swept all away with thee. Our father is gone; I am dead in regard to thee; thou thyself hast perished: our foes exult; that mother, who is none, is mad with joy,—she of whom thou didst oft send me secret messages, thy heralds, saying that thou thyself wouldst appear as an avenger. But our evil fortune, thine and mine, hath reft all that away, and hath sent thee forth unto me thus,—no more the form that I loved so well, but ashes and an idle shade.

Ah me, ah me! O piteous dust! Alas, thou dear one, sent on a dire journey, how hast undone me,—undone me indeed, O brother mine!

Therefore take me to this thy home, me who am as nothing, to thy nothingness, that I may dwell with thee henceforth below; for when thou wert on earth, we shared alike; and now I fain would die, that I may not be parted from thee in the grave. For I see that the dead have rest from pain.

Ch. Bethink thee, Electra, thou art the child of mortal sire, and mortal was Orestes; therefore grieve not too much. This is a debt which all of us must pay.

Or. Alas, what shall I say? What words can serve me at this pass? I can restrain my lips no longer!

El. What hath troubled thee? Why didst thou say that?

Or. Is this the form of the illustrious Electra that I behold?

El. It is; and very grievous is her plight.

Or. Alas, then, for this miserable fortune!

El. Surely, sir, thy lament is not for *me?*

Or. O form cruelly, godlessly misused!

El. Those ill-omened words, sir, fit no one better than me.

Or. Alas for thy life, unwedded and all unblest!

El. Why this steadfast gaze, stranger, and these laments?

Or. How ignorant was I, then, of mine own sorrows!

El. By what that hath been said hast thou perceived this?

Or. By seeing thy sufferings, so many and so great.

El. And yet thou seest but a few of my woes.

Or. Could any be more painful to behold?

El. This, that I share the dwelling of the murderers.

Or. Whose murderers? Where lies the guilt at which thou hintest?

El. My father's;—and then I am their slave perforce.

Or. Who is it that subjects thee to this constraint?

El. A mother—in name; but no mother in her deeds.

Or. How doth she oppress thee? With violence or with hardship?

El. With violence, and hardships, and all manner of ill.

Or. And is there none to succour, or to hinder?

El. None. I *had* one; and thou hast shown me his ashes.

Or. Hapless girl, how this sight hath stirred my pity!

El. Know, then, that thou art the first who ever pitied me.

Or. No other visitor hath ever shared thy pain.

El. Surely thou art not some unknown kinsman?

Or. I would answer, if these were friends who hear us.

El. Oh, they are friends; thou canst speak without mistrust.

Or. Give up this urn, then, and thou shalt be told all.

El. Nay, I beseech thee be not so cruel to me, sir!

Or. Do as I say, and never fear to do amiss.

El. I conjure thee, rob me not of my chief treasure!

Or. Thou must not keep it.

El. Ah woe is me for thee, Orestes, if I am not to give thee burial!

Or. Hush!—no such word!—Thou hast no right to lament.

El. No right to lament for my dead brother?

Or. It is not meet for thee to speak of him thus.

El. Am I so dishonoured of the dead?

Or. Dishonoured of none:—but this is not thy part.

El. Yes, if these are the ashes of Orestes that I hold.

Or. They are not; a fiction clothed them with his name.

[*He gently takes the urn from her.*

El. And where is that unhappy one's tomb?

Or. There is none; the living have no tomb.

El. What sayest thou, boy? Or. Nothing that is not true.

El. The man is alive? Or. If there be life in me.

El. What? Art thou he? Or. Look at this signet, once our father's, and judge if I speak truth.

El. O blissful day! Or. Blissful, in very deed!

El. Is this thy voice? Or. Let no other voice reply.

El. Do I hold thee in my arms?

Or. As mayest thou hold me always!

El. Ah, dear friends and fellow-citizens, behold Orestes here, who was feigned dead, and now, by that feigning hath come safely home!

Ch. We see him, daughter; and for this happy fortune a tear of joy trickles from our eyes.

*str.*El. Offspring of him whom I loved best, thou hast come even now, thou hast come, and found and seen her whom thy heart desired!

Or. I am with thee;—but keep silence for a while.

El. What meanest thou?

Or. 'Tis better to be silent, lest some one within should hear.

El. Nay, by ever-virgin Artemis, I will never stoop to fear women, stay-at-homes, vain burdens of the ground!

Or. Yet remember that in women, too, dwells the spirit of battle; thou hast had good proof of that I ween.

El. Alas! ah me! Thou hast reminded me of my sorrow, one which, from its nature, cannot be veiled, cannot be done away with, cannot forget!

Or. I know this also; but when occasion prompts, then will be the moment to recall those deeds.

*ant.*El. Each moment of all time, as it comes, would be meet occasion for these my just complaints; scarcely now have I had my lips set free.

Or. I grant it; therefore guard thy freedom.

El. What must I do?

Or. When the season serves not, do not wish to speak too much.

El. Nay, who could fitly exchange speech for such silence, when thou hast appeared? For now I have seen thy face, beyond all thought and hope!

Or. Thou sawest it, when the gods moved me to come....

* * * * * * * *

El. Thou hast told me of a grace above the first, if a god hath indeed brought thee to our house; I acknowledge therein the work of heaven.

Or. I am loth, indeed, to curb thy gladness, but yet this excess of joy moves my fear.

*ep.*El. O thou who, after many a year, hast deigned thus to gladden mine eyes by thy return, do not, now that thou hast seen me in all my woe—

Or. What is thy prayer?

El. —do not rob me of the comfort of thy face; do not force me to forego it!

Or. I should be wroth, indeed, if I saw another attempt it.

El. My prayer is granted? Or. Canst thou doubt?

El. Ah, friends, I heard a voice that I could never have hoped to hear; nor could I have restrained my emotion in silence, and without a cry, when I heard it.

Ah me! But now I have thee; thou art come to me with the light of that dear countenance, which never, even in sorrow, could I forget.

Or. Spare all superfluous words; tell me not of our mother's wickedness, or how Aegisthus drains the wealth of our father's house by lavish luxury or aimless waste; for the story would not suffer thee to keep due limit. Tell me rather that which will serve our present need,—where we must show ourselves, or wait in ambush, that this our coming may confound the triumph of our foes.

And look that our mother read not thy secret in thy radiant face, when we twain have advanced into the house, but make lament, as for the feigned disaster; for when we have prospered, then there will be leisure to rejoice and exult in freedom.

El. Nay, brother, as it pleases thee, so shall be my conduct also; for all my joy is a gift from thee, and not mine own. Nor would I consent to win a great good for myself at the cost of the least pain to thee; for so should I ill serve the divine power that befriends us now.

But thou knowest how matters stand here, I doubt not: thou must have heard that Aegisthus is from home, but our mother within;—and fear not that she will ever see my face lit up with smiles; for mine old hatred of her hath sunk into my heart; and, since I have beheld thee, for very joy I shall never cease to weep. How indeed should I cease, who have seen thee come home this day, first as dead, and then in life? Strangely hast thou wrought on me; so that, if my father should return alive, I

136

should no longer doubt my senses, but should believe that I saw him. Now, therefore, that thou hast come to me so wondrously, command me as thou wilt; for, had I been alone, I should have achieved one of two things,—a noble deliverance, or a noble death.

Or. Thou hadst best be silent; for I hear some one within preparing to go forth.

El. (*to* Orestes *and* Pylades). Enter, sirs; especially as ye bring that which no one could repulse from these doors, though he receive it without joy.

Enter the Paedagogus.

Pae. Foolish and senseless children! Are ye weary of your lives, or was there no wit born in you, that ye see not how ye stand, not on the brink, but in the very midst of deadly perils? Nay, had I not kept watch this long while at these doors, your plans would have been in the house before yourselves; but, as it is, my care shielded you from that. Now have done with this long discourse, these insatiate cries of joy, and pass within; for in such deeds delay is evil, and 'tis well to make an end.

Or. What, then, will be my prospects when I enter?

Pae. Good; for thou art secured from recognition.

Or. Thou hast reported me, I presume, as dead?

Pae. Know that here thou art numbered with the shades.

Or. Do they rejoice, then, at these tidings? Or what say they?

Pae. I will tell thee at the end; meanwhile, all is well for us on their part,—even that which is not well.

El. Who is this, brother? I pray thee, tell me.

Or. Dost thou not perceive? El. I cannot guess.

Or. Knowest thou not the man to whose hands thou gavest me once?

El. What man? How sayest thou?

Or. By whose hands, through thy forethought, I was secretly conveyed forth to Phocian soil.

El. Is this he in whom, alone of many, I found a true ally of old, when our sire was slain?

Or. 'Tis he; question me no further.

El. O joyous day! O sole preserver of Agamemnon's house, how hast thou come? Art thou he indeed, who didst save my brother and myself from many sorrows? O dearest hands; O messenger whose feet were kindly servants! How couldst thou be with me so long, and remain unknown, nor give a ray of light, but afflict me by fables, while possessed of truths most sweet? Hail, father,—for 'tis a father that I seem to behold! All hail,—and know that I have hated thee, and loved thee, in one day, as never man before!

Pae. Enough, methinks; as for the story of the past, many are the circling nights, and days as many, which shall show it thee, Electra, in its fulness.

(*To Orestes and Pylades.*) But this is my counsel to you twain, who stand there—now is the time to act; now Clytaemnestra is alone,—no man is now within: but, if ye pause, consider that ye will have to fight, not with the inmates alone, but with other foes more numerous and better skilled.

Or. Pylades, this our task seems no longer to crave many words, but rather that we should enter the house forthwith,—first adoring the shrines of my father's gods, who keep these gates.

[Orestes *and* Pylades *enter the house, followed by the* Paedagogus.—Electra *remains outside.*

137

El. O King Apollo! graciously hear them, and hear me besides, who so oft have come before thine altar with such gifts as my devout hand could bring! And now, O Lycean Apollo, with such vows as I can make, I pray thee, I supplicate, I implore, grant us thy benignant aid in these designs, and show men how impiety is rewarded by the gods!

[Electra *enters the house.*

Ch. Behold how Ares moves onward, breathing deadly vengeance, against which none may strive!

Even now the pursuers of dark guilt have passed beneath yon roof, the hounds which none may flee. Therefore the vision of my soul shall not long tarry in suspense.

The champion of the spirits infernal is ushered with stealthy feet into the house, the ancestral palace of his sire, bearing keen-edged death in his hands; and Hermes, son of Maia, who hath shrouded the guile in darkness, leads him forward, even to the end, and delays no more.

[*Enter* Electra *from the house.*

str. El. Ah, dearest friends, in a moment the men will do the deed;—but wait in silence.

Ch. How is it?—what do they now?

El. She is decking the urn for burial, and those two stand close to her.

Ch. And why hast thou sped forth?

El. To guard against Aegisthus entering before we are aware.

Clytaemnestra (*within*). Alas! Woe for the house forsaken of friends and filled with murderers!

El. A cry goes up within:—hear ye not, friends?

Ch. I heard, ah me, sounds dire to hear, and shuddered!

Clyt. (*within*). O hapless that I am!—Aegisthus, where, where art thou?

El. Hark, once more a voice resounds!

Clyt. (*within*). My son, my son, have pity on thy mother!

El. Thou hadst none for him, nor for the father that begat him.

Ch. Ill-fated realm and race, now the fate that hath pursued thee day by day is dying,—is dying!

Clyt. (*within*). Oh, I am smitten!

El. Smite, if thou canst, once more!

Clyt. (*within*). Ah, woe is me again!

El. Would that the woe were for Aegisthus too!

Ch. The curses are at work; the buried live; blood flows for blood, drained from the slayers by those who died of yore.

[*Enter* Orestes *and* Pylades *from the house.*

ant. Behold, they come! That red hand reeks with sacrifice to Ares; nor can I blame the deed.

El. Orestes, how fare ye? Or. All is well within the house, if Apollo's oracle spake well.

El. The guilty one is dead? Or. Fear no more that thy proud mother will ever put thee to dishonour.

*　*　*　*　*　*　*　*

Ch. Cease; for I see Aegisthus full in view.

El. Rash boys, back, back! Or. Where see ye the man?

El. Yonder, at our mercy, he advances from the suburb, full of joy.

Ch. Make with all speed for the vestibule; that, as your first task prospered, so this again may prosper now.

Or. Fear not,—we will perform it. El. Haste, then, whither thou wouldst.

Or. See, I am gone. El. I will look to matters here.

[*Exeunt* Orestes *and* Pylades.

Ch. 'Twere well to soothe his ear with some few words of seeming gentleness, that he may rush blindly upon the struggle with his doom.

Enter Aegisthus.

Aeg. Which of you can tell me, where are those Phocian strangers, who, 'tis said, have brought us tidings of Orestes slain in the wreck of his chariot? Thee, thee I ask, yes, thee, in former days so bold,—for methinks it touches thee most nearly; thou best must know, and best canst tell.

El. I know assuredly; else were I a stranger to the fortune of my nearest kinsfolk.

Aeg. Where then may be the strangers? Tell me.

El. Within; they have found a way to the heart of their hostess.

Aeg. Have they in truth reported him dead?

El. Nay, not reported only; they have shown him.

Aeg. Can I, then, see the corpse with mine own eyes?

El. Thou canst, indeed; and 'tis no enviable sight.

Aeg. Indeed, thou hast given me a joyful greeting, beyond thy wont.

El. Joy be thine, if in these things thou findest joy.

Aeg. Silence, I say, and throw wide the gates, for all Mycenaeans and Argives to behold; that, if any of them were once buoyed on empty hopes from this man, now, seeing him dead, they may receive my curb, instead of waiting till my chastisement make them wise perforce!

El. No loyalty is lacking on my part; time hath taught me the prudence of concord with the stronger.

[*A shrouded corpse is disclosed.* Orestes *and* Pylades *stand near it.*

Aeg. O Zeus, I behold that which hath not fallen save by the doom of jealous Heaven; but, if Nemesis attend that word, be it unsaid!

Take all the covering from the face, that kinship, at least, may receive the tribute of lament from me also.

Or. Lift the veil thyself; not my part this, but thine, to look upon these relics, and to greet them kindly.

Aeg. 'Tis good counsel, and I will follow it.—(*To Electra*) But thou—call me Clytaemnestra, if she is within.

Or. Lo, she is near thee: turn not thine eyes elsewhere.

[Aegisthus *removes the face-cloth from the corpse.*

Aeg. O, what sight is this!

Or. Why so scared? Is the face so strange?

Aeg. Who are the men into whose mid toils I have fallen, hapless that I am?

Or. Nay, hast thou not discovered ere now that the dead, as thou miscallest them, are living?

Aeg. Alas, I read the riddle: this can be none but Orestes who speaks to me!

Or. And, though so good a prophet, thou wast deceived so long?

Aeg. Oh lost, undone! Yet suffer me to say one word...

El. In heaven's name, my brother, suffer him not to speak further, or to plead at length! When mortals are in the meshes of fate, how can such respite avail one who is to die? No,—slay him forthwith, and cast his corpse to the creatures from whom such as he should have burial, far from our sight! To me, nothing but this can make amends for the woes of the past.

Or. (*to*Aegisthus). Go in, and quickly; the issue here is not of words, but of thy life.

Aeg. Why take me into the house? If this deed be fair, what need of darkness? Why is thy hand not prompt to strike?

Or. Dictate not, but go where thou didst slay my father, that in the same place thou mayest die.

Aeg. Is this dwelling doomed to see all woes of Pelops' line, now, and in time to come?

Or. Thine, at least; trust my prophetic skill so far.

Aeg. The skill thou vauntest belonged not to thy sire.

Or. Thou bandiest words, and our going is delayed. Move forward! Aeg. Lead thou. Or. Thou must go first. Aeg. Lest I escape thee? Or. No, but that thou mayest not choose how to die; I must not spare thee any bitterness of death. And well it were if this judgment came straightway upon all who dealt in lawless deeds, even the judgment of the sword: so should not wickedness abound.

Ch. O house of Atreus, through how many sufferings hast thou come forth at last in freedom, crowned with good by this day's enterprise!

TRACHINIAE

PERSONS OF THE DRAMA.

Deianeira.
Nurse.
Hyllus,*son of Heracles and Deianeira.*
Messenger.
Lichas,*the herald of Heracles.*
Heracles.
An Old Man.
Chorus of Trachinian Maidens.
Scene: At Trachis, before the house of Heracles.

Heracles came in early manhood to Pleuron in Aetolia, where Deianeira, daughter of the King Oeneus, was being wooed by the river-god Achelous; he overthrew the monstrous suitor in combat, and married the fair maiden. As he went away with his bride, they came to the river Evenus, where Nessus carried travellers across. While conveying Deianeira over, he insulted her, and Heracles shot him with an arrow. The dying Centaur said to her: 'Thou hast been my last passenger, and I would fain show thee a grace. Take some of the blood that is clotted about my wound: it will be a love-charm for the soul of Heracles, and thou shalt never have cause to fear a rival.' And then he told her how to use it. This gift she secretly treasured.

The goddess Hera bore enmity to Heracles, as the son of her husband Zeus and Alcmena; and presently she made him a thrall to Eurystheus, king of Tiryns, who sent him on many perilous labours. Deianeira and her children now dwelt at Tiryns. There it befell that Heracles treacherously slew Iphitus, son of Eurytus, king of Oechalia in Euboea,—visiting the father's deed upon the son, for Eurytus had once done him a foul despite. Heracles and his family were then forced to leave Tiryns. A new home was given them at Trachis by the hero's kinsman, the good king Ceÿx. But Zeus was wroth with Heracles because he had slain Iphitus by guile; and doomed him to servitude under a barbarian mistress, the Lydian Omphale, for a year. So Heracles went away from Trachis, leaving his wife and children there: they did not know whither he had gone. When his year with Omphale was over, and he had been purged of blood-guilt, he fulfilled the oath that he had sworn to himself, to be avenged on Eurytus, the first cause of his dishonour. He gathered an army: he ravaged Oechalia with sword and fire; slew the king and the male folk; and sent a train of captive women to Trachis, among whom was Iole, the daughter of Eurytus.

It is at this moment that the play begins. Fifteen months have passed since Heracles left Trachis, and still Deianeira knows not where he is: she has not yet heard the news concerning Oechalia.

DEIANEIRA.

There is a saying among men, put forth of old, that thou canst not rightly judge whether a mortal's lot is good or evil, ere he die. But I, even before I have passed to the world of death, know well that my life is sorrowful and bitter; I, who in the house of my father Oeneus, while yet I dwelt at Pleuron, had such fear of bridals as never vexed any maiden of Aetolia. For my wooer was a river-god, Acheloüs, who in three shapes10 was ever asking me from my sire,—coming now as a bull in bodily form, now as a serpent with sheeny coils, now with trunk of man and front of ox, while from a shaggy beard the streams of fountain-water flowed abroad. With the fear of

141

such a suitor before mine eyes, I was always praying in my wretchedness that I might die, or ever I should come near to such a bed.

But at last, to my joy, came the glorious son of Zeus and Alcmena; who closed with him in combat, and delivered me. How the fight was waged, I cannot20 clearly tell, I know not; if there be any one who watched that sight without terror, such might speak: I, as I sat there, was distraught with dread, lest beauty should bring me sorrow at the last. But finally the Zeus of battles ordained well,—if well indeed it be: for since I have been joined to Heracles as his chosen bride, fear after fear hath haunted me on his account; one night30 brings a trouble, and the next night, in turn, drives it out. And then children were born to us; whom he has seen only as the husbandman sees his distant field, which he visits at seedtime, and once again at harvest. Such was the life that kept him journeying to and fro, in the service of a certain master.

But now, when he hath risen above those trials,—now it is that my anguish is sorest. Ever since he slew the valiant Iphitus, we have been dwelling here in40 Trachis, exiles from our home, and the guests of a stranger; but where he is, no one knows; I only know that he is gone, and hath pierced my heart with cruel pangs for him. I am almost sure that some evil hath befallen him; it is no short space that hath passed, but ten long months, and then five more,—and still no message from him. Yes, there has been some dread mischance;—witness that tablet which he left with me ere he went forth: oft do I pray to the gods that I may not have received it for my sorrow.

NURSE.

Deianeira, my mistress, many a time have I marked50 thy bitter tears and lamentations, as thou bewailedst the going forth of Heracles; but now,—if it be meet to school the free-born with the counsels of a slave, and if I must say what behoves thee,—why, when thou art so rich in sons, dost thou send no one of them to seek thy lord;—Hyllus, before all, who might well go on that errand, if he cared that there should be tidings of his father's welfare? Lo! there he comes, speeding towards the house with timely step; if, then, thou deemest that I speak in season, thou canst use at once my counsel,60 and the man.

Enter Hyllus.

De. My child, my son, wise words may fall, it seems, from humble lips; this woman is a slave, but hath spoken in the spirit of the free.

Hy. How, mother? Tell me, if it may be told.

De. It brings thee shame, she saith, that, when thy father hath been so long a stranger, thou hast not sought to learn where he is.

Hy. Nay, I know,—if rumour can be trusted.

De. And in what region, my child, doth rumour place him?

Hy. Last year, they say, through all the months, he70 toiled as bondman to a Lydian woman.

De. If he bore that, then no tidings can surprise.

Hy. Well, he has been delivered from that, as I hear.

De. Where, then, is he reported to be now,—alive, or dead?

Hy. He is waging or planning a war, they say, upon Euboea, the realm of Eurytus.

De. Knowest thou, my son, that he hath left with me sure oracles touching that land?

Hy. What are they, mother? I know not whereof thou speakest.

De. That either he shall meet his death, or, having80 achieved this task, shall have rest thenceforth, for all his days to come.

So, my child, when his fate is thus trembling in the scale, wilt thou not go to succour him? For we are saved, if he find safety, or we perish with him.

Hy. Ay, I will go, my mother; and, had I known the import of these prophecies, I had been there long since; but, as it was, my father's wonted fortune suffered me not to feel fear for him, or to be anxious overmuch.90 Now that I have the knowledge, I will spare no pains to learn the whole truth in this matter.

De. Go, then, my son; be the seeker ne'er so late, he is rewarded if he learn tidings of joy.

CHORUS.

str. 1.Thou whom Night brings forth at the moment when she is despoiled of her starry crown, and lays to rest in thy splendour, tell me, I pray thee, O Sun-god, tell me where abides Alcmena's son? Thou glorious lord of flashing light, say, is he threading the straits of the sea, or hath he found an abode on either continent? Speak, thou who seest as none else can see!

ant. 1.For Deianeira, as I hear, hath ever an aching heart; she, the battle-prize of old, is now like some bird lorn of its mate; she can never lull her yearning, nor stay her tears; haunted by a sleepless fear for her absent lord, she pines on her anxious, widowed couch, miserable in her foreboding of mischance.

str. 2.As one may see billow after billow driven over the wide deep by the tireless south-wind or the north, so the trouble of his life, stormy as the Cretan sea, now whirls back the son of Cadmus, now lifts him to honour. But some god ever saves him from the house of death, and suffers him not to fail.

ant. 2.Lady, I praise not this thy mood; with all reverence will I speak, yet in reproof. Thou dost not well, I say, to kill fair hope by fretting; remember that the son of Cronus himself, the all-disposing king, hath not appointed a painless lot for mortals. Sorrow and joy come round to all, as the Bear moves in his circling paths.

*ep.*Yea, starry night abides not with men, nor tribulation, nor wealth; in a moment it is gone from us, and another hath his turn of gladness, and of bereavement. So would I wish thee also, the Queen, to keep that prospect ever in thy thoughts; for when hath Zeus been found so careless of his children?

De. Ye have heard of my trouble, I think, and that hath brought you here; but the anguish which consumes my heart—ye are strangers to that; and never may ye learn it by suffering! Yes, the tender plant grows in those sheltered regions of its own; and the Sun-god's heat vexes it not, nor rain, nor any wind; but it rejoices in its sweet, untroubled being, till such time as the maiden is called a wife, and finds her portion of anxious thoughts in the night, brooding on danger to husband or to children. Such an one could understand the burden of my cares; she could judge them by her own.

Well, I have had many a sorrow to weep for ere now; but I am going to speak of one more grievous than them all.

When Heracles my lord was going from home on his last journey, he left in the house an ancient tablet, inscribed with tokens which he had never brought himself to explain to me before, many as were the ordeals to which he had gone forth. He had always departed as if to conquer, not to die. But now, as if he were a doomed man, he told me what portion of his substance I was to take for my dower, and how he would have his sons share their father's land amongst them. And he fixed the time; saying that, when a year and three months should have passed since he had left the country, then he was fated to die; or, if he should have survived that term, to live thenceforth an untroubled life.

Such, he said, was the doom ordained by the gods to be accomplished in the toils of Heracles; as the ancient oak at Dodona had spoken of yore, by the mouth of the two Peleiades. And this is the precise moment when the fulfilment of that word becomes due; so that I start up from sweet slumber, my friends, stricken with terror at the thought that I must remain widowed of the noblest among men.

Ch. Hush—no more ill-omened words; I see a man approaching, who wears a wreath, as if for joyous tidings.

Enter Messenger.

Me. Queen Deianeira, I shall be the first of messengers to free thee from fear. Know that Alcmena's son lives and triumphs, and from battle brings the firstfruits to the gods of this land.

De. What news is this, old man, that thou hast told me?

Me. That thy lord, admired of all, will soon come to thy house, restored to thee in his victorious might.

De. What citizen or stranger hath told thee this?

Me. In the meadow, summer haunt of oxen, Lichas the herald is proclaiming it to many: from him I heard it, and flew hither, that I might be the first to give thee these tidings, and so might reap some guerdon from thee, and win thy grace.

De. And why is *he* not here, if he brings good news?

Me. His task, lady, is no easy one; all the Malian folk have thronged around him with questions, and he cannot move forward: each and all are bent on learning what they desire, and will not release him until they are satisfied. Thus their eagerness detains him against his will; but thou shalt presently see him face to face.

De. O Zeus, who rulest the meads of Oeta, sacred from the scythe, at last, though late, thou hast given us joy! Uplift your voices, ye women within the house and ye beyond our gates, since now we are gladdened by the light of this message, that hath risen on us beyond my hope!

Let the maidens raise a joyous strain for the house, with songs of triumph at the hearth; and, amidst them, let the shout of the men go up with one accord for Apollo of the bright quiver, our Defender! And at the same time, ye maidens, lift up a paean, cry aloud to his sister, the Ortygian Artemis, smiter of deer, goddess of the twofold torch, and to the Nymphs her neighbours!

My spirit soars; I will not reject the wooing of the flute.—O thou sovereign of my soul! Lo, the ivy's spell begins to work upon me! Euoe!—even now it moves me to whirl in the swift dance of Bacchanals!

Praise, praise unto the Healer! See, dear lady, see! Behold, these tidings are taking shape before thy gaze.

144

De. I see it, dear maidens; my watching eyes had not failed to note yon company. [*Enter* Lichas, *followed by Captive Maidens.*]—All hail to the herald, whose coming hath been so long delayed!—if indeed thou bringest aught that can give joy.

LICHAS.

We are happy in our return, and happy in thy greeting, lady, which befits the deed achieved; for when a man hath fair fortune, he needs must win good welcome.

De. O best of friends, tell me first what first I would know,—shall I receive Heracles alive?

Li. I, certainly, left him alive and well,—in vigorous health, unburdened by disease.

De. Where, tell me—at home, or on foreign soil?

Li. There is a headland of Euboea, where to Cenaean Zeus he consecrates altars, and the tribute of fruitful ground.

De. In payment of a vow, or at the bidding of an oracle?

Li. For a vow, made when he was seeking to conquer and despoil the country of these women who are before thee.

De. And these—who are they, I pray thee, and whose daughters? They deserve pity, unless their plight deceives me.

Li. These are captives whom he chose out for himself and for the gods, when he sacked the city of Eurytus.

De. Was it the war against that city which kept him away so long, beyond all forecast, past all count of days?

Li. Not so: the greater part of the time he was detained in Lydia,—no free man, as he declares, but sold into bondage No offence should attend on the word, lady, when the deed is found to be of Zeus. So he passed a whole year, as he himself avows, in thraldom to Omphalè the barbarian. And so stung was he by that reproach, he bound himself by a solemn oath that he would one day enslave, with wife and child, the man who had brought that calamity upon him. Nor did he speak the word in vain; but, when he had been purged, gathered an alien host, and went against the city of Eurytus. That man, he said, alone of mortals, had a share in causing his misfortune. For when Heracles, an old friend, came to his house and hearth, Eurytus heaped on him the taunts of a bitter tongue and spiteful soul,—saying, 'Thou hast unerring arrows in thy hands, and yet my sons surpass thee in the trial of archery'; 'Thou art a slave,' he cried, 'a free man's broken thrall': and at a banquet, when his guest was full of wine, he thrust him from his doors.

Wroth thereat, when afterward Iphitus came to the hill of Tiryns, in search for horses that had strayed, Heracles seized a moment when the man's wandering thoughts went not with his wandering gaze, and hurled him from a tower-like summit. But in anger at that deed, Zeus our lord, Olympian sire of all, sent him forth into bondage, and spared not, because, this once, he had taken a life by guile. Had he wreaked his vengeance openly, Zeus would surely have pardoned him the righteous triumph; for the gods, too, love not insolence.

So those men, who waxed so proud with bitter speech, are themselves in the mansions of the dead, all of them, and their city is enslaved; while the women whom thou beholdest, fallen from happiness to misery, come here to thee; for such was thy lord's command, which I, his faithful servant, perform. He himself, thou mayest be sure,—so soon as he shall have offered holy sacrifice for his victory to Zeus from whom he sprang,—will be with thee. After all the fair tidings that have been told, this, indeed, is the sweetest word to hear.

Ch. Now, O Queen, thy joy is assured; part is with thee, and thou hast promise of the rest.

De. Yea, have I not the fullest reason to rejoice at these tidings of my lord's happy fortune? To such fortune, such joy must needs respond. And yet a prudent mind can see room for misgiving lest he who prospers should one day suffer reverse. A strange pity hath come over me, friends, at the sight of these illfated exiles, homeless and fatherless in a foreign land; once the daughters, perchance, of free-born sires, but now doomed to the life of slaves. O Zeus, who turnest the tide of battle, never may I see child of mine thus visited by thy hand; nay, if such visitation is to be, may it not fall while Deianeira lives! Such dread do I feel, beholding these.

[*To*Iolè.] Ah, hapless girl, say, who art thou? A maiden, or a mother? To judge by thine aspect, an innocent maiden, and of a noble race. Lichas, whose daughter is this stranger? Who is her mother, who her sire? Speak, I pity her more than all the rest, when I behold her; as she alone shows a due feeling for her plight.

Li. How should I know? Why should'st thou ask me? Perchance the offspring of not the meanest in yonder land.

De. Can she be of royal race? Had Eurytus a daughter?

Li. I know not; indeed, I asked not many questions.

De. And thou hast not heard her name from any of her companions?

Li. No, indeed, I went through my task in silence.

De. Unhappy girl, let me, at least, hear it from thine own mouth. It is indeed distressing not to know *thy* name.

Li. It will be unlike her former behaviour, then, I can tell thee, if she opens her lips: for she hath not uttered one word, but hath ever been travailing with the burden of her sorrow, and weeping bitterly, poor girl, since she left her wind-swept home. Such a state is grievous for herself, but claims our forbearance.

De. Then let her be left in peace, and pass under our roof as she wishes; her present woes must not be crowned with fresh pains at my hands; she hath enough already.—Now let us all go in, that thou mayest start speedily on thy journey, while I make all things ready in the house. [Lichas,*followed by the Captives, moves towards the house.*]

Me. (*coming nearer to*Deianeira). Ay, but first tarry here a brief space, that thou mayest learn, apart from yonder folk, whom thou art taking to thy hearth, and mayest gain the needful knowledge of things which have not been told to thee. Of these I am in full possession.

De. What means this? Why wouldest thou stay my departure?

Me. Pause and listen. My former story was worth thy hearing, and so will this one be, methinks.

De. Shall I call those others back? Or wilt thou speak before me and these maidens?

Me. To thee and these I can speak freely; never mind the others.

De. Well, they are gone;—so thy story can proceed.

Me. Yonder man was not speaking the straightforward truth in aught that he has just told. He has given false tidings now, or else his former report was dishonest.

De. How sayest thou? Explain thy whole drift clearly; thus far, thy words are riddles to me.

Me. I heard this man declare, before many witnesses, that for this maiden's sake Heracles overthrew Eurytus and the proud towers of Occhalia; Love, alone of the gods, wrought on him to do those deeds of arms,—not the toilsome servitude to Omphalè in Lydia, nor the death to which Iphitus was hurled. But now the herald has thrust Love out of sight, and tells a different tale.

Well, when he could not persuade her sire to give him the maiden for his paramour, he devised some petty complaint as a pretext, and made war upon her land,—that in which, as he said, this Eurytus bore sway,—and slew the prince her father, and sacked her city. And now, as thou seest, he comes sending her to this house not in careless fashion, lady, nor like a slave;—no, dream not of that,—it is not likely, if his heart is kindled with desire.

I resolved, therefore, O Queen, to tell thee all that I had heard from yonder man. Many others were listening to it, as I was, in the public place where the Trachinians were assembled; and they can convict him. If my words are unwelcome, I am grieved; but nevertheless I have spoken out the truth.

De. Ah me unhappy! In what plight do I stand? What secret bane have I received beneath my roof? Hapless that I am! Is she nameless, then, as her convoy sware?

Me. Nay, illustrious by name as by birth; she is the daughter of Eurytus, and was once called Iolè; she of whose parentage Lichas could say nothing, because, forsooth, he asked no questions.

Ch. Accursed, above other evil-doers, be the man whom deeds of treachery dishonour!

De. Ah, maidens, what am I to do? These latest tidings have bewildered me!

Ch. Go and inquire from Lichas; perchance he will tell the truth, if thou constrain him to answer.

De. Well, I will go; thy counsel is not amiss.

Me. And I, shall I wait here? Or what is thy pleasure?

De. Remain;—here he comes from the house of his own accord, without summons from me.

Enter Lichas.

Li. Lady, what message shall I bear to Heracles? Give me thy commands, for, as thou seest, I am going.

De. How hastily thou art rushing away, when thy visit had been so long delayed,—before we have had time for further talk.

Li. Nay, if there be aught that thou would'st ask, I am at thy service.

De. Wilt thou indeed give me the honest truth?

Li. Yes, be great Zeus my witness,—in anything that I know.

De. Who is the woman, then, whom thou hast brought?

Li. She is Euboean; but of what birth, I cannot say.

Me. Sirrah, look at me:—to whom art thou speaking, think'st thou?

Li. And thou — what dost thou mean by such a question?

Me. Deign to answer me, if thou comprehendest.

Li. To the royal Deianeira, unless mine eyes deceive me,—daughter of Oeneus, wife of Heracles, and my queen.

Me. The very word that I wished to hear from thee:—thou sayest that she is thy queen?

Li. Yes, as in duty bound.

Me. Well, then, what art thou prepared to suffer, if found guilty of failing in that duty?

Li. Failing in duty? What dark saying is this?

Me. 'Tis none; the darkest words are thine own.

Li. I will go,—I was foolish to hear thee so long.

Me. No, not till thou hast answered a brief question.

Li. Ask what thou wilt; thou art not taciturn.

Me. That captive, whom thou hast brought home—thou knowest whom I mean?

Li. Yes; but why dost thou ask?

Me. Well, saidst thou not that thy prisoner—she, on whom thy gaze now turns so vacantly—was Iolè, daughter of Eurytus?

Li. Said it to whom? Who and where is the man that will be thy witness to hearing this from me?

Me. To many of our own folk thou saidst it: in the public gathering of Trachinians, a great crowd heard thus much from thee.

Li. Ay—said they heard; but 'tis one thing to report a fancy, and another to make the story good.

Me. A fancy! Didst thou not say on thine oath that thou wast bringing her as a bride for Heracles?

Li. I? bringing a bride?—In the name of the gods, dear mistress, tell me who this stranger may be?

Me. One who heard from thine own lips that the conquest of the whole city was due to love for this girl: the Lydian woman was not its destroyer, but the passion which this maid has kindled.

Li. Lady, let this fellow withdraw: to prate with the brainsick befits not a sane man.

De. Nay, I implore thee by Zeus whose lightnings go forth over the high glens of Oeta, do not cheat me of the truth! For she to whom thou wilt speak is not ungenerous, nor hath she yet to learn that the human heart is inconstant to its joys. They are not wise, then, who stand forth to buffet against Love; for Love rules the gods as he will, and me; and why not another woman, such as I am? So I am mad indeed, if I blame my husband, because that distemper hath seized him; or this woman, his partner in a thing which is no shame to them, and no wrong to me. Impossible! No; if he taught thee to speak falsely, 'tis not a noble lesson that thou art learning; or if thou art thine own teacher in this, thou wilt be found cruel when it is thy wish to prove kind. Nay, tell me the whole truth. To a free-born man, the name of liar cleaves as a deadly brand. If thy hope is to escape detection, that, too, is vain; there are many to whom thou hast spoken, who will tell me.

And if thou art afraid, thy fear is mistaken. *Not* to learn the truth,—that, indeed, would pain me; but to know it—what is there terrible in that? Hath not Heracles wedded others erenow,—ay, more than living man,—and no one of them hath had harsh word or taunt from me; nor shall this girl, though her whole being should be absorbed in her passion; for indeed I felt a profound pity when I beheld her, because her beauty hath wrecked her life, and she, hapless one, all innocent, hath brought her fatherland to ruin and to bondage.

Well, those things must go with wind and stream.—To thee I say,—deceive whom thou wilt, but ever speak the truth to me.

Ch. Hearken to her good counsel, and hereafter thou shalt have no cause to complain of this lady; our thanks, too, will be thine.

Li. Nay, then, dear mistress,—since I see that thou thinkest as mortals should think, and canst allow for weakness,—I will tell thee the whole truth, and hide it not. Yes, it is even as yon man saith. This girl inspired that overmastering love which long ago smote through the soul of Heracles; for this girl's sake the desolate Oechalia, her home, was made the prey of his spear. And he,—it is just to him to say so,—never denied this,—never told me to conceal it. But I, lady, fearing to wound thy heart by such tidings, have sinned, if thou count this in any sort a sin.

Now, however, that thou knowest the whole story, for both your sakes,—for his, and not less for thine own,—bear with the woman, and be content that the words which thou hast spoken regarding her should bind thee still. For he, whose strength is victorious in all else, hath been utterly vanquished by his passion for this girl.

De. Indeed, mine own thoughts move me to act thus. Trust me, I will not add a new affliction to my burdens by waging a fruitless fight against the gods.—

But let us go into the house, that thou mayest receive my messages; and, since gifts should be meetly recompensed with gifts,—that thou mayest take these also. It is not right that thou shouldest go back with empty hands, after coming with such a goodly train.

Ch. Great and mighty is the victory which the Cyprian queen ever bears away. I stay not now to speak of the gods; I spare to tell how she beguiled the son of Cronus, and Hades, the lord of darkness, or Poseidon, shaker of the earth.

But, when this bride was to be won, who were the valiant rivals that entered the contest for her hand? Who went forth to the ordeal of battle, to the fierce blows and the blinding dust?

One was a mighty river-god, the dread form of a horned and four-legged bull, Acheloüs, from Oeniadae: the other came from Thebè, dear to Bacchus, with curved bow, and spears, and brandished club, the son of Zeus: who then met in combat, fain to win a bride: and the Cyprian goddess of nuptial joy was there with them, sole umpire of their strife.

Then was there clatter of fists and clang of bow, and the noise of a bull's horns therewith; then were there close-locked grapplings, and deadly blows from the forehead, and loud deep cries from both.

Meanwhile, she, in her delicate beauty, sat on the side of a hill that could be seen afar, awaiting the husband that should be hers.

[So the battle rages], as I have told; but the fair bride who is the prize of the strife abides the end in piteous anguish. And suddenly she is parted from her mother, as when a heifer is taken from its dam.

De. Dear friends, while our visitor is saying his farewell to the captive girls in the house, I have stolen forth to you,—partly to tell you what these hands have devised, and partly to crave your sympathy with my sorrow.

149

A maiden,—or, methinks, no longer a maiden, but a mistress,—hath found her way into my house, as a freight comes to a mariner,—a merchandise to make shipwreck of my peace. And now we twain are to share the same marriage-bed, the same embrace. Such is the reward that Heracles hath sent me,—he whom I called true and loyal,—for guarding his home through all that weary time. I have no thought of anger against him, often as he is vexed with this distemper. But then to live with her, sharing the same union—what woman could endure it? For I see that the flower of her age is blossoming, while mine is fading; and the eyes of men love to cull the bloom of youth, but they turn aside from the old. This, then, is my fear,—lest Heracles, in name my spouse, should be the younger's mate.

But, as I said, anger ill beseems a woman of understanding. I will tell you, friends, the way by which I hope to find deliverance and relief. I had a gift, given to me long ago by a monster of olden time, and stored in an urn of bronze; a gift which, while yet a girl, I took up from the shaggy-breasted Nessus,—from his life-blood, as he lay dying; Nessus, who used to carry men in his arms for hire across the deep waters of the Evenus, using no oar to waft them, nor sail of ship.

I, too, was carried on his shoulders,—when, by my father's sending, I first went forth with Heracles as his wife; and when I was in mid-stream, he touched me with wanton hands. I shrieked; the son of Zeus turned quickly round, and shot a feathered arrow; it whizzed through his breast to the lungs; and, in his mortal faintness, thus much the Centaur spake:—

'Child of aged Oeneus, thou shalt have at least this profit of my ferrying,—if thou wilt hearken,—because thou wast the last whom I conveyed. If thou gatherest with thy hands the blood clotted round my wound, at the place where the Hydra, Lerna's monstrous growth, hath tinged the arrow with black gall,—this shall be to thee a charm for the soul of Heracles, so that he shall never look upon any woman to love her more than thee.'

I bethought me of this, my friends—for, after his death, I had kept it carefully locked up in a secret place; and I have anointed this robe, doing everything to it as he enjoined while he lived. The work is finished. May deeds of wicked daring be ever far from my thoughts, and from my knowledge,—as I abhor the women who attempt them! But if in any wise I may prevail against this girl by love-spells and charms used on Heracles, the means to that end are ready;—unless, indeed, I seem to be acting rashly: if so, I will desist forthwith.

Ch. Nay, if these measures give any ground of confidence, we think that thy design is not amiss.

De. Well, the ground stands thus,—there is a fair promise; but I have not yet essayed the proof.

Ch. Nay, knowledge must come through action; thou canst have no test which is not fanciful, save by trial.

De. Well, we shall know presently:—for there I see the man already at the doors; and he will soon be going.—Only may my secret be well kept by you! While thy deeds are hidden, even though they be not seemly, thou wilt never be brought to shame.

Enter Lichas.

Li. What are thy commands? Give me my charge, daughter of Oeneus; for already I have tarried over long.

De. Indeed, I have just been seeing to this for thee, Lichas, while thou wast speaking to the stranger maidens in the house;—that thou shouldest take for me this long robe, woven by mine own hand, a gift to mine absent lord.

And when thou givest it, charge him that he, and no other, shall be the first to wear it; that it shall not be seen by the light of the sun, nor by the sacred precinct, nor by the fire at the hearth, until he stand forth, conspicuous before all eyes, and show it to the gods on a day when bulls are slain.

For thus had I vowed,—that if I should ever see or hear that he had come safely home, I would duly clothe him in this robe, and so present him to the gods, newly radiant at their altar in new garb.

As proof, thou shalt carry a token, which he will quickly recognise within the circle of this seal.

Now go thy way; and, first, remember the rule that messengers should not be meddlers; next, so bear thee that my thanks may be joined to his, doubling the grace which thou shalt win.

Li. Nay, if I ply this herald-craft of Hermes with any sureness, I will never trip in doing thine errand: I will not fail to deliver this casket as it is, and to add thy words in attestation of thy gift.

De. Thou mayest be going now; for thou knowest well how things are with us in the house.

Li. I know, and will report, that all hath prospered.

De. And then thou hast seen the greeting given to the stranger maiden—thou knowest how I welcomed her?

Li. So that my heart was filled with wondering joy.

De. What more, then, is there for thee to tell? I am afraid that it would be too soon to speak of the longing on my part, before we know if I am longed for there.

str. 1.Ch. O ye who dwell by the warm springs between haven and crag, and by Oeta's heights; O dwellers by the land-locked waters of the Malian sea, on the shore sacred to the virgin-goddess of the golden shafts, where the Greeks meet in famous council at the Gates;

ant. 1.Soon shall the glorious voice of the flute go up for you again, resounding with no harsh strain of grief, but with such music as the lyre maketh to the gods! For the son whom Alcmena bore to Zeus is hastening homeward, with the trophies of all prowess.

str. 2.He was lost utterly to our land, a wanderer over sea, while we waited through twelve long months, and knew nothing; and his loving wife, sad dweller with sad thoughts, was ever pining amid her tears. But now the War-god, roused to fury, hath delivered her from the days of her mourning.

ant. 2.May he come, may he come! Pause not the manyoared ship that carries him, till he shall have reached this town, leaving the island altar where, as rumour saith, he is sacrificing! Thence may he come, full of desire, steeped in love by the specious device of the robe, on which Persuasion hath spread her sovereign charm!

De. Friends, how I fear that I may have gone too far in all that I have been doing just now!

Ch. What hath happened, Deianeira, daughter of Oeneus?

De. I know not; but feel a misgiving that I shall presently be found to have wrought a great mischief, the issue of a fair hope.

Ch. It is nothing, surely, that concerns thy gift to Heracles?

De. Yea, even so. And henceforth I would say to all, act not with zeal, if ye act without light.

Ch. Tell us the cause of thy fear, if it may be told.

De. A thing hath come to pass, my friends, such that, if I declare it, ye will hear a marvel whereof none could have dreamed.

That with which I was lately anointing the festal robe,—a white tuft of fleecy sheep's wool,—hath disappeared,—not consumed by anything in the house, but self-devoured and self-destroyed, as it crumbled down from the surface of a stone. But I must tell the story more at length, that thou mayest know exactly how this thing befell.

I neglected no part of the precepts which the savage Centaur gave me, when the bitter barb was rankling in his side: they were in my memory, like the graven words which no hand may wash from a tablet of bronze. Now these were his orders, and I obeyed them:—to keep this unguent in a secret place, always remote from fire and from the sun's warm ray, until I should apply it, newly spread, where I wished. So had I done. And now, when the moment for action had come, I performed the anointing privily in the house, with a tuft of soft wool which I had plucked from a sheep of our homeflock; then I folded up my gift, and laid it, unvisited by sunlight, within its casket, as ye saw.

But as I was going back into the house, I beheld a thing too wondrous for words, and passing the wit of man to understand. I happened to have thrown the shred of wool, with which I had been preparing the robe, into the full blaze of the sunshine. As it grew warm, it shrivelled all away, and quickly crumbled to powder on the ground, like nothing so much as the dust shed from a saw's teeth where men work timber. In such a state it lies as it fell. And from the earth, where it was strewn, clots of foam seethed up, as when the rich juice of the blue fruit from the vine of Bacchus is poured upon the ground.

So I know not, hapless one, whither to turn my thoughts; I only see that I have done a fearful deed. Why or wherefore should the monster, in his deaththroes, have shown good will to me, on whose account he was dying? Impossible! No, he was cajoling me, in order to slay the man who had smitten him: and I gain the knowledge of this too late, when it avails no more. Yes, I alone—unless my foreboding prove false—I, wretched one, must destroy him! For I know that the arrow which made the wound did scathe even to the god Cheiron; and it kills all beasts that it touches. And since 'tis this same black venom in the blood that hath passed out through the wound of Nessus, must it not kill my lord also? I ween it must.

Howbeit, I am resolved that, if he is to fall, at the same time I also shall be swept from life; for no woman could bear to live with an evil name, if she rejoices that her nature is not evil.

Ch. Mischief must needs be feared; but it is not well to doom our hope before the event.

De. Unwise counsels leave no room even for a hope which can lend courage.

Ch. Yet towards those who have erred unwittingly, men's anger is softened; and so it should be towards thee.

De. Nay, such words are not for one who has borne a part in the ill deed, but only for him who has no trouble at his own door.

Ch. 'Twere well to refrain from further speech, unless thou would'st tell aught to thine own son; for he is at hand, who went erewhile to seek his sire.

Enter Hyllus.

Hy. O mother, would that one of three things had befallen thee! Would that thou wert dead,—or, if living, no mother of mine,—or that some new and better spirit had passed into thy bosom.

De. Ah, my son, what cause have I given thee to abhor me?

Hy. I tell thee that thy husband—yea, my sire— hath been done to death by thee this day!

De. Oh, what word hath passed thy lips, my child!

Hy. A word that shall not fail of fulfilment; for who may undo that which hath come to pass?

De. What saidst thou, my son? Who is thy warranty for charging me with a deed so terrible?

Hy. I have seen my father's grievous fate with mine own eyes; I speak not from hearsay.

De. And where didst thou find him,—where didst thou stand at his side?

Hy. If thou art to hear it, then must all be told.

After sacking the famous town of Eurytus, he went his way with the trophies and first-fruits of victory. There is a sea-washed headland of Euboea, Cape Cenaeum, where he dedicated altars and a sacred grove to the Zeus of his fathers; and there I first beheld him, with the joy of yearning love.

He was about to celebrate a great sacrifice, when his own herald, Lichas, came to him from home, bearing thy gift, the deadly robe; which he put on, according to thy precept; and then began his offering with twelve bulls, free from blemish, the firstlings of the spoil; but altogether he brought a hundred victims, great or small, to the altar.

At first, hapless one, he prayed with serene soul, rejoicing in his comely garb. But when the blood-fed flame began to blaze from the holy offerings and from the resinous pine, a sweat broke forth upon his flesh, and the tunic clung to his sides, at every joint, closeglued, as if by a craftsman's hand; there came a biting pain that racked his bones; and then the venom, as of some deadly, cruel viper, began to devour him.

Thereupon he shouted for the unhappy Lichas,—in no wise to blame for thy crime,—asking what treason had moved him to bring that robe; but he, all-unknowing, hapless one, said that he had brought the gift from thee alone, as it had been sent. When his master heard it, as a piercing spasm clutched his lungs, he caught him by the foot, where the ankle turns in the socket, and hurled him at a surf-beaten rock in the sea; and he made the white brain to ooze from the hair, as the skull was dashed to splinters, and blood scattered therewith.

But all the people lifted up a cry of awe-struck grief, seeing that one was frenzied, and the other slain; and no one dared to come before the man. For the pain dragged him to earth, or made him leap into the air, with yells and shrieks, till the cliffs rang around, steep headlands of Locris, and Euboean capes.

But when he was spent with oft throwing himself on the ground in his anguish, and oft making loud lament,—cursing his fatal marriage with thee, the vile one, and his alliance with Oeneus,—saying how he had found in it the ruin of his life,—then, from out of the shrouding altar-smoke, he lifted up his wildly-rolling eyes, and saw me in the great crowd, weeping. He turned his gaze on me, and called me: 'O son, draw near; do not fly from my trouble, even though thou must share my death. Come, bear me forth, and set me, if thou canst, in a place where no man shall see me; or, if thy pity forbids that, at least convey me with all speed out of this land, and let me not die where I am.'

That command sufficed; we laid him in mid-ship, and brought him—but hardly brought him—to this shore, moaning in his torments. And ye shall presently behold him, alive, or lately dead.

Such, mother, are the designs and deeds against my sire whereof thou hast been found guilty. May avenging Justice and the Erinys visit thee for them! Yes, if it be right, that is my prayer: and right it is,—for I have seen thee trample on the right, by slaying the noblest man in all the world, whose like thou shalt see nevermore!

[Deianeira *moves towards the house.*

Ch. (*to*Deianeira). Why dost thou depart in silence? Knowest thou not that such silence pleads for thine accuser?

Hy. Let her depart. A fair wind speed her far from my sight! Why should the name of mother bring her a semblance of respect, when she is all unlike a mother in her deeds? No, let her go,—farewell to her; and may such joy as she gives my sire become her own!

str. 1.Ch. See, maidens, how suddenly the divine word of the old prophecy hath come upon us, which said that, when the twelfth year should have run through its full tale of months, it should end the series of toils for the true-born son of Zeus! And that promise is wafted surely to its fulfilment. For how shall he who beholds not the light have toilsome servitude any more beyond the grave?

ant. 1.If a cloud of death is around him, and the doom wrought by the Centaur's craft is stinging his sides, where cleaves the venom which Thanatos begat and the gleaming serpent nourished, how can he look upon to-morrow's sun,—when that appalling Hydra-shape holds him in its grip, and those murderous goads, prepared by the wily words of black-haired Nessus, have started into fury, vexing him with tumultuous pain?

str. 2.Of such things this hapless lady had no foreboding; but she saw a great mischief swiftly coming on her home from the new marriage. Her own hand applied the remedy; but for the issues of a stranger's counsel, given at a fatal meeting,—for these, I ween, she makes despairing lament, shedding the tender dew of plenteous tears. And the coming fate foreshadows a great misfortune, contrived by guile.

ant. 2.Our streaming tears break forth: alas, a plague is upon him more piteous than any suffering that foemen ever brought upon that glorious hero.

Ah, thou dark steel of the spear foremost in battle, by whose might yonder bride was lately borne so swiftly from Oechalia's heights! But the Cyprian goddess, ministering in silence, hath been plainly proved the doer of these deeds.

First Semi-Chorus. Is it fancy, or do I hear some cry of grief just passing through the house? What is this?

Second Semi.-Ch. No uncertain sound, but a wail of anguish from within: the house hath some new trouble.

Ch. And mark how sadly, with what a cloud upon her brow, that aged woman approaches, to give us tidings.

Enter Nurse, *from the house.*

Nu. Ah, my daughters, great, indeed, were the sorrows that we were to reap from the gift sent to Heracles!

Ch. Aged woman, what new mischance hast thou to tell?

Nu. Deianeira hath departed on the last of all her journeys, departed without stirring foot.

Ch. Thou speakest not of death?

Nu. My tale is told.

Ch. Dead, hapless one?

Nu. Again thou hearest it.

Ch. Hapless, lost one! Say, what was the manner of her death?

Nu. Oh, a cruel deed was there!

Ch. Speak, woman, how hath she met her doom?

Nu. By her own hand hath she died.

Ch. What fury, what pangs of frenzy have cut her off by the edge of a dire weapon? How contrived she this death, following death,—all wrought by her alone?

Nu. By the stroke of the sword that makes sorrow.

Ch. Sawest thou that violent deed, poor helpless one?

Nu. I saw it; yea, I was standing near.

Ch. Whence came it? How was it done? Oh, speak!

Nu. 'Twas the work of her own mind and her own hand.

Ch. What dost thou tell us?

Nu. The sure truth.

Ch. The first-born, the first-born of that new bride is a dread Erinys for this house!

Nu. Too true; and, hadst thou been an eye-witness of the action, verily thy pity would have been yet deeper.

Ch. And could a woman's hand dare to do such deeds?

Nu. Yea, with dread daring; thou shalt hear, and then thou wilt bear me witness.

When she came alone into the house, and saw her son preparing a deep litter in the court, that he might go back with it to meet his sire, then she hid herself where none might see; and, falling before the altars, she wailed aloud that they were left desolate; and, when she touched any household thing that she had been wont to use, poor lady, in the past, her tears would flow; or when, roaming hither and thither through the house, she beheld the form of any well-loved servant, she wept, hapless one, at that sight, crying aloud upon her own fate, and that of the household which would thenceforth be in the power of others.

But when she ceased from this, suddenly I beheld her rush into the chamber of Heracles. From a secret place of espial, I watched her; and saw her spreading coverings on the couch of her lord. When she had done this, she sprang thereon, and sat in the middle of the bed; her tears burst forth in burning streams, and thus she spake: 'Ah, bridal bed and bridal chamber mine, farewell now and for ever; never more shall ye receive me to rest upon this couch.' She said no more, but with a vehement hand loosed her robe, where the gold-wrought brooch lay above her breast, baring all her left side and arm. Then I ran with all my strength, and warned her son of her intent. But lo, in the space between my going and our return, she had driven a two-edged sword through her side to the heart.

At that sight, her son uttered a great cry; for he knew, alas, that in his anger he had driven her to that deed; and he had learned, too late, from the servants in the house that she had acted without knowledge, by the prompting of the Centaur. And now the youth, in his misery, bewailed her with all passionate lament; he knelt, and showered kisses on her lips; he threw himself at her side upon the ground, bitterly crying that he had rashly smitten her with a slander,—weeping, that he must now live bereaved of both alike,—of mother and of sire.

Such are the fortunes of this house. Rash indeed, is he who reckons on the morrow, or haply on days beyond it; for to-morrow is not, until to-day is safely past.

str. 1.Ch. Which woe shall I bewail first, which misery is the greater? Alas, 'tis hard for me to tell.

ant. 1.One sorrow may be seen in the house; for one we wait with foreboding: and suspense hath a kinship with pain.

str. 2.Oh that some strong breeze might come with wafting power unto our hearth, to bear me far from this land, lest I die of terror, when I look but once upon the mighty son of Zeus!

For they say that he is approaching the house in torments from which there is no deliverance, a wonder of unutterable woe.

ant. 2.Ah, it was not far off, but close to us, that woe of which my lament gave warning, like the nightingale's piercing note!

Men of an alien race are coming yonder. And how, then, are they bringing him? In sorrow, as for some loved one, they move on their mournful, noiseless march.

Alas, he is brought in silence! What are we to think; that he is dead, or sleeping?

*Enter*Hyllus*and an* Old Man, *with attendants, bearing*Heracles*upon a litter.*

Hy. Woe is me for thee, my father, woe is me for thee, wretched that I am! Whither shall I turn? What can I do? Ah me!

Old Man (*whispering*). Hush, my son! Rouse not the cruel pain that infuriates thy sire! He lives, though prostrated. Oh, put a stern restraint upon thy lips!

Hy. How sayest thou, old man—is he alive?

Old Man (*whispering*). Thou must not awake the slumberer! Thou must not rouse and revive the dread frenzy that visits him, my son!

Hy. Nay, I am crushed with this weight of misery—there is madness in my heart!

HERACLES (*AWAKING*).

O Zeus, to what land have I come? Who are these among whom I lie, tortured with unending agonies? Wretched, wretched that I am! Oh, that dire pest is gnawing me once more!

Old Man (*to*Hyllus). Knew I not how much better it was that thou shouldest keep silence, instead of scaring slumber from his brain and eyes?

Hy. Nay, I cannot be patient when I behold this misery.

He. O thou Cenaean rock whereon mine altars rose, what a cruel reward hast thou won me for those fair offerings,—be Zeus my witness! Ah, to what ruin hast thou brought me, to what ruin! Would that I had never beheld thee for thy sorrow! Then had I never come face to face with this fiery madness, which no spell can soothe! Where is the charmer, where is the cunning healer, save Zeus alone, that shall lull this plague to rest? I should marvel, if he ever came within my ken!

str. 1.Ah!

Leave me, hapless one, to my rest—leave me to my last rest!

str. 2.Where art thou touching me? Whither wouldst thou turn me? Thou wilt kill me, thou wilt kill me! If there be any pang that slumbers, thou hast aroused it!

It hath seized me,—oh, the pest comes again!— Whence are ye, most ungrateful of all the Greeks? I wore out my troublous days in ridding Greece of pests, on the deep and in all forests; and now, when I am stricken, will no man succour me with merciful fire or sword?

ant. 1.Oh, will no one come and sever the head, at one fierce stroke, from this wretched body? Woe, woe is me!

Old Man. Son of Heracles, this task exceeds my strength,—help thou,—for strength is at thy command, too largely to need my aid in his relief.

Hy. My hands are helping; but no resource, in myself or from another, avails me to make his life forget its anguish:—such is the doom appointed by Zeus!

str. 3.He. O my son, where art thou? Raise me,—take hold of me,—thus, thus! Alas, my destiny!

ant. 2.Again, again the cruel pest leaps forth to rend me, the fierce plague with which none may cope!

O Pallas, Pallas, it tortures me again! Alas, my son, pity thy sire,—draw a blameless sword, and smite beneath my collar-bone, and heal this pain wherewith thy godless mother hath made me wild! So may I see her fall,—thus, even thus, as she hath destroyed me!

ant. 3.Sweet Hades, brother of Zeus, give me rest, give me rest,—end my woe by a swiftly-sped doom!

Ch. I shudder, friends, to hear these sorrows of our lord; what a man is here, and what torments afflict him!

He. Ah, fierce full oft, and grievous not in name alone, have been the labours of these hands, the burdens borne upon these shoulders! But no toil ever laid on me by the wife of Zeus or by the hateful Eurystheus was like unto this thing which the daughter of Oeneus, fair and false, hath fastened upon my back,—this woven net of the Furies, in which I perish! Glued to my sides, it hath eaten my flesh to the inmost parts; it is ever with me, sucking the channels of my breath; already it hath drained my fresh life-blood, and my whole body is wasted, a captive to these unutterable bonds.

Not the warrior on the battle-field, not the Giants' earth-born host, nor the might of savage beasts, hath ever done unto me thus,—not Hellas, nor the land of the alien, nor any land to which I have come as a deliverer: no, a woman, a weak woman, born not to the strength of man, all alone hath vanquished me, without stroke of sword!

Son, show thyself my son indeed, and do not honour a mother's name above a sire's: bring forth the woman that bare thee, and give her with thine own hands into my hand, that I may know of a truth which sight grieves thee most,—my tortured frame, or hers, when she suffers her righteous doom!

Go, my son, shrink not—and show thy pity for me, whom many might deem pitiful,—for me, moaning and weeping like a girl;—and the man lives not who can say that he ever saw me do thus before; no, without complaining I still went whither mine evil fortune led. But now, alas, the strong man hath been found a woman.

Approach, stand near thy sire, and see what a fate it is that hath brought me to this pass; for I will lift the veil. Behold! Look, all of you, on this miserable body; see how wretched, how piteous is my plight!

Ah, woe is me!

The burning throe of torment is there anew, it darts through my sides—I must wrestle once more with that cruel, devouring plague!

O thou lord of the dark realm, receive me! Smite me, O fire of Zeus! Hurl down thy thunderbolt, O King, send it, O father, upon my head! For again the pest is consuming me; it hath blazed forth, it hath started into fury! O hands, my hands, O shoulders and breast and trusty arms, ye, now in this plight, are the same whose force of old subdued the dweller in Nemea, the scourge of herdsmen, the lion, a creature that no man might approach or confront; ye tamed the Lernaean Hydra, and that monstrous host of double form, man joined to steed, a race with whom none may commune, violent, lawless, of surpassing might; ye tamed the Erymanthian beast, and the three-headed whelp of Hades underground, a resistless terror, offspring of the dread Echidna; ye tamed the dragon that guarded the golden fruit in the utmost places of the earth.

These toils and countless others have I proved, nor hath any man vaunted a triumph over my prowess. But now, with joints unhinged and with flesh torn to shreds, I have become the miserable prey of an unseen destroyer,—I, who am called the son of noblest mother,—I, whose reputed sire is Zeus, lord of the starry sky.

But ye may be sure of one thing:—though I am as nought, though I cannot move a step, yet she who hath done this deed shall feel my heavy hand even now: let her but come, and she shall learn to proclaim this message unto all, that in my death, as in my life, I chastised the wicked!

Ch. Ah, hapless Greece, what mourning do I foresee for her, if she must lose this man!

Hy. Father, since thy pause permits an answer, hear me, afflicted though thou art. I will ask thee for no more than is my due. Accept my counsels, in a calmer mood than that to which this anger stings thee: else thou canst not learn how vain is thy desire for vengeance, and how causeless thy resentment.

He. Say what thou wilt, and cease; in this my pain I understand nought of all thy riddling words.

Hy. I come to tell thee of my mother,—how it is now with her, and how she sinned unwittingly.

He. Villain! What—hast thou dared to breathe her name again in my hearing,—the name of the mother who hath slain thy sire?

Hy. Yea, such is her state that silence is unmeet.

He. Unmeet, truly, in view of her past crimes.

Hy. And also of her deeds this day,—as thou wilt own.

He. Speak,—but give heed that thou be not found a traitor.

Hy. These are my tidings. She is dead, lately slain.

He. By whose hand? A wondrous message, from a prophet of ill-omened voice!

Hy. By her own hand, and no stranger's.

He. Alas, ere she died by mine, as she deserved!

Hy. Even thy wrath would be turned, couldst thou hear all.

He. A strange preamble; but unfold thy meaning.

Hy. The sum is this;—she erred, with a good intent.

He. Is it a good deed, thou wretch, to have slain thy sire?

Hy. Nay, she thought to use a love-charm for thy heart, when she saw the new bride in the house; but missed her aim.

He. And what Trachinian deals in spells so potent?

Hy. Nessus the Centaur persuaded her of old to inflame thy desire with such a charm.

He. Alas, alas, miserable that I am! Woe is me, I am lost,—undone, undone! No more for me the light of day! Alas, now I see in what a plight I stand! Go, my son,—for thy father's end hath come,—summon, I pray thee, all thy brethren; summon, too, the hapless Alcmena, in vain the bride of Zeus,—that ye may learn from my dying lips what oracles I know.

Hy. Nay, thy mother is not here; as it chances, she hath her abode at Tiryns by the sea. Some of thy children she hath taken to live with her there, and others, thou wilt find, are dwelling in Thebè's town. But we who are with thee, my father, will render all service that is needed, at thy bidding.

He. Hear, then, thy task: now is the time to show what stuff is in thee, who art called my son.

It was foreshown to me by my Sire of old that I should perish by no creature that had the breath of life, but by one that had passed to dwell with Hades. So I have been slain by this savage Centaur, the living by the dead, even as the divine will had been foretold.

And I will show thee how later oracles tally therewith, confirming the old prophecy. I wrote them down in the grove of the Selli, dwellers on the hills, whose couch is on the ground; they were given by my Father's oak of many tongues; which said that, at the time which liveth and now is, my release from the toils laid upon me should be accomplished. And I looked for prosperous days; but the meaning, it seems, was only that I should die; for toil comes no more to the dead.

Since, then, my son, those words are clearly finding their fulfilment, thou, on thy part, must lend me thine aid. Thou must not delay, and so provoke me to bitter speech: thou must consent and help with a good grace, as one who hath learned that best of laws, obedience to a sire.

Hy. Yea, father,—though I fear the issue to which our talk hath brought me,—I will do thy good pleasure.

He. First of all, lay thy right hand in mine.

Hy. For what purpose dost thou insist upon this pledge?

He. Give thy hand at once—disobey me not!

Hy. Lo, there it is: thou shalt not be gainsaid.

He. Now, swear by the head of Zeus my sire!

Hy. To do what deed? May this also be told?

He. To perform for me the task that I shall enjoin.

Hy. I swear it, with Zeus for witness of the oath.

He, And pray that, if thou break this oath, thou mayest suffer.

Hy. I shall not suffer, for I shall keep it:—yet so I pray.

He. Well, thou knowest the summit of Oeta, sacred to Zeus?

Hy. Ay; I have often stood at his altar on that height.

159

He. Thither, then, thou must carry me up with thine own hands, aided by what friends thou wilt; thou shalt lop many a branch from the deep-rooted oak, and hew many a faggot also from the sturdy stock of the wild-olive; thou shalt lay my body thereupon, and kindle it with flaming pine-torch.

And let no tear of mourning be seen there; no, do this without lament and without weeping, if thou art indeed my son. But if thou do it not, even from the world below my curse and my wrath shall wait on thee for ever.

Hy. Alas, my father, what hast thou spoken? How hast thou dealt with me!

He. I have spoken that which thou must perform; if thou wilt not, then get thee some other sire, and be called my son no more!

Hy. Woe, woe is me! What a deed dost thou require of me, my father,—that I should become thy murderer, guilty of thy blood!

He. Not so, in truth, but healer of my sufferings, sole physician of my pain!

Hy. And how, by enkindling thy body, shall I heal it?

He. Nay, if that thought dismay thee, at least perform the rest.

Hy. The service of carrying thee shall not be refused.

He. And the heaping of the pyre, as I have bidden?

Hy. Yea, save that I will not touch it with mine own hand. All else will I do, and thou shalt have no hindrance on my part.

He. Well, so much shall be enough.—But add one small boon to thy large benefits.

Hy. Be the boon never so large, it shall be granted.

He. Knowest thou, then, the girl whose sire was Eurytus?

Hy. It is of Iolè that thou speakest, if I mistake not.

He. Even so. This, in brief, is the charge that I give thee, my son. When I am dead, if thou wouldest show a pious remembrance of thine oath unto thy father, disobey me not, but take this woman to be thy wife. Let no other espouse her who hath lain at my side, but do thou, O my son, make that marriage-bond thine own. Consent: after loyalty in great matters, to rebel in less is to cancel the grace that had been won.

Hy. Ah me, it is not well to be angry with a sick man: but who could bear to see him in such a mind?

He. Thy words show no desire to do my bidding.

Hy. What! When she alone is to blame for my mother's death, and for thy present plight besides? Lives there the man who would make such a choice, unless he were maddened by avenging fiends?

Better were it, father, that I too should die, rather than live united to the worst of our foes!

He. He will render no reverence, it seems, to my dying prayer.—Nay, be sure that the curse of the gods will attend thee for disobedience to my voice.

Hy. Ah, thou wilt soon show, methinks, how distempered thou art!

He. Yea, for thou art breaking the slumber of my plague.

Hy. Hapless that I am! What perplexities surround me!

He. Yea, since thou deignest not to hear thy sire.

Hy. But must I learn, then, to be impious, my father?

He. 'Tis not impiety, if thou shalt gladden my heart.

Hy. Dost thou command me, then, to do this deed, as a clear duty?

He. I command thee,—the gods bear me witness!

Hy. Then will I do it, and refuse not,—calling upon the gods to witness thy deed. I can never be condemned for loyalty to thee, my father.

He. Thou endest well; and to these words, my son, quickly add the gracious deed, that thou mayest lay me on the pyre before any pain returns to rend or sting me.

Come, make haste and life me! This, in truth, is rest from troubles; this is the end, the last end, of Heracles!

Hy. Nothing, indeed, hinders the fulfilment of thy wish, since thy command constrains us, my father.

He. Come, then, ere thou arouse this plague, O my stubborn soul, give me a curb as of steel on lips set like stone to stone, and let no cry escape them; seeing that the deed which thou art to do, though done perforce, is yet worthy of thy joy!

Hy. Lift him, followers! And grant me full forgiveness for this; but mark the great cruelty of the gods in the deeds that are being done. They beget children, they are hailed as fathers, and yet they can look upon such sufferings.

No man foresees the future; but the present is fraught with mourning for us, and with shame for the powers above, and verily with anguish beyond compare for him who endures this doom.

Maidens, come ye also, nor linger at the house; ye who have lately seen a dread death, with sorrows manifold and strange: and in all this there is nought but Zeus.

PHILOCTETE

PERSONS OF THE DRAMA.

Odysseus.
Neoptolemus.
Philoctetes.
Merchant (*a follower of Neoptolemus in disguise*).
Heracles.
Chorus of Sailors *belonging to the ship of Neoptolemus.*

Scene: On the north-east coast of Lemnos, near the promontory of Mount Hermaeum. A rocky cliff rises steeply from the sea-shore (cp. 1000 ff.): in it is seen the cave of Philoctetes.

When Heracles was burned, by his own command, on Mount Oeta, the funeral-pile was kindled, at his prayer, by the youthful Philoctetes, son of Poeas, King of Malis. It was to Philoctetes that Heracles bequeathed the bow and arrows which he himself had received from Apollo.

Many years afterwards, Philoctetes came with seven ships to join the Greek armada which Agamemnon led against Troy. An oracle had enjoined that, in the course of their voyage, the Greeks should offer sacrifice to a deity named Chryse, whose altar was on a small island in the Aegean. Philoctetes alone knew where this altar was; he had once visited it in company with Heracles: and he guided the Greeks thither. The altar of Chryse stood in a sacred precinct under the open sky. As Philoctetes approached it, followed by the Greek chiefs, he was bitten in the foot by a serpent. His cries of pain made it impossible to perform the religious rites, which required the absence of all ill-omened sounds; and a noisome odour from the wound rendered the sufferer's presence a distress to his ship-mates. They conveyed him to the neighbouring coast of Lemnos; and there, at the bidding of the Atreidae, Odysseus put him ashore in his sleep, with only a scanty dole of food. The Greeks then sailed away to Troy. Lemnos was an uninhabited island. Philoctetes had his bow and arrows, and, though he could not crawl far from his cave, contrived to subsist by shooting birds.

Ten years had passed since the Greek chiefs did this inhuman deed. They were still besieging Troy. Achilles had fallen; Ajax had died by his own hand; and the Greeks were despondent. Their prophet Calchas told them that, if they wished to learn the destiny of Ilium, they must consult a Trojan seer, Helenus, son of Priam. Helenus was made prisoner by a stratagem of Odysseus; and then declared that, before the Greeks could prevail, two things must be done. First, Philoctetes must be brought back from Lemnos: Troy could never fall, until the invincible arrows of Heracles were launched against its defenders. Secondly, Neoptolemus, the youthful son of Achilles, must come from the island of Scyros, and must receive his due heritage, the armour wrought for his father by the God Hephaestus; which, after that hero's death, had been awarded by the chiefs to Odysseus.

The Greeks obeyed these precepts. Phoenix and Odysseus went to Scyros, and brought the young Neoptolemus to Troy, where his father's armour was duly given to him. Odysseus then set out for Lemnos, accompanied by Neoptolemus,—each chief sailing in his own ship. At the moment when the play begins, they have just landed on the north-east coast of Lemnos.

ODYSSEUS.

This is the shore of the sea-girt land of Lemnos, untrodden of men and desolate. O thou whose sire was the noblest of the Greeks, true-bred son of Achilles, Neoptolemus,—here, long ago, I put ashore the Malian, the son of Poeas, (having charge from my chiefs so to do,)—his foot all ulcerous with a gnawing sore,—when neither drink-offering nor sacrifice could be attempted10 by us in peace, but with his fierce, ill-omened cries he filled the whole camp continually, shrieking, moaning. But what need to speak of that? 'Tis no time for many words, lest he learn that I am here, and I waste the whole plan whereby I think to take him anon.

Come, to work!—'tis for thee to help in what remains, and to seek where in this region is a cave with twofold mouth, such that in cold weather either front offers a sunny seat, but in summer a breeze wafts20 sleep through the tunnelled grot. And a little below, on the left hand, perchance thou wilt see a spring, if it hath not failed.

Move thither silently, and signify to me whether he still dwells in this same place, or is to be sought elsewhere,—that so our further course may be explained by me, and heard by thee, and sped by the joint work of both.

NEOPTOLEMUS.

King Odysseus, the task that thou settest lies not far off; methinks I see such a cave as thou hast described.

Od. Above thee, or below? I perceive it not.

Ne. Here, high up;—and of footsteps not a sound.

Od. Look that he be not lodged there, asleep.30

Ne. I see an empty chamber,—no man therein.

Od. And no provision in it for man's abode?

Ne. Aye, a mattress of leaves, as if for some one who makes his lodging here.

Od. And all else is bare? Nought else beneath the roof?

Ne. Just a rude cup of wood, the work of a sorry craftsman; and this tinder-stuff therewith.

Od. His is the household store whereof thou tellest.

Ne. Ha! Yes, and here are some rags withal, drying in the sun,—stained with matter from some grievous sore.

Od. The man dwells in these regions, clearly, and40 is somewhere not far off; how could one go far afield, with foot maimed by that inveterate plague? No, he hath gone forth in quest of food, or of some soothing herb, haply, that he hath noted somewhere. Send thine attendant, therefore, to keep watch, lest the foe come on me unawares; for he would rather take me than all the Greeks beside.

Ne. Enough, the man is going, and the path shall be watched.—And now, if thou wouldst say more, proceed. [*Exit* Attendant, *on the spectators' left.*

Od.50 Son of Achilles, thou must be loyal to thy mission,—and not with thy body alone. Shouldst thou hear some new thing, some plan unknown to thee till now, thou must help it; for to help is thy part here.

Ne. What is thy bidding?

Od. Thou must beguile the mind of Philoctetes by a story told in thy converse with him. When he asks thee who and whence thou art, say, the son of Achilles,—there must be no deception touching that; but thou art homeward bound,—thou hast left the fleet of the Achaean warriors, and hast conceived a deadly hatred60 for them; who, when they had moved thee by their prayers to come from home, deemed thee not worthy of the arms of Achilles,—deigned not to give them to thee when thou camest and didst claim them by right,—but made them over to Odysseus. Of

163

me, say what thou wilt,—the vilest of vile reproaches;—thou wilt cost me no pang by that;—but if thou fail to do this deed, thou wilt bring sorrow on all our host. For if yon man's bow is not to be taken, never canst thou sack the realm of Dardanus.

70 And mark why thine intercourse with him may be free from mistrust or danger, while mine cannot. *Thou* hast come to Troy under no oath to any man, and by no constraint; nor hadst thou part in the earlier voyage: but none of these things can I deny. And so, if he shall perceive me while he is still master of his bow, I am lost, and thou, as my comrade, wilt share my doom. No; the thing that must be plotted is just this,—how thou mayest win the resistless arms by stealth. I well know, my son, that by nature thou art not apt to utter80 or contrive such guile; yet, seeing that victory is a sweet prize to gain, bend thy will thereto; our honesty shall be shown forth another time. But now lend thyself to me for one little knavish day, and then, through all thy days to come, be called the most righteous of mankind.

Ne. When counsels pain my ear, son of Laertes, then I abhor to aid them with my hand. It is not in my nature to compass aught by evil arts,—nor was it, as men say, in my sire's. But I am ready to take the90 man by force,—not by fraud;—for, having the use of one foot only, he cannot prevail in fight against us who are so many. And yet, having been sent to act with thee, I am loth to be called traitor. But my wish, O King, is to do right and miss my aim, rather than succeed by evil ways.

Od. Son of brave sire, time was when I too, in my youth, had a slow tongue and a ready hand: but now, when I come forth to the proof, I see that words, not deeds, are ever the masters among men.

Ne. What, then, is thy command? What, but that I should lie?

Od. I say that thou art to take Philoctetes by guile.

Ne. And why by guile rather than by persuasion?

Od. He will never listen; and by force thou canst not take him.

Ne. Hath he such dread strength to make him bold?

Od. Shafts inevitable, and winged with death.

Ne. None may dare, then, e'en to approach that foe?

Od. No, unless thou take him by guile, as I say.

Ne. Thou thinkest it no shame, then, to speak falsehoods?

Od. No, if the falsehood brings deliverance.

Ne. And how shall one have the face to speak those words?

Od. When thy deed promises gain, 'tis unmeet to shrink.

Ne. And what gain is it for me, that he should come to Troy?

Od. With these shafts alone can Troy be taken.

Ne. Then *I* am not to be the conqueror, as ye said?

Od. Neither thou apart from these, nor these from thee.

Ne. 'Twould seem that we must try to win them, if it stands thus.

Od. Know that, if thou dost this thing, two prizes are thine.

Ne. What are they? Tell me, and I will not refuse the deed.

Od. Thou wilt be called at once wise and valiant.

Ne. Come what may, I'll do it, and cast off all shame.

Od. Art thou mindful, then, of the counsels that I gave?

Ne. Be sure of it,—now that once I have consented.

Od. Do thou, then, stay here, in wait for him; but I will go away, lest I be espied with thee, and will send our watcher back to the ship. And, if ye seem to be tarrying at all beyond the due time, I will send that same man hither again, disguised as the captain of a merchant-ship, that secrecy may aid us; and then, my son, as he tells his artful story, take such hints as may help thee from the tenor of his words.

Now I will go to the ship, having left this charge with thee; and may speeding Hermes, the lord of stratagem, lead us on, and Victory, even Athena Polias, who saves me ever!

[*Exit* Odysseus, *on the spectators' left.*

CHORUS.

str. 1. A stranger in a strange land, what am I to hide, what am I to speak, O Master, before a man who will be swift to think evil? Be thou my guide: his skill excels all other skill, his counsel hath no peer, with whom is the sway of the godlike sceptre given by Zeus. And to thee, my son, that sovereign power hath descended from of old; tell me, therefore, wherein I am to serve thee.

syst. 1. Ne. For the present,—as haply thou wouldst behold the place where he abides on ocean's verge,—survey it fearlessly: but when the dread wayfarer, who hath left this dwelling, shall return, come forward at my beck from time to time, and try to help as the moment may require.

ant. 1. Ch. Long have I been careful of that care, my prince,—that mine eye should be watchful for thy good, before all else. And now tell me, in what manner of shelter hath he made his abode? In what region is he? 'Twere not unseasonable for me to learn, lest he surprise me from some quarter. What is the place of his wandering, or of his rest? Where planteth he his steps, within his dwelling, or abroad?

syst. 2. Ne. Here thou seest his home, with its two portals,—his rocky cell.

Ch. And its hapless inmate,—whither is he gone?

Ne. I doubt not but he is trailing his painful steps somewhere near this spot, in quest of food. For rumour saith that in this fashion he lives, seeking prey with his winged shafts, all-wretched that he is; and no healer of his woe draws nigh unto him.

str. 2. Ch. I pity him, to think how, with no man to care for him, and seeing no companion's face, suffering, lonely evermore, he is vexed by fierce disease, and bewildered by each want as it arises. How, how doth he endure in his misery? Alas, the dark dealings of the gods! Alas, hapless races of men, whose destiny exceeds due measure!

ant. 2. This man,—noble, perchance, as any scion of the noblest house,—reft of all life's gifts, lies lonely, apart from his fellows, with the dappled or shaggy beasts of the field, piteous alike in his torments and his hunger, bearing anguish that finds no cure; while the mountain nymph, babbling Echo, appearing afar, makes answer to his bitter cries.

syst. 3. Ne. Nought of this is a marvel to me. By heavenly ordinance, if such as I may judge, those first sufferings came on him from relentless Chrysè; and the woes that now he bears, with none to tend him, surely he bears by the providence of some god, that so he should not bend against Troy the resistless shafts divine, till the time be fulfilled when, as men say, Troy is fated by those shafts to fall.

str. 3. Ch. Hush, peace, my son! Ne. What now? Ch. A sound rose on the air, such as might haunt the lips of a man in weary pain.—From this point it came, I think,—or this.—It smites, it smites indeed upon my ear—the voice of one who creeps

165

painfully on his way; I cannot mistake that grievous cry of human anguish from afar,—its accents are too clear.

ant. 3.Then turn thee, O my son— Ne. Say, whither?— Ch. —to new counsels: for the man is not far off, but near; not with music of the reed he cometh, like shepherd in the pastures,—no, but with far-sounding moan, as he stumbles, perchance, from stress of pain, or as he gazes on the haven that hath no ship for guest: loud is his cry, and dread.

*Enter*Philoctetes,*on the spectators' right.*

Ph. O strangers!

Who may ye be, and from what country have ye put into this land, that is harbourless and desolate? What should I deem to be your city or your race?

The fashion of your garb is Greek,—most welcome to my sight,—but I fain would hear your speech: and do not shrink from me in fear, or be scared by my wild looks; nay, in pity for one so wretched and so lonely, for a sufferer so desolate and so friendless, speak to me, if indeed ye have come as friends.—Oh, answer! 'Tis not meet that I should fail of this, at least, from you, or ye from me.

Ne. Then know this first, good Sir, that we are Greeks,—since thou art fain to learn that.

Ph. O well-loved sound! Ah, that I should indeed be greeted by such a man, after so long a time! What quest, my son, hath drawn thee towards these shores, and to this spot? What enterprise? What kindliest of winds? Speak, tell me all, that I may know who thou art.

Ne. My birthplace is the seagirt Scyros; I am sailing homeward; Achilles was my sire; my name is Neoptolemus:—thou know'st all.

Ph. O son of well-loved father and dear land, foster-child of aged Lycomedes, on what errand hast thou touched this coast? Whence art thou sailing?

Ne. Well, it is from Ilium that I hold my present course.

Ph. What? Thou wast not, certainly, our shipmate at the beginning of the voyage to Ilium.

Ne. Hadst thou, indeed, a part in that emprise?

Ph. O my son, then thou know'st not who is before thee?

Ne. How should I know one whom I have never seen before?

Ph. Then thou hast not even heard my name, or any rumour of those miseries by which I was perishing?

Ne. Be assured that I know nothing of what thou askest.

Ph. O wretched indeed that I am, O abhorred of heaven, that no word of this my plight should have won its way to my home, or to any home of Greeks! No, the men who wickedly cast me out keep their secret and laugh, while my plague still rejoices in its strength, and grows to more!

O my son, O boy whose father was Achilles, behold, I am he of whom haply thou hast heard as lord of the bow of Heracles,—I am the son of Poeas, Philoctetes, whom the two chieftains and the Cephallenian king foully cast upon this solitude, when I was wasting with a fierce disease, stricken down by the furious bite of the destroying serpent; with that plague for sole companion, O my son, those men put me out here, and were gone,—when from sea-girt Chrysè they touched at this coast with their fleet. Glad, then, when they saw me asleep—after much tossing on the waves—in the shelter of a cave upon the shore, they abandoned me,—first putting out a few rags,—good enough for such a wretch,—and a scanty dole of food withal:—may Heaven give them the like!

Think now, my son, think what a waking was mine, when they had gone, and I rose from sleep that day! What bitter tears started from mine eyes,—what miseries were those that I bewailed when I saw that the ships with which I had sailed were all gone, and that there was no man in the place,—not one to help, not one to ease the burden of the sickness that vexed me,—when, looking all around, I could find no provision, save for anguish—but of that a plenteous store, my son!

So time went on for me, season by season; and, alone in this narrow house, I was fain to meet each want by mine own service. For hunger's needs this bow provided, bringing down the winged doves; and, whatever my string-sped shaft might strike, I, hapless one, would crawl to it myself, trailing my wretched foot just so far; or if, again, water had to be fetched,—or if (when the frost was out, perchance, as oft in winter) a bit of fire-wood had to be broken,—I would creep forth, poor wretch, and manage it. Then fire would be lacking; but by rubbing stone on stone I would at last draw forth the hidden spark; and this it is that keeps life in me from day to day. Indeed, a roof over my head, and fire therewith, gives all that I want—save release from my disease.

Come now, my son, thou must learn what manner of isle this is. No mariner approaches it by choice; there is no anchorage; there is no sea-port where he can find a gainful market or a kindly welcome. This is not a place to which prudent men make voyages. Well, suppose that some one has put in against his will; such things may oft happen in the long course of a man's life. These visitors, when they come, have compassionate words for me; and perchance, moved by pity, they give me a little food, or some raiment: but there is one thing that no one will do, when I speak of it,—take me safe home; no, this is now the tenth year that I am wearing out my wretched days, in hunger and in misery, feeding the plague that is never sated with my flesh.

Thus have the Atreidae and the proud Odysseus dealt with me, my son: may the Olympian gods some day give them the like sufferings, in requital for mine!

Ch. Methinks I too pity thee, son of Poeas, in like measure with thy former visitors.

Ne. And I am myself a witness to thy words,—I know that they are true; for I have felt the villainy of the Atreidae and the proud Odysseus.

Ph. What, hast thou, too, a grief against the accursed sons of Atreus,—a cause to resent ill-usage?

Ne. Oh that it might be mine one day to wreak my hatred with my hand, that so Mycenae might learn, and Sparta, that Scyros also is a mother of brave men!

Ph. Well said, my son! Now wherefore hast thou come in this fierce wrath which thou denouncest against them?

Ne. Son of Poeas, I will speak out—and yet 'tis hard to speak—concerning the outrage that I suffered from them at my coming. When fate decreed that Achilles should die—

Ph. Ah me! Tell me no more, until I first know this—say'st thou that the son of Peleus is dead?

Ne. Dead,—by no mortal hand, but by a god's; laid low, as men say, by the arrow of Phoebus.

Ph. Well, noble alike are the slayer and the slain! I scarce know, my son, which I should do first,—inquire into thy wrong, or mourn the dead.

Ne. Methinks thine own sorrows, unhappy man, are enough for thee, without mourning for the woes of thy neighbour.

Ph. Thou sayest truly.—Resume thy story, then, and tell me wherein they did thee a despite.

Ne. They came for me in a ship with gaily decked prow,—princely Odysseus, and he who watched over my father's youth,—saying, (whether truly or falsely, I know not,) that since my father had perished, fate now forbad that the towers of Troy should be taken by any hand but mine.

Saying that these things stood thus, my friend, they made me pause not long ere I set forth in haste,—chiefly through my yearning towards the dead, that I might see him before burial,—for I had never seen him; then, besides, there was a charm in their promise, if, when I went, I should sack the towers of Troy.

It was now the second day of my voyage, when, sped by breeze and oar, I drew nigh to cruel Sigeum. And when I landed, straightway all the host thronged around me with greetings, vowing that they saw their lost Achilles once more alive.

He, then, lay dead; and I, hapless one, when I had wept for him, presently went to the Atreidae,—to friends, as I well might deem,—and claimed my father's arms, with all else that had been his. O, 'twas a shameless answer that they made! 'Seed of Achilles, thou canst take all else that was thy sire's; but of those arms another man now is lord,—the son of Laertes.' The tears came into my eyes,—I sprang up in passionate anger, and said in my bitterness,—'Wretch! What, have ye dared to give my arms to another man, without my leave?' Then said Odysseus,—for he chanced to be near,—'Yea, boy, this award of theirs is just; I saved the arms and their master at his need.' Then straightway, in my fury, I began to hurl all manner of taunts at him, and spared not one, if I was indeed to be robbed of my arms by *him*. At this point,—stung by the abuse, though not prone to wrath,—he answered,—'Thou wast not here with us, but absent from thy duty. And since thou must talk so saucily, thou shalt never carry those arms back to Scyros.'

Thus upbraided, thus insulted, I sail for home, despoiled of mine own by that worst offspring of an evil breed, Odysseus. And yet he, I think, is less to blame than the rulers. For an army, like a city, hangs wholly on its leaders; and when men do lawless deeds, 'tis the counsel of their teachers that corrupts them. My tale is told; and may the foe of the Atreidae have the favour of Heaven, as he hath mine!

*str.*Ch. Goddess of the hills, all-fostering Earth, mother of Zeus most high, thou through whose realm the great Pactolus rolls golden sands,—there also, dread Mother, I called upon thy name, when all the insults of the Atreidae were being heaped upon this man,—when they were giving his sire's armour, that peerless marvel, to the son of Lartius—hear it, thou immortal one, who ridest on bull-slaughtering lions!

Ph. It seems that ye have come to me, friends, well commended by a common grief; and your story is of a like strain with mine, so that I can recognise the work of the Atreidae and of Odysseus. For well I know that he would lend his tongue to any base pretext, to any villainy, if thereby he could hope to compass some dishonest end. No, 'tis not at this that I wonder, but rather that the elder Ajax, if he was there, could endure to see it.

Ne. Ah, friend, he was no more; I should never have been thus plundered while he lived.

Ph. How sayest thou? What, is he, too, dead and gone?

Ne. Think of him as of one who sees the light no more.

Ph. Woe is me! But the son of Tydeus, and the offspring of Sisyphus that was bought by Laertes—they will not die; for they ought not to live

Ne. Not they, be sure of it; no, they are now prospering full greatly in the Argive host.

Ph. And what of my brave old friend, Nestor of Pylos,—is he not alive? *Their* mischiefs were often baffled by his wise counsels.

Ne. Aye, he has trouble now; death has taken Antilochus, the son that was at his side.

Ph. Ah me! These two, again, whom thou hast named, are men of whose death I had least wished to hear. Alas! What are we to look for, when these have died, and, here again, Odysseus lives,—when he, in their place, should have been numbered with the dead?

Ne. A clever wrestler he; but even clever schemes, Philoctetes, are often tripped up.

Ph. Now tell me, I pray thee, where was Patroclus in this thy need,—he whom thy father loved so well?

Ne. He, too, was dead. And to be brief, I would tell thee this,—war takes no evil man by choice, but good men always.

Ph. I bear thee witness;—and for that same reason I will ask thee how fares a man of little worth, but shrewd of tongue and clever—

Ne. Surely this will be no one but Odysseus?—

Ph. I meant not him:—but there was one Thersites, who could never be content with brief speech, though all men chafed:—know'st thou if he is alive?

Ne. I saw him not, but heard that he still lives.

Ph. It was his due. No evil thing has been known to perish; no, the gods take tender care of such, and have a strange joy in turning back from Hades all things villainous and knavish, while they are ever sending the just and the good out of life. How am I to deem of these things, or wherein shall I praise them, when, praising the ways of the gods, I find that the gods are evil?

Ne. Son of Oetean sire, I, at least, shall be on my guard henceforth against Ilium and the Atreidae, nor look on them save from afar; and where the worse man is stronger than the good,—where honesty fails and the dastard bears sway,—among such men will I never make my friends. No, rocky Scyros shall suffice for me henceforth, nor shall I ask a better home.

Now to my ship! And thou, son of Poeas, farewell,—heartily farewell; and the gods deliver thee from thy sickness, even as thou wouldst! But we must be going, so that we may set forth whenever the god permits our voyage.

Ph. Do ye start now, my son?

Ne. Aye, prudence bids us watch the weather near our ship, rather than from afar.

Ph. Now by thy father and by thy mother, my son—by all that is dear to thee in thy home—solemnly I implore thee, leave me not thus forlorn, helpless amid these miseries in which I live,—such as thou seest, and many as thou hast heard! Nay, spare a passing thought to me.—Great is the discomfort, I well know, of such a freight;—yet bear with it: to noble minds baseness is hateful, and a good deed is glorious. Forsake this task, and thy fair name is sullied; perform it, my son, and a rich meed of glory will be thine, if I return alive to Oeta's land. Come, the trouble lasts not one whole day:—make the effort—take and thrust me where thou wilt, in hold, in prow, in stern,—wherever I shall least annoy my ship-mates.

O consent, by the great Zeus of suppliants, my son,—be persuaded! I supplicate thee on my knees, infirm as I am, poor wretch, and maimed! Nay, leave me not thus desolate, far from the steps of men! Nay, bring me safely to thine own home, or to Euboea, Chalcodon's seat; and thence it will be no long journey for me to Oeta, and the Trachinian heights, and the fair-flowing Spercheius, that thou mayest show me to my beloved sire; of whom I have long feared that he may have gone from me. For often did I summon him by those who came, with imploring prayers that he would himself send a ship, and fetch me home. But either he is dead, or else, methinks, my messengers—as was likely—made small account of my concerns, and hastened on their homeward voyage.

Now, however—since in thee I have found one who can carry at once my message and myself—do thou save me, do thou show me mercy,—seeing how all human destiny is full of the fear and the peril that good fortune may be followed by evil. He who stands clear of trouble should beware of dangers; and when a man lives at ease, then it is that he should look most closely to his life, lest ruin come on it by stealth.

*ant.*Ch. Have pity, O king; he hath told of a struggle with sufferings manifold and grievous; may the like befall no friend of mine! And if, my prince, thou hatest the hateful Atreidae, then, turning their misdeed to this man's gain, I would waft him in thy good swift ship to the home for which he yearns, that so thou flee the just wrath of Heaven.

Ne. Beware lest, though now, as a spectator, thou art pliant, yet, when wearied of his malady by consorting with it, thou be found no longer constant to these words.

Ch. No, verily: never shalt thou have cause to utter that reproach against me!

Ne. Nay, then, it were shame that the stranger should find me less prompt than thou art to serve him at his need.—Come, if it please you, let us sail: let the man set forth at once; our ship, for her part, will carry him, and will not refuse.—Only may the gods convey us safely out of this land, and hence to our haven, wheresoever it be!

Ph. O most joyful day! O kindest friend—and ye, good sailors—would that I could prove to you in deeds what love ye have won from me! Let us be going, my son, when thou and I have made a solemn farewell to the homeless home within,—that thou mayest e'en learn by what means I sustained life, and how stout a heart hath been mine. For I believe that the bare sight would have deterred any other man from enduring such a lot; but I have been slowly schooled by necessity to patience.

[*Neoptolemus is about to follow Philoctetes into the cave.*

Ch. Stay, let us give heed:—two men are coming, one a seaman of thy ship, the other a stranger: ye should hear their tidings before ye go in.

*Enter*Merchant,*on the spectators' left, accompanied by a Sailor.*

Me. Son of Achilles, I asked my companion here,—who, with two others, was guarding thy ship,—to tell me where thou mightest be,—since I have fallen in with

170

thee, when I did not expect it, by the chance of coming to anchor off the same coast. Sailing, in trader's wise, with no great company, homeward bound from Ilium to Peparethus with its cluster-laden vines,—when I heard that the sailors were all of thy crew, I resolved not to go on my voyage in silence, without first giving thee my news, and reaping guerdon due. Thou knowest nothing, I suspect, of thine own affairs— the new designs that the Greeks have regarding thee,—nay, not designs merely, but deeds in progress, and no longer tarrying.

Ne. Truly, Sir, the grace shown me by thy forethought, if I be not unworthy, shall live in my grateful thoughts. But tell me just what it is whereof thou hast spoken,— that I may learn what strange design on the part of the Greeks thou announcest to me.

Me. Pursuers have started in quest of thee with ships,—the aged Phoenix and the sons of Theseus.

Ne. To bring me back by force, or by fair words?

Me. I know not; but I have come to tell thee what I have heard.

Ne. Can Phoenix and his comrades be showing such zeal on such an errand, to please the Atreidae?

Me. The errand is being done, I can assure thee,—and without delay.

Ne. Why, then, was not Odysseus ready to sail for this purpose, and to bring the message himself? Or did some fear restrain him?

Me. Oh, he and the son of Tydeus were setting forth in pursuit of another man, as I was leaving port.

Ne. Who was this other in quest of whom Odysseus himself was sailing?

Me. There was a man... But tell me first who that is yonder,—and whatever thou sayest, speak not loud.

Ne. Sir, thou seest the renowned Philoctetes.

Me. Ask me no more, then, but convey thyself with all speed out of this land.

Ph. What is he saying, my son? Why is the sailor trafficking with thee about me in these dark whispers?

Ne. I know not his meaning yet; but whatever he would say he must say openly to thee and me and these.

Me. Seed of Achilles, do not accuse me to the army of saying what I should not; I receive many benefits from them for my services,—as a poor man may.

Ne. I am the foe of the Atreidae, and this man is my best friend, because he hates them. Since, then, thou hast come with a kindly purpose towards me, thou must not keep from us any part of the tidings that thou hast heard.

Me. See what thou doest, my son.

Ne. I am well aware.

Me. I will hold thee accountable.

Ne. Do so, but speak.

Me. I obey. 'Tis in quest of this man that those two are sailing whom I named to thee,—the son of Tydeus and mighty Odysseus,—sworn to bring him, either by winning words or by constraining force. And all the Achaeans heard this plainly from Odysseus,—for his confidence of success was higher than his comrade's.

Ne. And wherefore, after so long a time, did the Atreidae turn their thoughts towards this man, whom long since they had cast forth? What was the yearning that came to them,—what compulsion, or what vengeance, from gods who requite evil deeds?

Me. I can expound all that to thee,—since it seems that thou hast not heard it. There was a seer of noble birth, a son of Priam,—by name Helenus; whom this man, going forth by night,—this guileful Odysseus, of whom all shameful and dishonouring words are spoken,—made his prisoner; and, leading him in bonds, showed him publicly to the Achaeans, a goodly prize: who then prophesied to them whatso else they asked, and that they should never sack the towers of Troy, unless by winning words they should bring this man from the island whereon he now dwells.

And the son of Laertes, when he heard the seer speak thus, straightway promised that he would bring this man and show him to the Achaeans,—most likely, he thought, as a willing captive,—but, if reluctant, then by force; adding that, should he fail in this, whoso wished might have his head.—Thou hast heard all, my son, and I commend speed to thee, and to any man for whom thou carest.

Ph. Hapless that I am! Hath he, that utter pest, sworn to bring me by persuasion to the Achaeans? As soon shall I be persuaded, when I am dead, to come up from Hades to the light, as his father came!

Me. I know nothing about that:—but I must go to ship, and may Heaven be with you both for all good.

[*Exit* Merchant.

Ph. Now is not this wondrous, my son, that the offspring of Laertes should have hoped, by means of soft words, to lead me forth from his ship and show me amidst the Greeks? No! sooner would I hearken to that deadliest of my foes, the viper which made me the cripple that I am! But there is nothing that *he* would not say, or dare; and now I know that he will be here. Come, my son, let us be moving, that a wide sea may part us from the ship of Odysseus. Let us go: good speed in good season brings sleep and rest, when toil is o'er.

Ne. We will sail, then, as soon as the head-wind falls; at present it is adverse.

Ph. 'Tis ever fair sailing, when thou fleest from evil.

Ne. Nay, but this weather is against them also.

Ph. No wind comes amiss to pirates, when there is a chance to steal, or to rob by force.

Ne. Well, let us be going, if thou wilt,—when thou hast taken from within whatever thou needest or desirest most.

Ph. Aye, there are some things that I need,—though the choice is not large.

Ne. What is there that will not be found on board my ship?

Ph. I keep by me a certain herb, wherewith I can always best assuage this wound, till it is wholly soothed.

Ne. Fetch it, then. Now, what else wouldst thou take?

Ph. Any of these arrows that may have been forgotten, and may have slipped away from me,—lest I leave it to be another's prize.

Ne. Is that indeed the famous bow which thou art holding?

Ph. This, and no other, that I carry in my hand.

Ne. Is it lawful for me to have a nearer view of it,—to handle it and to salute it as a god?

Ph. To thee, my son, this shall be granted, and anything else in my power that is for thy good.

Ne. I certainly long to touch it,—but my longing is on this wise;—if it be lawful, I should be glad; if not, think no more of it.

Ph. Thy words are reverent, and thy wish, my son, is lawful; for thou alone hast given to mine eyes the light of life,—the hope to see the Oetean land,—to see mine aged father and my friends,—thou who, when I lay beneath the feet of my foes, hast lifted me beyond their reach. Be of good cheer; the bow shall be thine, to handle, and to return to the hand that gave it; thou shalt be able to vaunt that, in reward of thy kindness, thou, alone of mortals, hast touched it; for 'twas by a good deed that I myself won it.

Ne. I rejoice to have found thee, and to have gained thy friendship; for whosoever knows how to render benefit for benefit must prove a friend above price.—Go in, I pray thee.

Ph. Yes, and I will lead thee in; for my sick estate craves the comfort of thy presence. [*They enter the cave.*

str. 1.Ch. I have heard in story, but seen not with mine eyes, how he who once came near the bed of Zeus was bound upon a swift wheel by the almighty son of Cronus; but of no other mortal know I, by hearsay or by sight, that hath encountered a doom so dreadful as this man's; who, though he had wronged none by force or fraud, but lived at peace with his fellow-men, was left to perish thus cruelly.

Verily I marvel how, as he listened in his solitude to the surges that beat around him, he kept his hold upon a life so full of woe;

ant. 1.where he was neighbour to himself alone,—powerless to walk,—with no one in the land to be near him while he suffered, in whose ear he could pour forth the lament, awaking response, for the plague that gnawed his flesh and drained his blood;—no one to assuage the burning flux, oozing from the ulcers of his envenomed foot, with healing herbs gathered from the bounteous earth, so often as the torment came upon him.

Then would he creep this way or that, with painful steps, like a child without kindly nurse, to any place whence his need might be supplied, whenever the devouring anguish abated;

str. 2.gathering not for food the fruit of holy Earth, nor aught else that we mortals gain by toil; save when haply he found wherewith to stay his hunger by winged shafts from his swift-smiting bow. Ah, joyless was his life, who for ten years never knew the gladness of the wine-cup, but still bent his way towards any stagnant pool that he could descry as he gazed around him.

ant. 2.But now, after those troubles, he shall be happy and mighty at the last; for he hath met with the son of a noble race, who in the fulness of many months bears him on sea-cleaving ship to his home, haunt of Malian nymphs, and to the banks of the Spercheius; where, above Oeta's heights, the lord of the brazen shield drew near to the gods, amid the splendour of the lightnings of his sire.

Ne. I pray thee, come on. Why art thou so silent? Why dost thou halt, as if dismayed, without a cause?

Ph. Alas, alas!

Ne. What is the matter?

Ph. Nothing serious:—go on, my son.

Ne. Art thou in pain from the disease that vexes thee?

Ph. No indeed,—no, I think I am better just now.—Ye gods!

Ne. Why groanest thou thus, and callest on the gods?

Ph. That they may come to us with power to save and soothe.—Ah me!—ah me!

Ne. What ails thee? Speak,—persist not in this silence:—'tis plain that something is amiss with thee.

Ph. I am lost, my son—I can never hide my trouble from you:—ah, it pierces me, it pierces! O misery,—O wretched that I am! I am undone, my son—it devours me.—Oh, for the gods' love, if thou hast a sword ready to thy hand, strike at my heel,—shear it off straightway—heed not my life! Quick, quick, my son!

Ne. And what new thing hath come on thee so suddenly, that thou bewailest thyself with such loud laments?

Ph. Thou knowest, my son. Ne. What is it? Ph. Thou knowest, boy. Ne. What is the matter with thee? I know not. Ph. How canst thou help knowing? Oh, oh!

Ne. Dread, indeed, is the burden of the malady.

Ph. Aye, dread beyond telling. Oh, pity me!

Ne. What shall I do? Ph. Forsake me not in fear. This visitant comes but now and then,—when she hath been sated, haply, with her roamings.

Ne. Ah, hapless one! Hapless, indeed, art thou found in all manner of woe! Shall I take hold of thee, or lend thee a helping hand?

Ph. No, no:—but take this bow of mine, I pray thee,—as thou didst ask of me just now,—and keep it safe till this present access of my disease is past. For indeed sleep falls on me when this plague is passing away, nor can the pain cease sooner; but ye must allow me to slumber in peace. And if meanwhile those men come, I charge thee by Heaven that in no wise, willingly or unwillingly, thou give up this bow to them,—lest thou bring destruction at once on thyself and on me, who am thy suppliant.

Ne. Have no fears as to my caution. The bow shall pass into no hands but thine and mine.—Give it to me, and may good luck come with it!

Ph. There it is, my son:—and pray the jealous gods that it may not bring thee troubles, such as it brought to me and to him who was its lord before me.

Ne. Ye gods, grant this to us twain! Grant us a voyage prosperous and swift, whithersoever the god approves and our purpose tends!

Ph. Nay, my son, I fear that thy prayers are vain; for lo, once more the dark blood oozes drop by drop from the depths, and I look for worse to come. Ah me, oh, oh! Thou hapless foot, what torment wilt thou work for me! It creeps on me,—it is drawing near! Woe, woe is me! Ye know it now:—flee not, I pray you!

O Cephallenian friend, would that this anguish might cleave to thee, and transfix thy breast! Ah me! Ah me! O ye chieftains twain, Agamemnon, Menelaus, would that ye, instead of me, might have this malady upon you, and for as long! Ah me, ah me! O Death, Death, when I am thus ever calling thee, day by day, why canst thou never come? O my son, generous youth, come, seize me, burn me up, true-hearted friend, in yonder fire, famed as Lemnian:—I, too, once deemed it lawful to do the same unto the son of Zeus, for the meed of these same arms, which are now in thy keeping. What sayest thou, boy,—what sayest thou? Why art thou silent? Where are thy thoughts, my son?

Ne. I have long been grieving in my heart for thy load of pain.

Ph. Nay, my son, have good hope withal; this visitor comes sharply, but goes quickly. Only, I beseech thee, leave me not alone.

Ne. Fear not, we will remain. Ph. Thou wilt remain? Ne. Be sure of it.

Ph. Well, I do not ask to put thee on thine oath, my son.

Ne. Rest satisfied: 'tis not lawful for me to go without thee.

Ph. Thy hand for pledge! Ne. I give it—to stay.

Ph. Now take me yonder, yonder— Ne. Whither meanest thou? Ph. Up yonder—

Ne. What is this new frenzy? Why gazest thou on the vault above us?

Ph. Let me go, let me go! Ne. Whither? Ph. Let me go, I say!

Ne. I will not. Ph. Thou wilt kill me, if thou touch me.

Ne. There, then—I release thee, since thou art calmer.

Ph. O Earth, receive me as I die, here and now! This pain no longer suffers me to stand upright.

Ne. Methinks sleep will come to him ere long: see, his head sinks backward; yes, a sweat is bathing his whole body, and a thin stream of dark blood hath broken forth from his heel.

Come, friends, let us leave him in quietness, that he may fall on slumber.

*str.*Ch. Sleep, stranger to anguish, painless Sleep, come, at our prayer, with gentle breath, come with benison, O king, and keep before his eyes such light as is spread before them now; come, I pray thee, come with power to heal!

O son, bethink thee where thou wilt stand, and to what counsels thou wilt next turn our course. Thou seest how 'tis now! Why should we delay to act? Opportunity, arbiter of all action, oft wins a great victory by one swift stroke.

*mes.*Ne. Nay, though he hears nothing, I see that in vain have we made this bow our prize, if we sail without him. His must be the crown; 'tis he that the god bade us bring. 'Twere a foul shame for us to boast of deeds in which failure hath waited on fraud.

*ant.*Ch. Nay, my son, the god will look to that. But when thou answerest me again, softly, softly whisper thy words, my son: for sick men's restless sleep is ever quick of vision.

But, I pray thee, use thine utmost care to win that prize, that great prize, by stealth. For if thou maintain thy present purpose towards this man,—thou knowest of what purpose I speak,—a prudent mind can foresee troubles most grievous.

*ep.*Now, my son, now the wind is fair for thee:—sightless and helpless, the man lies stretched in darkness,—sleep in the heat is sound,—with no command of hand or foot, but reft of all his powers, like unto one who rests with Hades.

Take heed, look if thy counsels be seasonable: so far as my thoughts can seize the truth, my son, the best strategy is that which gives no alarm.

Ne. Hush, I say, and let not your wits forsake you:—yon man opens his eyes, and lifts his head.

Ph. Ah, sunlight following on sleep,—ah, ye friendly watchers, undreamed of by my hopes! Never, my son, could I have dared to look for this,—that thou shouldest have patience to wait so tenderly upon my sufferings, staying beside me, and helping to relieve me. The Atreidae, certainly, those valiant chieftains, had no heart to bear this burden so lightly. But thy nature, my son, is noble, and of noble breed; and so thou hast made little of all this, though loud cries and noisome odours vexed thy senses.

And now, since the plague seems to allow me a space of forgetfulness and peace at last, raise me thyself, my son, set me on my feet, so that, when the faintness shall at length release me, we may set forth to the ship, and delay not to sail.

Ne. Right glad am I to see thee, beyond my hope, living and breathing, free from pain; for, judged by the sufferings that afflict thee, thy symptoms seemed to speak of death.—But now lift thyself; or, if thou prefer it, these men will carry thee; the trouble would not be grudged, since thou and I are of one mind.

Ph. Thanks, my son,—and help me to rise, as thou sayest:—but do not trouble these men, that they may not suffer from the noisome smell before the time. It will be trial enough for them to live on board with me.

Ne. So be it.—Now stand up, and take hold of me thyself.

Ph. Fear not, the old habit will help me to my feet.

Ne. Alack! What am I to do next?

Ph. What is the matter, my son? Whither strays thy speech?

Ne. I know not how I should turn my faltering words.

Ph. Faltering? Wherefore? Say not so, my son.

Ne. Indeed, perplexity has now brought me to that pass.

Ph. It cannot be that the offence of my disease hath changed thy purpose of receiving me in thy ship?

Ne. All is offence when a man hath forsaken his true nature, and is doing what doth not befit him.

Ph. Nay, thou, at least, art not departing from thy sire's example in word or deed, by helping one who deserves it.

Ne. I shall be found base; this is the thought that torments me.

Ph. Not in thy present deeds; but the presage of thy words disquiets me.

Ne. O Zeus, what shall I do? Must I be found twice a villain,—by disloyal silence, as well as by shameful speech?

Ph. If my judgment errs not, yon man means to betray me, and forsake me, and go his way!

Ne. Forsake thee—no; but take thee, perchance, on a bitter voyage—that is the pain that haunts me.

Ph. What meanest thou, my son? I understand not.

Ne. I will tell thee all. Thou must sail to Troy, to the Achaeans and the host of the Atreidae.

Ph. Oh, what hast thou said? Ne. Lament not, till thou learn—

Ph. Learn what? What would'st thou do to me?

Ne. Save thee, first, from this misery,—then go and ravage Troy's plains with thee.

Ph. And this is indeed thy purpose? Ne. A stern necessity ordains it; be not wroth to hear it.

Ph. I am lost, hapless one,—betrayed! What hast thou done unto me, stranger? Restore my bow at once!

Ne. Nay, I cannot: duty and policy alike constrain me to obey my chiefs.

Ph. Thou fire, thou utter monster, thou hateful masterpiece of subtle villainy,—how hast thou dealt with me,—how hast thou deceived me! And thou art not ashamed to look upon me, thou wretch,—the suppliant who turned to thee for pity? In taking my bow, thou hast despoiled me of my life. Restore it, I beseech thee,—

restore it, I implore thee, my son! By the gods of thy fathers, do not rob me of my life! Ah me! No—he speaks to me no more; he looks away,—he will not give it up!

O ye creeks and headlands, O ye wild creatures of the hills with whom I dwell, O ye steep cliffs! to you—for to whom else can I speak?—to you, my wonted listeners, I bewail my treatment by the son of Achilles: he swore to convey me home,—to Troy he carries me: he clinched his word with the pledge of his right hand,—yet hath he taken my bow,—the sacred bow, once borne by Heracles son of Zeus,—and keeps it, and would fain show it to the Argives as his own.

He drags me away, as if he had captured a strong man,—and sees not that he is slaying a corpse, the shadow of a vapour, a mere phantom. In my strength he would not have taken me,—no, nor as I am, save by guile. But now I have been tricked, unhappy that I am. What shall I do? Nay, give it back,—return, even now, to thy true self! What sayest thou? Silent? Woe is me, I am lost!

Ah, thou cave with twofold entrance, familiar to mine eyes, once more must I return to thee,—but disarmed, and without the means to live. Yes, in yon chamber my lonely life shall fade away; no winged bird, no beast that roams the hills shall I slay with yonder bow; rather I myself, wretched one, shall make a feast for those who fed me, and become a prey to those on whom I preyed; alas, I shall render my life-blood for the blood which I have shed,—the victim of a man who seemed innocent of evil! Perish!—no, not yet, till I see if thou wilt still change thy purpose;—if thou wilt not, mayest thou die accurs'd!

Ch. What shall we do? It now rests with thee, O prince, whether we sail, or hearken to yon man's prayer.

Ne. A strange pity for him hath smitten my heart,—and not now for the first time, but long ago.

Ph. Show mercy, my son, for the love of the gods, and do not give men cause to reproach thee for having ensnared me.

Ne. Ah me, what shall I do? Would I had never left Scyros!—so grievous is my plight.

Ph. Thou art no villain; but thou seemest to have come hither as one schooled by villains to a base part. Now leave that part to others, whom it befits, and sail hence,—when thou hast given me back mine arms.

Ne. What shall we do, friends? Odysseus (*appearing suddenly from behind the cave*). Wretch, what art thou doing? Back with thee—and give up this bow to me!

Ph. Ah, who is this? Do I hear Odysseus?

Od. Odysseus, be sure of it—me, whom thou beholdest.

Ph. Ah me, I am betrayed,—lost! He it was, then, that entrapped me and robbed me of mine arms.

Od. I, surely, and no other: I avow it.

Ph. Give back my bow,—give it up, my son.

Od. That shall he never do, even if he would. And moreover thou must come along with it, or they will bring thee by force.

Ph. What, thou basest and boldest of villains,—are these men to take *me* by force?

Od. Unless thou come of thy free will.

Ph. O Lemnian land, and thou all-conquering flame whose kindler is Hephaestus,—is this indeed to be borne, that yonder man should take me from thy realm by force?

Od. 'Tis Zeus, let me tell thee, Zeus, who rules this land,—Zeus, whose pleasure this is; and I am his servant.

Ph. Hateful wretch, what pleas thou canst invent! Sheltering thyself behind gods, thou makest those gods liars.

Od. Nay, true prophets.—Our march must begin.

Ph. Never! Od. But I say, Yes. There is no help for it.

Ph. Woe is me! Plainly, then, my father begat me to be a slave and no free man.

Od. Nay, but to be the peer of the bravest, with whom thou art destined to take Troy by storm, and raze it to the dust.

Ph. No, never,—though I must suffer the worst,—while I have this isle's steep crags beneath me!

Od. What would'st thou do? Ph. Throw myself straightway from the rock and shatter this head upon the rock below!

Od. Seize him, both of you! Put it out of his power!

Ph. Ah, hands, how ill ye fare, for lack of the bow that ye loved to draw,—yon man's close prisoners! O thou who canst not think one honest or one generous thought, how hast thou once more stolen upon me, how hast thou snared me,— taking this boy for thy screen, a stranger to me,—too good for thy company, but meet for mine,—who had no thought but to perform thy bidding, and who already shows remorse for his own errors and for my wrongs. But thy base soul, ever peering from some ambush, had well trained him,—all unapt and unwilling as he was,—to be cunning in evil.

And now, wretch, thou purposest to bind me hand and foot, and take me from this shore where thou didst fling me forth, friendless, helpless, homeless,—dead among the living!

Alas!

Perdition seize thee! So have I often prayed for thee. But, since the gods grant nothing sweet to me, thou livest and art glad, while life itself is pain to me, steeped in misery as I am,—mocked by thee and by the sons of Atreus, the two chieftains, for whom thou doest this errand. Yet thou sailedst with them only when brought under their yoke by stratagem and constraint; but I—thrice-wretched that I am— joined the fleet of mine own accord, with seven ships, and then was spurned and cast out—by *them*, as thou sayest, or, as they say, by thee.

And now, why would ye take me? why carry me with you? for what purpose? I am nought; for you, I have long been dead. Wretch abhorred of heaven, how is it that thou no longer findest me lame and noisome? How, if I sail with you, can ye burn sacrifices to the gods, or make drink-offerings any more? That was thy pretext for casting me forth.

Miserably may ye perish!—and perish ye shall, for the wrong that ye have wrought against me, if the gods regard justice. But I know that they regard it; for ye would never have come on this voyage in quest of one so wretched, unless some heaven-sent yearning for me had goaded you on.

O, my fatherland, and ye watchful gods, bring your vengeance, bring your vengeance on them all,—at last though late,—if in my lot ye see aught to pity! Yes, a piteous life is mine; but, if I saw those men overthrown, I could dream that I was delivered from my plague.

Ch. Bitter with his soul's bitterness are the stranger's words, Odysseus; he bends not before his woes.

Od. I could answer him at length, if leisure served; but now I can say one thing only. Such as the time needs, such am I. Where the question is of just men and good, thou wilt find no man more scrupulous. Victory, however, is my aim in every field,—save with regard to thee: to thee, in this case, I will gladly give way.

Yes, release him, lay no finger upon him more,—let him stay here.—Indeed, we have no further need of thee, now that these arms are ours; for Teucer is there to serve us, well-skilled in this craft, and I, who deem that I can wield this bow no whit worse than thou, and point it with as true a hand. What need, then, of thee? Pace thy Lemnos, and joy be with thee! We must be going. And perchance thy treasure will bring to me the honour which ought to have been thine own.

Ph. Ah, unhappy that I am, what shall I do? Shalt *thou* be seen among the Argives graced with the arms that are mine?

Od. Bandy no more speech with me—I am going.

Ph. Son of Achilles, wilt thou, too, speak no more to me, but depart without a word?

Od. (*to*Ne.). Come on! Do not look at him, generous though thou art, lest thou mar our fortune.

Ph. (*to*Chorus). Will ye also, friends, indeed leave me thus desolate, and show no pity?

Ch. This youth is our commander; whatsoever he saith to thee, that answer is ours also.

Ne. (*to*Chorus). I shall be told by my chief that I am too soft-hearted; yet tarry ye here, if yon man will have it so, until the sailors have made all ready on board, and we have offered our prayers to the gods. Meanwhile, perhaps, he may come to a better mind concerning us.—So we two will be going: and ye, when we call you, are to set forth with speed.

[*Exeunt*Odysseus*and*Neoptolemus.

str. 1.Ph. Thou hollow of the caverned rock, now hot, now icy cold,—so, then, it was my hapless destiny never to leave thee! No, thou art to witness my death also. Woe, woe is me! Ah, thou sad dwelling, so long haunted by the pain of my presence, what shall be my daily portion henceforth? Where and whence, wretched that I am, shall I find a hope of sustenance? Above my head, the timorous doves will go on their way through the shrill breeze; for I can arrest their flight no more.

Ch. 'Tis thou, 'tis thou thyself, ill-fated man, that hast so decreed; this fortune to which thou art captive comes not from without, or from a stronger hand: for, when it was in thy power to show wisdom, thy choice was to reject the better fate, and to accept the worse.

ant. 1.Ph. Ah, hapless, hapless then that I am, and broken by suffering; who henceforth must dwell here in my misery, with no man for companion in the days to come, and waste away,—woe, woe, is me,—no longer bringing food to my home, no longer gaining it with the winged weapons held in my strong hands.

But the unsuspected deceits of a treacherous soul beguiled me. Would that I might see him, the contriver of this plot, doomed to my pangs, and for as long a time!

Ch. Fate, heaven-appointed fate hath come upon thee in this,—not any treachery to which my hand was lent. Point not at me thy dread and baneful curse! Fain indeed am I that thou shouldest not reject my friendship.

str. 2.Ph. Ah me, ah me! And sitting, I ween, on the marge of the white waves, he mocks me, brandishing the weapon that sustained my hapless life, the weapon which no other living man had borne! Ah, thou well-loved bow, ah, thou that hast been torn from loving hands, surely, if thou canst feel, thou seest with pity that the comrade of Heracles is now to use thee nevermore! Thou hast found a new and wily master; by him art thou wielded; foul deceits thou seest, and the face of that abhorred foe by whom countless mischiefs, springing from vile arts, have been contrived against me,—be thou, O Zeus, my witness!

Ch. It is the part of a man ever to assert the right; but, when he hath done so, to refrain from stinging with rancorous taunts. Odysseus was but the envoy of the host, and, at their mandate, achieved a public benefit for his friends.

ant. 2.Ph. Ah, my winged prey, and ye tribes of brighteyed beasts that this place holds in its upland pastures, start no more in flight from your lairs; for I bear not in my hands those shafts which were my strength of old,—ah, wretched that I now am! Nay, roam at large,—the place hath now no more terrors for you,—no more! Now is the moment to take blood for blood,—to glut yourselves at will on my discoloured flesh! Soon shall I pass out of life; for whence shall I find the means to live? Who can feed thus on the winds, when he no longer commands aught that life-giving earth supplies?

Ch. For the love of the gods, if thou hast any regard for a friend who draws near to thee in all kindness, approach him! Nay, consider, consider well,—it is in thine own power to escape from this plague. Cruel is it to him on whom it feeds; and time cannot teach patience under the countless woes that dwell with it.

Ph. Again, again, thou hast recalled the old pain to my thoughts,—kindest though thou art of all who have visited this shore! Why hast thou afflicted me? What hast thou done unto me!

Ch. How meanest thou? Ph. If it was thy hope to take me to that Trojan land which I abhor.

Ch. Nay, so I deem it best. Ph. Leave me, then—begone!

Ch. Welcome is thy word, right welcome,—I am not loth to obey.—Come, let us be going, each to his place in the ship! [*They begin to move away.*

Ph. By the Zeus who hears men's curses, depart not, I implore you! Ch. Be calm.

Ph. Friends, in the gods' name, stay! Ch. Why dost thou call?

Ph. Alas, alas! My doom, my doom! Hapless, I am undone! O foot, foot, what shall I do with thee, wretched that I am, in the days to come?—O friends, return!

Ch. What would'st thou have us do, different from the purport of thy former bidding?

Ph. 'Tis no just cause for anger if one who is distraught with stormy pain speaks frantic words.

Ch. Come, then, unhappy man, as we exhort thee.

Ph. Never, never,—of that be assured—no, though the lord of the fiery lightning threaten to wrap me in the blaze of his thunderbolts! Perish Ilium, and the men before its walls, who had the heart to spurn me from them, thus crippled! But oh, my friends, grant me one boon!

180

Ch. What would'st thou ask?

Ph. A sword, if ye can find one, or an axe, or any weapon,—oh, bring it to me!

Ch. What rash deed would'st thou do?

Ph. Mangle this body utterly,—hew limb from limb with mine own hand! Death, death is my thought now—

Ch. What means this? Ph. I would seek my sire—

Ch. In what land? Ph. In the realm of the dead; he is in the sunlight no more. Ah, my home, city of my fathers! Would I might behold thee,—misguided, indeed, that I was, who left thy sacred stream, and went forth to help the Danai, mine enemies!—Undone—undone!

Ch. Long since should I have left thee, and should now have been near my ship, had I not seen Odysseus approaching, and the son of Achilles, too, coming hither to us.

*Enter*Neoptolemus,*followed by*Odysseus.

Od. Wilt thou not tell me on what errand thou art returning in such hot haste?

Ne. To undo the fault that I committed before.

Od. A strange saying; and what was the fault?

Ne. When, obeying thee and all the host—

Od. What deed didst thou, that became thee not?

Ne. When I ensnared a man with base fraud and guile.

Od. Whom? Alas!—canst thou be planning some rash act?

Ne. Rash,—no: but to the son of Poeas—

Od. What wilt thou do? A strange fear comes over me...

Ne. —from whom I took this bow, to him again—

Od. Zeus! what would'st thou say? Thou wilt not give it back?

Ne. Yea, I have gotten it basely and without right.

Od. In the name of the gods, sayest thou this to mock me?

Ne. If it be mockery to speak the truth.

Od. What meanest thou, son of Achilles? What hast thou said?

Ne. Must I repeat the same words twice and thrice?

Od. I should have wished not to hear them at all.

Ne. Rest assured that I have nothing more to say.

Od. There is a power, I tell thee, that shall prevent thy deed.

Ne. What meanest thou? Who is to hinder me in this?

Od. The whole host of the Achaeans,—and I for one.

Ne. Wise though thou be, thy words are void of wisdom.

Od. Thy speech is not wise, nor yet thy purpose.

Ne. But if just, that is better than wise.

Od. And how is it just, to give up what thou hast won by my counsels? Ne. My fault hath been shameful, and I must seek to retrieve it.

Od. Hast thou no fear of the Achaean host, in doing this?

Ne. With justice on my side, I do not fear thy terrors.

[Od. But I will compel thee.]

Ne. Nay, not even to thy force do I yield obedience.

Od. Then we shall fight, not with the Trojans, but with thee.

Ne. Come, then, what must. Od. Seest thou my right hand on my sword-hilt? Ne. Nay, thou shalt see me doing the same, and that promptly.

181

Od. Well, I will take no more heed of thee; but I will go and tell this to all the host, and by them thou shalt be punished.

Ne. Thou hast come to thy senses; and if thou art thus prudent henceforth, perchance thou mayest keep clear of trouble.

[*Exit* Odysseus.

But thou, O son of Poeas, Philoctetes, come forth, leave the shelter of thy rocky home!

Ph. (*within*). What means this noise of voices once more rising beside my cave? Why do you call me forth? What would ye have of me, sirs?

[*He appears at the mouth of the cave, and sees* Neoptolemus.

Ah me! this bodes no good. Can ye have come as heralds of new woes for me, to crown the old?

Ne. Fear not, but hearken to the words that I bring.

Ph. I am afraid. Fair words brought me evil fortune once before, when I believed thy promises.

Ne. Is there no room, then, for repentance?

Ph. Even such wast thou in speech, when seeking to steal my bow,—a trusty friend, with treason in his heart.

Ne. But not so now;—and I fain would learn whether thy resolve is to abide here and endure, or to sail with us.

Ph. Stop, speak no more! All that thou canst say will be said in vain.

Ne. Thou art resolved? Ph. More firmly, believe me, than speech can tell.

Ne. Well, I could have wished that thou hadst listened to my words; but if I speak not in season, I have done. Ph. Aye, thou wilt say all in vain.

Never canst thou win the amity of my soul, thou who hast taken the stay of my life by fraud, and robbed me of it,—and then hast come here to give me counsel— thou most hateful offspring of a noble sire! Perdition seize you all, the Atreidae first, and next the son of Laertes, and thee! Ne. Utter no more curses; but receive these weapons from my hand.

Ph. What sayest thou? Am I being tricked a second time?

Ne. No, I swear it by the pure majesty of Zeus most high!

Ph. O welcome words,—if thy words be true!

Ne. The deed shall soon prove the word:—come, stretch forth thy right hand, and be master of thy bow!

[*As he hands the bow and arrows to Philoctetes,* Odysseus *suddenly appears.*

Od. But I forbid it—be the gods my witnesses—in the name of the Atreidae and all the host!

Ph. My son, whose voice was that? Did I hear Odysseus? Od. Be sure of it,—and thou seest him at thy side,—who will carry thee to the plains of Troy perforce, whether the son of Achilles will or no.

Ph. But to thy cost, if this arrow fly straight.

[*Bends his bow.*

Ne. (*seizing his arm*). Ah, for the gods' love, forbear—launch not thy shaft!

Ph. Unhand me, in Heaven's name, dear youth!

Ne. I will not. Ph. Alas! why hast thou disappointed me of slaying my hated enemy with my bow!

Ne. Nay, it suits not with my honour, nor with thine. [*Exit* Odysseus.

182

Ph. Well, thou mayest be sure of one thing,—that the chiefs of the host, the lying heralds of the Greeks, though brave with words, are cowards in fight.

Ne. Good; the bow is thine; and thou hast no cause of anger or complaint against me.

Ph. I grant it; and thou hast shown the race, my son, from which thou springest,—no child, thou, of Sisyphus, but of Achilles, whose fame was fairest when he was with the living, as it is now among the dead.

Ne. Sweet to me is thy praise of my sire, and of myself; but hear the boon that I am fain to win from thee. Men must needs bear the fortunes given by the gods; but when they cling to self-inflicted miseries, as thou dost, no one can justly excuse or pity them. Thou hast become intractable; thou canst tolerate no counsellor; and if one advise thee, speaking with good will, thou hatest him, deeming him a foe who wishes thee ill. Yet I will speak, calling Zeus to witness, who hears men's oaths; and do thou mark these words, and write them in thy heart.

Thou sufferest this sore plague by a heaven-sent doom, because thou didst draw near to Chrysè's watcher, the serpent, secret warder of her home, that guards her roofless sanctuary. And know that relief from this grievous sickness can never be thy portion, so long as the sun still rises in the east and sets in the west, until thou come, of thine own free will, to the plains of Troy, where thou shalt meet with the sons of Asclepius, our comrades, and shalt be eased of this malady; and, with this bow's aid and mine, shalt achieve the capture of the Ilian towers.

I will tell thee how I know that these things are so ordained. We have a Trojan prisoner, Helenus, foremost among seers; who saith plainly that all this must come to pass; and further, that this present summer must see the utter overthrow of Troy: or else he is willing that his life be forfeit, if this his word prove false.

Now, therefore, that thou knowest this, yield with a good grace; 'tis a glorious heightening of thy gain, to be singled out as bravest of the Greeks,—first, to come into healing hands,—then to take the Troy of many tears, and so to win a matchless renown.

Ph. O hateful life, why, why dost thou keep me in the light of day, instead of suffering me to seek the world of the dead? Ah me, what shall I do? How can I be deaf to this man's words, who hath counselled me with kindly purpose? But shall I yield, then? How, after doing that, shall I come into men's sight, wretched that I am? Who will speak to me? Ye eyes that have beheld all my wrongs, how could ye endure to see me consorting with the sons of Atreus, who wrought my ruin, or with the accursed son of Laertes?

It is not the resentment for the past that stings me,— I seem to foresee what I am doomed to suffer from these men in the future; for, when the mind hath once become a parent of evil, it teaches men to be evil thenceforth. And in thee, too, this conduct moves my wonder. It behoved thee never to revisit Troy thyself, and to hinder me from going thither; seeing that those men have done thee outrage, by wresting from thee the honours of thy sire; [they, who in their award of thy father's arms, adjudged the hapless Ajax inferior to Odysseus:]—after that, wilt thou go to fight at their side,—and wouldest thou constrain me to do likewise?

Nay, do not so, my son; but rather, as thou hast sworn to me, convey me home; and, abiding in Scyros thyself, leave those evil men to their evil doom. So shalt thou

183

win double thanks from me, as from my sire, and shalt not seem, through helping bad men, to be like them in thy nature.

Ne. There is reason in what thou sayest; nevertheless, I would have thee put thy trust in the gods and in my words, and sail forth from this land with me, thy friend.

Ph. What! to the plains of Troy, and to the abhorred son of Atreus,—with this wretched foot?

Ne. Nay, but to those who will free thee and thine ulcered limb from pain, and will heal thy sickness.

Ph. Thou giver of dire counsel, what canst thou mean?

Ne. What I see is fraught with the best issue for us both.

Ph. Hast thou no shame that the gods should hear those words?

Ne. Why should a man be ashamed of benefiting his friends?

Ph. Is this benefit to the Atreidae, or for me?

Ne. For thee, I ween: I am thy friend, and speak in friendship.

Ph. How so, when thou would'st give me up to my foes?

Ne. Prithee, learn to be less defiant in misfortune.

Ph. Thou wilt ruin me, I know thou wilt, with these words.

Ne. I will not; but I say that thou dost not understand.

Ph. Do I not know that the Atreidae cast me out?

Ne. They cast thee out, but look if they will not restore thee to welfare.

Ph. Never,—if I must first consent to visit Troy.

Ne. What am I to do, then, if my pleading cannot win thee to aught that I urge? The easiest course for me is that I should cease from speech, and that thou shouldest live, even as now, without deliverance.

Ph. Let me bear the sufferings that are my portion; but the promise which thou madest to me, with hand laid in mine,—to bring me home,—that promise do thou fulfil, my son; and tarry not, nor speak any more of Troy; for the measure of my lamentation is full.

Ne. If thou wilt, let us be going. Ph. O generous word!

Ne. Now plant thy steps firmly. Ph. To the utmost of my strength.

Ne. But how shall I escape blame from the Achaeans? Ph. Heed it not.

Ne. What if they ravage my country? Ph. I will be there—

Ne. And what help wilt thou render? Ph. With the shafts of Heracles—

Ne. What is thy meaning?— Ph. —I will keep them afar. Ne. Take thy farewell of this land, and set forth.

Heracles *appears above them.*

He. Nay, not yet, till thou hast hearkened unto my words, son of Poeas: know that the voice of Heracles soundeth in thine ears, and thou lookest upon his face.

For thy sake have I come from the heavenly seats, to show thee the purposes of Zeus, and to stay the journey whereon thou art departing; give thou heed unto my counsel.

First I would tell thee of mine own fortunes,—how, after enduring many labours to the end, I have won deathless glory, as thou beholdest. And for thee, be sure, the destiny is ordained that through these thy sufferings thou shouldest glorify thy life.

Thou shalt go with yon man to the Trojan city, where, first, thou shalt be healed of thy sore malady; then, chosen out as foremost in prowess of the host, with my bow shalt thou slay Paris, the author of these ills; thou shalt sack Troy; the prize of valour shall be given to thee by our warriors; and thou shalt carry the spoils to thy home, for the joy of Poeas thy sire, even to thine own Oetaean heights. And whatsoever spoils thou receivest from that host, thence take a thank-offering for my bow unto my pyre.

(And these my counsels are for thee also, son of Achilles; for thou canst not subdue the Trojan realm without his help, nor he without thine: ye are as lions twain that roam together; each of you guards the other's life.)

For the healing of thy sickness, I will send Asclepius to Troy; since it is doomed to fall a second time before mine arrows. But of this be mindful, when ye lay waste the land,—that ye show reverence towards the gods. All things else are of less account in the sight of our father Zeus; for piety dies not with men; in their life and in their death, it is immortal.

Ph. Ah, thou whose accents I had yearned to hear, thou whose form is seen after many days, I will not disobey thy words!

Ne. I, too, consent.

He. Tarry not long, then, ere ye act; for occasion urges, and the fair wind yonder at the stern.

Ph. Come, then, let me greet this land, as I depart. Farewell, thou chamber that hast shared my watches, farewell, ye nymphs of stream and meadow, and thou, deep voice of the sea-lashed cape,—where, in the cavern's inmost recess, my head was often wetted by the southwind's blasts, and where oft the Hermaean mount sent an echo to my mournful cries, in the tempest of my sorrow!

But now, O ye springs, and thou Lycian fount, I am leaving you,—leaving you at last,—I, who had never attained to such a hope!

Farewell, thou sea-girt Lemnos; and speed me with fair course, for my contentment, to that haven whither I am borne by mighty fate, and by the counsel of friends, and by the all-subduing god who hath brought these things to fulfilment.

Ch. Now let us all set forth together, when we have made our prayer to the Nymphs of the sea, that they come to us for the prospering of our return.

www.ingramcontent.com/pod-product-compliance
Lightning Source LLC
Chambersburg PA
CBHW060319050426
42449CB00011B/2560